# Global Advertising, Attitudes and Audiences

# Routledge Advances in Management and Business Studies

*For a full list of titles in this series, please visit www.routledge.com*

# Global Advertising, Attitudes and Audiences

Tony Wilson

R Routledge
Taylor & Francis Group

NEW YORK AND LONDON

First published 2011
by Routledge
270 Madison Avenue, New York, NY 10016

Simultaneously published in the UK
by Routledge
2 Park Square, Milton Park, Abingdon, Oxon OX14 4RN

*Routledge is an imprint of the Taylor & Francis Group, an informa
business*

© 2011 Taylor & Francis

Typeset in Sabon by Taylor & Francis Books

*Library of Congress Cataloging in Publication Data*
Wilson, Tony.
Global advertising, attitudes and audiences / by Tony Wilson. -- 1st ed.
p. cm. -- (Routledge advances in management and business studies;44)
Includes bibliographical references and index.
ISBN 978-0-415-87597-4
1. Advertising. 2. Telemarketing. I. Title.
HF5823.W52 2010
659--dc22
2010005071

ISBN13: 978-0-415-87597-4 (hbk)
ISBN13: 978-0-203-84634-6 (ebk)

# Contents

# Acknowledgements and Co-Researchers

*To the striving students of Sarawak*
*—we succeeded in making sense!—*
*and Siow Ai Wei (Jenny) who supported it all.*

Norsita Lin Binti Ahmad is Senior Researcher, Digi Telecommunications Sdn. Bhd., Malaysia.

Azizah Hamzah is professor in the Faculty of Arts and Social Sciences, Universiti Malaya, Malaysia. She is the author of many articles in English and Malay and five monographs including, most recently, *Women in Malaysia: Breaking Boundaries and Asia's High Technology Projects* (Kuala Lumpur: Universiti Malaya Press).

Kiranjit Kaur is associate professor at the Faculty of Communication and Media Studies, Universiti Teknologi MARA, Malaysia. Her current areas of research are in public relations management, media ethics, media and gender, media audiences and new media technologies. She is also Director of the Institute of Journalism Studies, a university Center of Excellence.

Khor Yoke Lim is associate professor of health communication in the School of Communication at Universiti Sains Malaysia (University of Science, Malaysia). She has published widely on ethnicity, women and health, and is currently working with the author on a Royal Melbourne Institute of Technology University project about branding the banking industry.

Tan Huey Pyng lectures at the Faculty of Arts and Social Science, Universiti Tunku Abdul Rahman (Malaysian Chinese Association). She recently published with the author in *Consumption, Markets, and Culture* and *Information, Communication and Society* (Taylor and Francis journals).

Rabaah Tudin lectures at the Faculty of Economics and Business, Universiti Malaysia Sarawak. Her current research interests and diverse publishing are in studies of consumer behavior, entrepreneurship, human resource development and services marketing.

# Introduction

"A brand is the sign of a slave."

(Husserl, 1985: 167)

In the commercial spaces between television programs or on cyberspace Internet pages, marketing maps out branded landscapes for consumption. Whether metaphorical or more literal in their accounts, these visual stories perennially celebrate product use as a known aspect or moment of living. "We have shared some great moments, good food and fun times. You have been part of our many achievements. We have always been there together" (McDonald's Malaysia website).

We view these media narratives as people (embodied beings), as consenting or skeptical consumers who are also citizens with our established and remembered patterns of practice and perception forming our familiar everyday life-world. Like people everywhere else, McDonald's "guests" are interpretive: they implicitly classify their eating experiences as instantiating types of always already familiar phenomena ("fun times" or otherwise) and anticipate events accordingly.

Where appropriately addressed by advertisers, media marketing's model recipients become absorbed in these "storied" forms of life on screen for the (re)creative conjoining of people, places and products. Audiences perceive these narrative programs of purchasing meaning (wherein people buying become "life-loving") from informed horizons of expecting content. Knowledgeable about screen marketing, consumers implicitly anticipate a finalizing tag line: they are explicitly surprised should it be absent. Media users make intelligible these narratives reproducing previous patterns.

As audiences articulating sense from an often elliptically edited sequence of events, their game like goal is generating knowledge—to produce from their horizons of understanding these value-laden screen stories an intelligible space and time. Adding meaning to their lives or to the person they are, advertising's model consumers appropriate or gain a purchase in/on these places.

Such audio-visually branded spaces and times or "brandscapes" (Sherry, 1986)[1] are sketched out in narrative accounts on television and websites of comfortable consumption in which intended audiences immerse themselves.[2]

Fast food restaurant media brandscapes are thus digital agora[3] or gathering places, screened as familiar if special spaces and times, life-worlds of trusted support for consumer citizens—often shown therein as close companions in playful (ludic) accomplishment. These *McDonaldized* agora form "regular" sites for projected stories of self confirmation.[4]

The branding narratives which we consider in this volume can be more enigmatic and even contradictory. As extended stories, their ambiguous accounts or "ambi-branding" (Brown, 2006) of agora on screen show consumers thought-provoking events ranging from an implausible Chinese singing in Tamil to an impossibly soaring basketball player and an inverted sampan sinking. But audiences are supported in reconciling such antinomies on condition that they give credence to aspirational advertising for products which can render these worlds coherent and comfortable.

The idea that branding constructs agoric places on screen whose products enable them to be "comfortable for gathering purposes" was suggested by an Indian female student at the University of Science, Malaysia, where I conducted focus groups with a Chinese colleague. Marketed brandscapes (as represented by transnational coffee shop advertising) facilitate multiple forms of *gathering by people* for the intrinsic pleasure of being together or for more instrumental purposes (preparing for work). Screen images encourage enthusiastic product use which may or may not occur in practice.

But (as another student pointed out) consumers can also *gather their thoughts* together or articulate them in personal narratives of reflection over a coffee in a branded shopping landscape after a busy week. Branding's goal here and more widely is to convince potential customers of a certain product-oriented creative caring for their comfort in agreeable agora. Purchasers will enjoy recreative (immersive) reliable circumstances—in a marketed ludic life-world where product use is familiar (because regular), dependably supporting anticipated narratives in which identity is formed.

Branding builds on screen forms of life as space and time for bonding. Brandscapes are an elliptically edited assembling (Lury, 2009) of cultural practice sketched in stories which absorbed audiences articulate into narratives of aspirational activity—events to be emulated. Images of Coffee Bean comfortable consumption or Pizza Hut sensation on screen are thereby integrated into small familiar worlds. Immersed in these stories consumers identify with inhabitants already present in these media places—or respond with irritation. We line up together—or absent our alienated selves.

In parallel mode, across shopping malls and other precincts urging purchasing, branded agora take material shape, promising their acquisitive audiences pleasure after entry. People "discover" citizenship in reflecting upon the conditions of their consumption. From fast food restaurants to higher education "shops," travel agents to telecommunications providers, representation in media marketing is realized by audiences—or found depleted in substance. Consumer citizens commence and conclude personal narratives of delight or disillusionment we consider in this volume.

In consumer and cultural studies, the concept of a business-oriented branded landscape allows "theory of everything" to be constructed in which the political economy of producing places is integrated with accounts of their reception in the processes of audience perception and purchase. We can see how corporations shape space and time on marketing screens and plazas for profit. Studies of branded agora show buyers immersing themselves, consorting in consensus with existing consumers on enjoyable eating—or passing by, perhaps walking swiftly on from this spatiotemporal zoning for meals in anger. We drink at—or distance ourselves from—Starbucks.

Entering some of our many surrounding mall or media brandscapes, we both absorb and are absorbed by their agora. We have anticipated and articulate their life-worlds in narratives after entry to be familiar, regular "comfort zones." We substantiate their sense, appropriating or at other times becoming alienated from their constructed routine consumption. *Global Advertising, Attitudes and Audiences* explores these narrative screen representations, their material instantiation and reception.

We are guided by philosophical psychology or the philosophy of mind in studying marketing. Undertaking research with Asian consumers and writing about its results, we are distant from the Scottish philosopher Hume and his argument that constant conjunction (here of screen content and consumer attitude) is no less than causality. Critical of this far reaching illusion, instead we shall follow Husserl and the subsequent philosophical hermeneutics of Heidegger, Gadamer, Habermas and Ricoeur. Their view that human existence is fundamentally interpretive informs our regarding audience consumers as drawing continually on their collective cultural memory (located on horizons of understanding) in producing meaning for media branding. Putting this point starkly, media advertising has no sense without an interpretive audience who aligns with or declares their distance from its prescriptive narratives. Consumers produce the meaning of marketing.

*Global Advertising* is *not* an argument against statistical methods in marketing. Rather, its focus is on the conceptual presuppositions of using those methods. Nor is the book dismissive of inductivism (or generalizing) as underwriting the employment of statistical sampling across wide populations, though we are aware that the logic of generalizing is never conclusive. *Global Advertising* sets out consumer centered theory of what we shall call interpretive inductivism.

Chapter One locates these thoughts on branding and responses in a wider context of audience and consumer studies. Three phases and thirty years of media user theory are integrated to produce a philosophical psychology of buyers responding to brandscapes, of audiences in agora:

i) Audiences as Passive Spectators—European Structuralist and US Effects Studies (despite their evident differences) assumed audience acquiescence in screen content.

ii) Audiences as Political Respondents—the work of the Birmingham (UK) Centre for Contemporary Cultural Studies presented viewers as being capable of expressing ideological distance from media constructions of contemporary nationhood.

iii) Audiences as Projecting Meaning—drawing on European Reception Theory, audience studies (particularly in work on the consumer) attended to the question: how do we understand media narrative—not least in marketing? How do watching buyers make sense of brandscapes?

As in fast food marketing, these "product worlds" are places associated primarily with convenient predictability or comfortable creative play, regulated recreation. In recounting the process of gaining a purchase, such spaces and times of fun and familiarity are ludic life-worlds.

Brandscapes are multi-dimensional. On screen media (principally television and Internet advertising), they are two-dimensional, constructed by marketing narratives. In shopping malls they take three-dimensional shape. Whether engaging with mall or media agora, people's responses have the same structure. Immersing themselves in branded shopping or screen "territory" of which they always already have generic knowledge, consumers anticipate events: they articulate "storied" accounts of these occasions (e.g. in chatting or blogs)[5] and appropriate or derive reviving narratives informing lives. Or they distance themselves from agora in identity defining alienated criticism.

Chapter One discusses further the substantial use of hermeneutic and reception theory by advertising research when investigating how buyers interpret branding. Paradoxically, unlike English audience studies which in the 1980s reduced European philosophy to structuralism, American consumer theory mobilizes French and German phenomenology to understand the process of purchasing. Here, the *Journal of Consumer Research* is a first place of reference.

How do we negotiate our understanding of the world—and of media marketing in particular? Phenomenologists (Heidegger, Huizinga, Husserl) answer by pointing to a process of informed inference guided by our intrinsic interest in establishing intelligibility. Our absorption is equally our anticipating sense. Immersed in a continuing mental play of meaning formation, consumers articulate coherent screen content: their aim fundamentally is making sense of mediated marketing.

Albeit accused of being intellectually insular, Birmingham English audience theory (Morley, 1980) has become a paradigmatic perspective in analyzing our responses to screen content. We interpret programs actively and differently and do not passively receive a predetermined meaning as a caused consequence of viewing. Philosophically guided consumer research argues that re-reading this theory anew through the prism of hermeneutic phenomenology can provide us with a closely specified sense of the substantial cognitive element previously only implicitly characterizing this model of media use. In short, audience understanding is a time-taking goal-oriented process.

The structured activity of making sense of screen events has seven aspects or "moments" (from the simultaneous to the sequential) which we consider to be at the core of consumers' responses to branding. Interested in further internationalizing media studies, our discussion in these chapters reflects on inflections of this singular cognitive route wherein real audiences arrive at multi-cultural readings of screen marketing a shopping mall from its eateries to education.

Consumers challenge the "bulldozing homogenization effects of globaliza-tion" (Askegaard, 2006: 92).We focus on screen texts of transnational and S.E. Asian national marketing to explore the less-apparent "coming into being" of Chinese, Indian and Malay responses as consumers and citizens. Following Schroeder (2002: 115–40) one can say that if media marketing presents person and product identity, it is articulated and appropriated through individuating cultural difference. In reflecting on this process of reading screens we render global a psychology of gaining a purchase.

Chapter Two focuses on Western fast food brandscapes, relating moments in their corporate production to aspects of Asian responses in blogs and focus groups. Frying forms a fat issue. Through analyzing multiple multi-cultural reactions to five culinary agora represented in cyber-space and television, we see that these branded virtual landscapes and their material embodiment function as familiar *ludic life-worlds*, consumption spaces in which (partici-pants said) people "hang out"—suspended paradoxically from life in an agoric safe place for gathering or swift "go-getting."

Branded ludic landscapes are regulated "regular" places which support consumers in an extended cognitively rich release from external daily demands, a play-like production of selves. Alongside such intrinsic enjoyment, fast food spaces and times are seen as used instrumentally (and intensively) in less game-like mode for convenience.

Global brandscapes circulate a certain celebrating "together" of familiarity. Their ludic landscapes are long term agora. "We have always been there together" during these "good times when we get together" (McDonald's and Kentucky Fried Chicken Malaysian website "home pages"). "Our" egalitarian eating is focused on consuming internationally identical (Coffee Bean) or locally hybridized (Pizza Hut) products. Asian marketing and mall consumers in online blogs or our focus groups perceive such Western claims to cultural proximity in food and friendship with varying degrees of assent. Chinese and Malay females defined their difference in Kuala Lumpur: meals with Occidental origins will "never get better than home."

Chapters Three through to the Conclusion explore the idea of brandscapes as "ludic life-worlds," following the process of their reception by consumer citizens. In Chapter Four (Advertising Academia), for instance, higher education is seen to be marketed as international destination for personal discovery, multiple brandscaping for the brain. People are offered an immersive (friendly, supportive) experience of study (as creative mental play) and sport (physical play), the chance to construct campus-located narratives driven by the development of self for subsequent employment and gain. We consider, in consumer focus groups and blogs, audience articulation and appropriation of—or alienation from—education branding of agora on Internet and in TV advertisement.

The Appendix: Constructing Marketed Meaning from Consumer Culture draws substantially on focus group data in the author's (co-researched with Tan Huey Pyng) "Television's Glocal Advertising in Veridical Product Narrative," *Consumption, Markets and Culture* 9(1): 45–62. He acknowledges permission from the Taylor and Francis journal (http://informaworld.com) to include sections of this article in the present publication.

# 1 Audiences Articulating Advertising

"Modern marketing" could be "modern culture par excellence. Its success in becoming—for all institutions—the principal mode of relating with their constituents is a testimony to the centrality of marketing in contemporary culture."
(Firat and Dholakia, 2006: 124)

If marketing is now culturally central how is it mediated through television and Internet screens which are equally perceptually pivotal in modern times? How does it address consumers leading them to buy brands? What is the communicative logic of this situation? How can we understand the process of media persuading us to purchase product? Why do audiences align with or become alienated from advertising on screen? Continuing this spatial metaphor, how does global branding become culturally close to local consumers? For they clearly have differing perspectives on the world (or occupy distant horizons of understanding its content). In seeking to respond to these geographically oriented questions we remember Fischer and Sherry's remark (2007) while presenting Consumer Culture Theory that the "geography of contemporary consumption, as it must, will be re-written and re-mapped continuously" (3).

As a book on media branding, this volume is about *understanding the reasons* why everyday audiences form attitudes rather than *explaining the causes* of those value judgments. Relationships between evaluative belief and eventual buying abstracted by theory elsewhere are placed back within cultural horizons (or an informing context) where people link product and person in a process of articulating identities for both screen and self. Recognizing and interpreting such phenomena needs to conceptually precede inductive (generalizing) statistical description. We shall attend to the time-taking process wherein *both* consumer and market researcher understand "data."

Consumers articulate (sometimes persuasive) narrative about media branded products, appropriating these branding stories to shape their horizons of self understanding for a *reason*. They are not *caused* to do so as an effect of screen content. Rather, drawing on their always already existing awareness of narrative and other cultural forms to assemble the meaning of a sometimes enigmatic branding story, they identify (or align) with people's product use therein. Consumers thereby generate narratives of (would-be) guidance from generic information and find them appropriate. Or they distance (alienate) themselves from narrative content (and form) in distrust.

*Global Advertising* considers Asian consumer responses to global and local screen marketing and shopping malls which are argued to be analogous in their modes of immersing audiences. How shoppers understand and incorporate both mall and media marketing into their daily lives is immensely culturally varied but essentially identical. We focus on their interpreting and identifying (with) marketing brands on screen from banks and fast food to universities, nations to telecommunications. Our research participant discourse (or speech) displaying the prolonged cognitive process wherein consumers make sense of advertising and branding and integrate them with living is emphasized as fundamentally important in our analyzing marketing.

Often, the story of selling through screens is couched in terms of influencing consumer *attitudes* towards a brand or product. Like some communication studies (e.g. in cultivation theory), marketing research can consider this to be a causal chain, a narrative in which powerful advertising will have the effect of bringing about buying behavior. The success (or strength) of this connection, it is said, can be quantitatively measured. In this chapter we shall discuss some initial instances of consumer discourse (or talk) to conclude that such a linking of events between screen and purchase is a myth with caused or causal *attitudes* a core fiction at the heart of this methodological delusion.

Replacing such a narrative of passive purchasing, we shall argue instead, consumers actively *appropriate* media advertising. They both identify the meaning of content (i.e. recognize it) and identify (i.e. align) with characters on screen, with the latter's activity providing reasons for purchase. As a contributor to my early consumer research asserted, "they are doing that, why not us?" Or, resisting the rational momentum of advertising's sought for agreement, consumers are critical, becoming *alienated* (Brecht, 1978) or discovering their distance from marketing on screen.[1]

So how do audiences form attitudes? Can they be said to do so actively and rationally? Or are attitudes the passive caused consequences of much media watching? Do we cultivate screen content as meaningful narrative or do the media cultivate our perceptions as audiences? More specifically, in consumer responses to advertising are attitudes towards products produced by screen branding? Or are they arrived at through audiences articulating the meaning of media marketing? Do consumers construct their conceptions of products or are both built for them? And when we have answered these questions about the structure of consuming, how do we statistically evaluate our data? For the abstractions of hermeneutics precede but do not displace quantitative assessment.

In *Global Advertising*, we refer to researchers for whom audiences or consumers are passive recipients of perceptual content (of what used to be called "sense data") as *Inductive Causalists*. Constructing what could be called an "inductive statistical apparatus" (ISA) of measurement, these investigators focus on generalizing or generating statistical accounts of data (such as events on screen and audience behavior). Highly correlated "data" are elevated to the status of being linked as cause and effect by a connecting "mechanism" about which speculation can take place. Inductivists of this persuasion are thus to be considered would-be *Causalists* seeking a more or less complex chain of cause and effect occurrence between "variables" like "media-use" and "audience attitudes":

> media-use variables, then, are endogenous—that is, subject to the influence of causally prior variables. Conversely (...) there is ample evidence for effects of media-use variables on beliefs, attitudes, and behavior—the components of personal and social identity.
>
> (Slater, 2007: 282).

The underlying issue here is: are the data discovered to be primarily conceptualized or described in terms belonging to the world view of researcher or researched? For studies pursued quantitatively nonetheless rest on a qualitative base as calculations concerning the world.

*Interpretivists* (as I shall call them) assume that audience consumers (actively) construct (narrative) sense for that which they see: research investigates this process of producing meaning as it occurs over time within responses to the screen. People draw on their cultural background to generate understanding of media events. Hence interpretivists can be referred to as *Culturalists*. Consumer interpreted branding narratives incorporate reasons for aligning or identifying with product use. Given their qualitatively subtle focus, the issue is mathematical measurement: how are such data quantified? Interpretivism needs a statistical package to "triangulate" its findings.

I paint this initial presentation of philosophy and research method with a broad brush. For distinguishing in practice between inductivists and interpretivists can be difficult. Researchers may be statistically inclined but equally seek to categorically accommodate as the foundation of their measurement an audience's articulating meaning for marketing on screen. Moreover, my distinction relates to a broader methodological struggle occurring between Positivists and Phenomenology over conceptualizing the nature of human and social inquiry. Considered as philosophers of science, the first group of theorists link causal judgment about observable events with universal natural law.

Media cultivation theory is a clear candidate for the inductivist would-be causalist category. Television's "images cultivate the dominant tendencies of our culture's beliefs, ideologies and world views": here "the 'size' of a (program's) 'effect' is far less critical than the direction of its steady contribution" (Gerbner et al., 1980: 14). Surprisingly, "despite four decades of (media) cultivation research demonstrating a reliable, albeit small, cultivation relationship, questions remain about the mechanisms that link exposure to perception" conclude Bilandzic and Busselle (2008: 508).

Nonetheless, these latter authors assert inductively that where "transportation" or "losing one's self in a (screen) narrative" occurs, "repeated highly transportive experiences contribute to the overall cultivation effect by adjusting the viewers' worldviews after each exposure": thus the "constant presence of stories with similar messages may be absorbed by audiences and alter their understanding of social reality" (ibid.: 508, 509). Such "adjusted," "absorbed" and "altered" audiences are surely passive recipients of the media's "worldviews" in their "understanding (of) social reality" as a caused consequence of continuing screen "exposure."[2]

Similarly, a "mechanism" is proposed in a discussion of the brand–consumer relationship. While in this instance the latter may not entirely involve an audience's conscious attention the "automatic processes" proposed would surely exclude the relationship being one of reason-giving. Here, frequently perceived coffee branding ("repeated exposures to a brand") is conceptualized as "driving (an) effect" on consumers "via automatic processes (...) (as an) underlying mechanism":

> On any given morning, one might pass several people with Starbucks coffee in hand. What are the effects of such repeated exposures to a brand? (...) (We) focus on situations during which these effects occur via automatic processes (whose) ease of processing (characterizes the) underlying mechanism driving this effect.
>
> (Ferraro et al., 2009: 729, 731)

In the inductivist causalist camp, more or less determinate *mechanisms* link screen (or shop front) content with the formation of audience and consumer evaluative beliefs or attitudes. Such a causalist model of attaching attitudes must be attractive to positivists. For conceptualizing attitude formation in its sequential and statistical terms can present the process as conforming to laws and hence the *deductive-nomological* model of explanation at the heart of positivism. Here, being able to predict on the basis of positive correlation (preferably the constant conjunction of observable events) leads inexorably to the capacity to explain: explanation is symmetrical with prediction.

In a definitive editorial recommendation establishing the "Primary of Theory" for the *European Journal of Marketing*, Lee and Greenley (2008) write with approval that:

> one of the truly great theorists in marketing, Shelby Hunt, described theory as "a systematically related set of statements, including some law-like generalizations, that is empirically testable (...) a systematized structure capable of both explaining and predicting phenomena."
>
> (Hunt, 1991: 4)

Inductivist causalist theory is implicitly engaged in "lawlike generalization." A propositional causal candidate for nomological (law) status would be that,

other circumstances being equal, when repeated consumer exposures to satisfied Brand X coffee drinkers ("with Brand X coffee in hand") take place a
favorable consumer attitude towards that brand of coffee will result.

From the perspective of the interpretive or culturalist model, however, the
perception of agents as passive inherent in this theory of attitude formation is
unacceptable. For consumers actively recognize, anticipate and articulate
advertising's prescriptive screen narrative from its elliptical or indeterminate
elements by drawing on a wider knowledge of generic textual type.

In the present volume, the causal formation of attitudes is replaced by a
cognitively active audience's alignment with (or distancing alienation from) a
text's prescriptive meaning. "We are like them." Such "borrowing" to attach
oneself to the significance of a global brand is premised upon viewer identification or alignment with narrative agent made possible by local cultural
similarities to media content. Successful world marketing is particularly
glocal.

Connections between branding and buying are not the main focus of a book
on audiences forming attitudes. But the latter are considered in marketing as
the basis of predictable behavior:

> Why does the attitude concept maintain its unparalleled popularity? One
> possible answer is that the concept is central to the observer's dream: "If
> only I knew your attitude, I could predict your thoughts and behavior."
>
> (Schwarz, 2006: 20)

Again this nexus is of interest to positivists as potentially nomological since
they consider prediction of effects is allowed by knowledge of law-governed
causal events. However, attitudes are evaluative beliefs, not events: and in any
case predicting economic decision-making or buying has drawn on theory of
reasoned action rather than causal models implying participant passivity
(Lunt, 1995). The philosophical or conceptual assumptions of predicting need
certainly not be positivist.[3]

*Global Advertising* does not purport, then, to discuss the relationship
between consumer attitude and action (buying). However, the volume ven-
tures to consider how audiences relate their perception of marketing narrative
to themselves, connecting content to conception of the self. We will discuss,
that is, how encultured consumers articulate and appropriate meaning from
screen media and shopping malls (whose spaces, I shall argue, are structurally
similar). In this emphasis on cultural and narrative intricacy my perspective
clearly differs from (for instance) the economic theory of reasoned action and
preference in purchasing [as set out by Ajzen (1988)].

Within interpretive theory guided by philosophical insights from phenomenology, the audience of consumer citizens who view media marketing are
found always already located upon habitual "horizons" of concrete being and
cultural understanding upon which they rarely turn to focus. Shaping the
perceptual process, these generic frameworks of comprehension within which

we continually interpret new experience as instantiating an already known ("pre-cognitive") type are thus semi-effaced or half-hidden. Nonetheless, situated on these sites of sense-making, recognizing the world as exemplifying categories of which they are aware, people continually anticipate (or "project") events. Pursuing a "hermeneutic circle of understanding" they attempt to articulate occurrence into coherent narrative. Audiences shape into a story elliptical segments on screen.

In screen theory of the last century, contradictory texts constructed by the political avant-garde were considered to bring about an alienated revolutionary audience critical of capitalism (see Wilson, 1993). The passive workers were (re)produced as active instruments of historical change.

Now, incorporating political diversity, hermeneutic media marketing theory can show how consumers seek in the cognitive play of their responses to provide apparently conflicting elements (or antinomies) of advertising with coherent narrative meaning. Irresolvable contradiction and complexity may be read still as distancing. But products can be branded as the source of coherence.

In talking to them and learning during focus groups and interviews of their responses, we attempt to bring consumer consciousness a little closer to discern in more detail the structure of their understanding marketing on media. One Malaysian television branding narrative for Coca-Cola features a vigorously edited ball game occupying a city centre street. During our research on responses a Chinese male viewer was concerned to reconcile the apparent contradiction between the vigorous demands of outdoor basketball he sees on screen and constricting enclosure of the body by *baju kurung* Malay dress worn by one of the players:

> it's controversial [the scenes before the female are "outdoor" look—activism, while the Malay female looks like an "indoor" girl, walking slow and wearing *baju kurung*, which (means) she can't play basketball like the other female does. However, she can still play it] kind of breaking the rules.

The "Malay female" drinking Coca-Cola is seen by this Chinese viewer (as enabling him) to resolve the contradiction between basketball and *baju kurung*, the conflict between energetic creativity and encompassing constraint! Thereby freed by viewers from the tyranny of paradox, elliptical marketing stories offer audiences who align themselves with such action, powerful reasons to appropriate a drink or other mode of dynamism as an aspect of their life-worlds. Contradictions can be resolved by bringing advertised artifacts into the branding narrative—demonstrating their value (or foregrounding their potency) as problem resolving products. Going along with this outcome, in so identifying or consensually connecting with content, consumers transform a moment (aspect) of their living. They have produced and now purchase "refreshing" meaning.

"Don't you just love this country?" asks Malaysian oil company television branding of those consumers who gain a paradox resolving purchase of/on its narrative meaning celebrating cultural diversity rather than divergence. For they see multi-culturalism supporting Chinese singing Tamil!

In (actively) articulating the narrative meaning of media branding as (after all) coherent, consumers come to comprehend (their reading of) its evaluative message: they complete an appropriately prescriptive reading of the latter's (not too) indeterminate elements. Coke resolves conflict with innovation, rendering the impossible possible, "breaking the rules"! And Malaysia's national oil company can be integrated by the consumer into a branding narrative supporting its multi-cultural society, enabling a Chinese to express his happiness in Tamil song. "Don't you just love this country?" where opposites are reconciled in contradictions becoming a creative resource.

> The first time I see it I feel a bit surprised because I thought that the person who is singing is not a Chinese. But when I know the Chinese (is) singing a Tamil song it is not really a surprise because Malaysia is a multi-cultural country.
>
> (female Chinese)

Branding messages ("Don't you just love this country?") can thus address a consumer who has already constructed a persuasive narrative from the more or less fragmented content (edited and elliptical elements) of media marketing (or the sights and sounds of a mall). For always already having positioned themselves as readers on a cultural horizon of comprehension from which screened stories are identified as instantiating types (or generic), audiences absorb themselves in such advertising and anticipate its selling (or project a prescriptive narrative).

Reading "to and fro" across the text in the playlike construction of sense, moving through this hermeneutic circle of understanding, viewers articulate from its apparent contradictions a coherent story. In such a consumer constructed narrative, for instance, family members far away from each other can gain nonetheless greater intimacy as purchasers of a cellphone product—in using which, indeed, "distance should bring you closer."

The story of resolution a consumer has shaped out of the text's edited elements, then, constitutes not a *cause* of, but a *reason* for her or his aligning (identifying) with the marketing maxim ("purchase the product because distance should bring you closer"). Thus appropriating prescriptive narrative and product the audience emerges to understand themselves as telco users.

Shaping sense from screen media and making sense of shopping malls, I argue in the penultimate chapter, are analogous. Both involve immersion and menu assisted inference. While television has program guides, most malls have purchasing directories (maps): both support audience consumers in anticipating, articulating and appropriating narratives of involvement.

A Malaysian mall's space and time is structured annually by multiple religious festivals. However, visitors we interviewed and some who weblogged indicate intrinsic pleasures and instrumental duties of a more secular character ranging from bibliophile buying to supermarket shopping. Becoming absorbed in a mall, whatever the particular cultural moments enjoyed, can be characterized as a consumer's brief, temporary "metaphorical migration" (Morley, 2000: 204).

In setting out a phenomenology of audience consumer responses to immersive mall and media, I am arguing for theory which despite being "universalist" nonetheless provides the "theoretical space within which one can allow for, and then investigate, differential readings, interpretations, or responses on the part of the audience" (Morley, 1995: 304). Throughout the following pages, Chinese, Indian, Malay and audiences of other ethnicity in Malaysia speak of their comprehending, consensual agreement with or contesting alienation from advertised spaces.

## FROM MECHANISM OF ATTITUDE FORMATION TO ARTICULATING MEANING FROM TEXT

Audiences are cognitively *active* in appropriating marketing for their lives (sometimes becoming critical citizens in the process). Consumer attitudes (to products and their purchasing) are not *passive* effects of powerful advertising much like gases expanding are a result of heating or lead to containers fracturing. The causalist alignment of methodology in studying communication and science requires a mythic connecting chain of successively impacting events, in which "attitudes" play a central role, leading from marketing screen content to consumers securing products. This stimulus–response model of the relationship between brand, attitude and behavior has similarities to early psychology's study of rats. Repeated exposure to product marketing or potential meals (a platform for prediction) causes effects via "automatic processes" or "underlying mechanisms."

"Attitude-events" are a far from effective story from causalist marketing theory. Real attitudes are not a "mechanized" occurrence which have in their turn effects but are (in principle) rationally defensible evaluative beliefs which logically (because of their conceptual category) can have no causal efficacy. Passing "several people with Starbucks coffee in hand," we may identify with their (presumed) pleasure—a reason (far from an "underlying mechanism") for our deciding subsequently to appropriate this practice to grace our morning going to work.

Inductivist causalist or positivist *attitudes* have three problems. First, they traditionally have been defined behaviorally, as a "predisposition to behave": a favorable attitude to a brand is likely to lead to its purchase. Here, "attitudes represent underlying general predispositions to respond that manifest themselves as consistent behaviors in different situations. Attitude theorists generally posited a causal relationship between the latent variable—attitude—and overt behavior" (Grunig, 1982: 171–2). This interpretation of "attitude" clearly supports prediction of subsequent behavior but is distant from everyday understanding of the term as referring to subjective belief.

Secondly, attitudes should be regarded by marketing researchers as evaluative beliefs held for reasons: I view product "x" unfavorably because I consider it to be environmentally harmful. Their expression in the discourse of consumer response constructs our perspective on the world. But if attitudes are beliefs they are not events featuring in a chain of cause and effect holding between screen and audience action, marketing content and consumer behavior. Beliefs and their sub-species, attitudes, cannot be characterized as an effect of screen stimulation. Rather, my believing may endure over time [although reference to an attitude does not describe an "internal mental state" (Potter and Wetherell, 1987: 45)]. It is an appropriate topic for reason giving defense.

Finally, pared down attitudes are invariably attributed by inductivist "scientific" investigators without referring to research participants' culturally specific or local beliefs. ("Evaluate your response from 1–5"!) Statistically quantifying and systematically generalizing about relationships between advertising and consumers unavoidably elides detail, glossing over or omitting particular responses to screen content. But this does not entail silencing subjectivity: a conceptual path or logical link between investigator and investigated perceptions of marketing must be retained.[4]

In short, "attitude-events" are a fundamental category mistake in managing those marketing studies which pursue a positivistic methodology. Throughout research undertaken from the latter perspective, advertising is said to cause or change consumer attitudes—its effect. Within this scenario of conjoined events, viewers are presented as passive, succumbing to screens.

In *Global Advertising*, instead, active audiences appropriate advertising to form beliefs about themselves and their circumstances. Rather than appropriation being a causal consequence of screen content, it is part of a prolonged cognitive process in which absorbed consumers draw on what they see and hear to construct an interpretation of these mediated events for their lives in a "dynamic process of always becoming" (Elliott and Davies, 2006: 168) selves in societal space and time.

A telecommunications branding narrative which will be considered later in this volume shows that "any place that you are, (the company) is there to help you, to assist you" (female Indian). If this is to be convincing marketing, of course, particularly in a transnational context, the advertising itself must be sufficiently culturally appropriate to travel and support a favorable audience response. In studying the passage and procuring of such subjectivity we shall draw upon phenomenology rather than an earlier positivistic methodology for marketing where consumers' understanding of themselves is largely ignored. For hermeneutic phenomenology (recognizing and establishing audience understanding as a process) allows us to acknowledge the local conceptual and linguistic complexity in which consumers are always already immersed: we are also able to accommodate this detail within a globally applicable theory of their responses to marketing on screen or in shopping mall. Quantifying such data later for the purpose of statistical enumeration abstracts from but nonetheless can respect their initial qualitative description by audiences.

Within causalist marketing studies, attitudes are events, preferably quantifiable effects of advertising. But the first minutes of a focus group or interview show that participant attitudes to a product are frequently culturally complex beliefs containing evaluations of product properties. In our research on fast food Internet branding, Asian students responded in terms evoking distance from their diverse perspectives in Malaysia to Coffee Bean's resolutely Western website online:

> viewing screen content, even the "price (of the cake) is too painful to look at" (female Indian): "culturally I don't find it close because I'm a Chinese" (male): it "doesn't welcome me," it "looks very generic" (female Malay): "it doesn't build that relationship you would want to build with your company" (female Indian).

We shall focus on local horizons of understanding global branding, consumer constructions (or reception) of media marketing content traveling often from West to East: fast food, higher education, telecommunications and tourist destination advertising. Marketing on screen can take concrete shape in shopping malls: we consider their exploration as immersive recreation or duty. Our methodology develops in detail marketing's productive use of reader reception theory. For the latter model of understanding texts, drawing on phenomenology, has become "one of the driving forces of the 'postmodern turn' in marketing and consumer research" (Brown, 2004: 209).

Media marketing reception theory (that is, inspired by hermeneutic phenomenology—or philosophically founded accounts of the process wherein people come to understand the world) holds that audiences of consumers engage with such selling on screen in a seven fold process of comprehension and consensus or criticism. Hermeneutics analyzes the "character of (audience) understanding as projection" (Heidegger, 1985: 218) in which cognitive "structural givens" are "actualized by the reader" (Mueller-Vollmer, 1985: 187) in viewing. We always already ("pre-cognitively" before making further judgment) see the world around us as instantiating types of phenomena and project or anticipate likely events accordingly. "Understanding" denotes or "covers all projection of meaning in a situation" (Ricoeur, 1981: 107).

Consumers, we shall show:

i) *Absorb* (marketing screen content)—immersing themselves while always already simultaneously

ii) *Anticipating* (its narrative)—or "projecting" likely events from a horizon of generic understanding of the text as an instance of a type so that they can

iii) *Articulate* (integrate content)—in a "hermeneutic circle" of understanding and intrinsic interest in the story they are constructing—enabling them to

iv) *Align* (with narrative agents)—identifying with their activity as a reason for

v) *Appropriating* (screen marketing)—to form consensually a scenario of "self as consumer" or they instead experience:

vi) *Alienation* (distance themselves)—in a "depth hermeneutics" of critical (citizenship invoking)

vii) *Analysis*—rejecting the text's transparent, apparently unproblematic, offer of "accommodation." *Apathy*—may be expressed by the tired or those traumatized by events elsewhere. But where such a response was signaled in our research (e.g. on place branding) it was thinly disguised alienation.

Understanding marketing processes our "anticipation of meaning" (Harindranath, 2009) from a perspective. This hybrid model of being a media user draws not only on an account of consumers "projecting" meaning (anticipating content from a horizon of understanding) in reception theory but from ideas about "identification" and its failure (alignment and alienation) in screen theory. We shall consider below how marketing reception theory brings together two non-positivist traditions of studying audiences and readers to form an account of consumer citizen responses to advertising.[5] Audiences of consumers simultaneously anticipate or infer narrative while absorbing or immersing themselves in screen content. Thereby constructively active they are equally constrained by their position on necessarily limited cultural horizons of comprehension from whose content they draw in perceiving a meaning for marketing. Through articulating or integrating the stories of screen mediated advertising viewers entertain an intrinsic interest in identification *of* content. Aligning or identifying *with* characters they have thereby partially constructed becomes a rationale for "purchasing" meaning. Here marketing secures its prescribed reading ("We buy this brand!") in consumers positioning themselves with its perspective on products. Audiences appropriate these narrative scenarios—with a "fusion of cultural horizons" informing their identities in a "stylization of life." Or they become alienated, conceptually/culturally distancing their consuming selves to exhibit critical citizens in a discourse of depth hermeneutics analytical of perceived power. "Critique rests on the moment of *distanciation*" (Ricoeur, 1981: 110) (emphasis in the original).

*Global Advertising* aligns with theorists who take consumer culture seriously on board ship. Like Schembri and Sandberg's earlier (2002) work on the "interpretive approach" to consumption, marketing reception theory resists the investigator's "attitudinal construct" (193). Instead, it defines branded selling and service in terms of experience interpreted within the consumer's diverse horizons of understanding, as contributing to the latter's culturally shaped sensibility. We thereby "aspire towards putting consumer experience back into consumer research" (195).

In these pages we follow Beckett and Nayak (2008) to acknowledge marketing's "attempt to subjectivize the consumer through the construction of forms of identity with which consumers are encouraged to identify" (300). Marketing narratives bear prescriptive readings as stories of product-enhanced existence, scenarios of self-immersion for audiences interpreting and identifying with persons of interest on screen as "active participants in production and consumption" (305). Media marketing aligns implied audience consumers with its narrative agents, so that the former (after identifying) appropriates the latter's product-oriented activity. A necessary but not sufficient condition of media audiences connecting to such advertising's *mise-en-scène* is that the latter be experienced as culturally close, enabling consumers both to comprehend and consent, to recognize and be recruited. Real consumers move away from marketing seen as misanthropic.

Marketing reception theory argues against positivist managerialism for whom successful advertising is instrumental in *causing* favorable attitudes. Instead, employing phenomenology's model of the interpreting consumer, marketing narratives are read here as providing *reasons* for audiences to appropriate the former's product focused scenarios to shape consumer lives. Discourses of "cause" and "reason" are distinct: causes have effects, whereas reasons *justify*.

## INDUCTIVIST ATTITUDES AND INTERPRETIVIST APPROPRIATION/ALIENATION

Inductivist causalist communication studies draw their understanding of research method from a particular account of scientific thought. According to the latter dubious narrative, the relationship between screen events, audiences and their behavior is deductive-nomological: that is to say, as in studying the physical world, these events and subsequent behavior are considered to invariably bear a symmetrical law-based predictive and explanatory relationship to each other. Just as a scientist can assert that (other things being equal) wherever gases are heated they expand, so it would be claimed increased advertising of a product causes or leads to its augmented acquisition.

In the terms adopted by this marketing pseudo-science, audience attitudes are a core link in the mythical causal chain: they constitute the responses to screen stimuli within the media–attitude–behavior sequence. But in this "happy marketing" scenario there is a fundamental fault. Attitudes cannot fill their conceptual role because, as argued, they are not events but beliefs: "one's 'attitude' suggests a more stable end-state" (Nabi and Krcmar, 2004: 295).[6]

A person's attitudes are sensibly said to be "held" (Bilandzic and Busselle, 2008: 508) or even "strengthened" (ibid.: 512): fundamental "attitudes provide a more holistic perspective for interpreting a film" (ibid.: 526). Selection of media content is argued to result in "maintenance of various attitudes" (Slater, 2007: 289). Yet the positivist myth of attitudes as predictable events analogous to the latter's occurrence in the hard sciences continues to appear: one researcher is "examining whether exposure to television network news programming can predict racial attitudes" (Dixon, 2008: 321). A research focus on predicting events can reduce data avowedly discerned ("attitudes") to questionnaire responses ("judgments"). "Although no empirically-robust meta-analysis of documented attitudes towards the police exists, many investigations have pointed to the role of socio-demographic factors in predicting such judgments" (Weatherall et al., 2007: 139). Attitudes are relational beliefs evaluating a conceptually constructed focus of thought [although it is possible to display a "disinterested attitude" (Charters, 2006: 247)], not caused events.

Instead a phenomenology of 'indigenous understanding' (Hutchinson et al., 2008) can come to the aid of positivism. Attitudes are a type or genre of belief. Establishing their content through talk (as in focus groups or interviews) sets out our perspectives on objects, persons or places—the cultural *horizons of understanding* from which we view.[7] In a *fusion of horizons* (Gadamer, 1975) audiences articulate advertising's perspectives evaluating a product-enhanced life. They project (or anticipate and achieve) a meaning for marketing on screen. In doing so we are *aligning* (or identifying) with narrative agents also making sense of the events in which they are immersed. We can *appropriate* the latter's mediated behavior as a scenario adding meaning to our lives—or become *alienated*, distancing ourselves from questionable marketing discourses on screen. In either case, our thought "actively" engages with media content—rather than being passively caused.

In short, attitudes are how we see our surroundings, construe our context—evaluatively. When successful in communicating, media marketing shares with consumers would be "persuasive readings" or evaluative perspectives on products. Consumers articulate, appropriate or are critically alienated from a media marketed package of meaning. This cultural fusion of horizons functions as a basis for people's deciding to upgrade life—the focus for a media psychology of persuasion. Writing about consumer responses to product placement in television sitcoms, Stern and Russell argue that the "presence of numerous placed products ensures that the plot includes a consumption scenario aimed at persuading consumers to develop favorable product attitudes" (2004: 373). "Persuasion" leading to "favorable product attitudes" does not consist of media causes and consumer effects. Rather it is a reason-giving process in which audiences respond to culturally close content by aligning with narrative agents on screen, appropriating (purchasing conceptually) the latter's mediated behavior as adding meaning to consumer lives, to the person they are.

Consumers consent (rather than being caused) to share media advertising's horizons of understanding from which a product-enhanced life is evaluated. People appropriate marketing's preferred perspectives through "intricate" interpretive processes (Ringberg and Reihlen, 2008: 173). They "buy" *modus operandi*. Our attitude can indeed be: on screen they are doing that, why not us?

Real attitudes, then, have no place in sequences of events relating product marketing to material purchases. They are beliefs open to justification not brought about by causes. Marketing can define "attitudes" in terms of events as propensities or tendencies to behave: this offers a basis for predicting purchasing activity. But reductive operationalizing of this tricky concept by relating it to that which is public and observable denies it a place in important subjective accounts of buying. Attitudes are private, albeit on occasion acquired through appropriation of shared media marketing. Attitudes are interpretive, horizons of understanding from which we view the world: they are our culturally informed perspectives. Ringberg and Reihlen complain that scales "used to measure attitudinal dispositions of informants do not reveal whether informants in fact make similar sense of stimuli": "little regard is given to the presence of divergent interpretive processes among consumers. Instead, such positivist research assumes that marketing communication is readily 'downloaded' and consumer reaction is based on their attitudinal variance (likings or dislikings)" (2008: 175, 176). However, "attitudinal" "reaction" brings interpretation to bear on "stimuli":

> interpretation and subsequent intersubjectivity (between sender and receiver) is an accomplishment that involves the receiver's interpretive strategies, which emerge in interaction between internalized socio-cultural patterning and cognitive (self-reflexive, creative) processes (ibid.: 177). Issues in interpretation lead to forming new horizons.

Attitudes are sometimes fundamental beliefs: they can form the frameworks within which we consider our lives. From the perspective of studies in political economy, these horizons of understanding serve interests: they are restricted or advanced by those in power for profit.

In summary, quantification rests on conceptualizing data, considered and shaped quite differently in the two analytical perspectives of positivism and phenomenology. Here we draw on research participants' horizons of understanding to write our "theorized storylines" (Maclaran and Hogg, 2008: 132). We shall aim in these pages at producing philosophically justified and theory engaged accounts of particular consumers reading media marketing. Our interpretations must fit the latter's articulating or interpreting of meaning: in turn, the empirical details of readings by the researched should enrich and enlighten the hermeneutic perspective involved in our writing.

## A Brief Philosophical Psychology of Media Marketing Consumption From Audience Absorption to Appropriation/Alienation

From the analytical perspective of hermeneutic media marketing reception theory, which we shall now outline more widely, consumers (who from time to time become a critical citizenry) construct or interpret advertising narratives drawing on their wider cultural awareness. Consenting audiences enter often branded space. The complex process of their cognitive response is as follows.

(i) Audiences *Absorb* Content

Consumers immerse themselves in the screen narratives of marketing as a (more or less) special "discursive space" (Wood, 2006: 84) and time of branding separate from their material (or three-dimensional) everyday activity. Their doing so is comparable to participating in play (ludic)—a disparate game-like involvement in distinct experience which distracts (or extracts) from mundane life. Audiences absorb themselves within a discursive "diversion" (Caillois, 1961: 9).

For example, a Malaysian television advertisement for Coca-Cola showed young people playing basketball in a busy Kuala Lumpur city centre street while drinking the global brew. Respondents in research groups watching this media marketing positioned themselves not only epistemologically but onto-logically (perceptually, but also absorbing themselves in the location). They shared the players' view of a world in which the watching audience becomes immersed: viewing Coca-Cola's advertising narrative "makes me feel like I'm one of them" (female Indian).

(ii) Audiences *Anticipate* Narrative

From the first moment of absorbing themselves in a media marketing nar-rative, consumers anticipate its likely development as an instance of a type of storytelling to which they are well accustomed. They "project," that is, the probable path of events on screen from a horizon of generic understanding, deploying in such understanding cultural discourses which they have accumulated. Interpretation is "working-out" "possibilities projected in understanding" (Heidegger, 1985: 221).

> Even the freshest and most original perception, whose ramifications still seem entirely unforeseeable, is what it truly was only when its consequences have been worked out, its connections with existing knowledge estab-lished, and when it has been absorbed into the medium of intersubjective understanding. (...) all cognition is first what it is only as re-cognition.
>
> (Gadamer, 1985: 279–80)

During our research on responses to a global telecommunications provider, media marketing its services in Malaysia, we showed one of the company's television advertisements featuring a search for the best household location to install a domestic Internet connection. When you initially see the narrative on screen, commented a female Chinese consumer (who was an event organizer outside her role as a research participant), "you won't know what happens next. So that you have to imagine first (...) you will think many things, 'Eh, what (are) they going to do?' (...) You will just watch it out. Eh, actually, what's going (to) happen?"

(iii) Audiences *Articulate* Stories

Pursuing a "hermeneutic circle" of understanding, consumers aim at assembling parts of the narrative together, relating confirmed projections to form a consistent story of events on screen. In doing so, they are guided by their wider generic awareness of the type of media marketing they are viewing and hence the likely integrated narrative to emerge from their interpretive activity. Responding to a Malaysian National Day television marketing nar-rative using the metaphor of building a boat to portray the necessity of long term goals in building a nation, a male Indian graduate student described his cognitive process of thinking through a coherent account of content:

> we have to watch it again and again and again (...) the message there, we cannot grab it easily. We have to think and then we have to do the link,

you know. And then we have to do our own conclusion, and finally we also think "Why, suddenly, the boat sinks?"

Initial anticipation of narrative on screen together with subsequently further articulating "indeterminate" content constitute a "filling-out" of the text or its "concretization." Ingarden writes:

> The places of indeterminacy are removed in the individual concretizations in such a way that a more or less close determination takes their place and, so to speak, "fills them out." This "filling-out" is, however, not sufficiently determined by the determinate features of the object and can thus vary with different concretizations.
>
> (Ingarden, 1985: 193).

Audiences then either:

(iv) *Align* (with narrative agents)

Consumers identify with the media marketing narrative agents they view on screen both in constructing a coherent account of diegetic (the story's) events and in attaining a brand or particular product with its connotation of accomplishment. *Doubly aligned*, they have gained multiple reasons for appropriating the surrounding scenario of attainment on show.

We absorb ourselves in brandscapes on screen media or set out in shopping malls. Within these spaces and times enabling immersive identification we can share people's "human interest" in pursuing coherent accounts of purchase: aligning with them "you want to see from the beginning to the end because there is human interest inside (...) to make you listen and hear what they say (...) the human interest inside the advertisement, that makes us really feel inside" (female Malay).

(v) and *Appropriate* (screen marketing)

Appropriating or consensually connecting to the marketing narrative on screen, audiences form an identity of consuming selves, *personae* focused on purchasing products/brands promoted. "Ultimately, what I appropriate is a proposed world," renovating "self-understanding in front of the work" (Ricoeur, 1981b:142–43) whether book or branding.

Aligning with an Internet address which "speaks to me personally," identifying with similarity on screen, a female Indian undergraduate research participant regards herself as both recognizing and being recognized by media marketing's address. She is enabled with good reason to "relate" to (appropriate) a hybrid Pizza Hut website to inform her identity (shape her shopping) "because I do like curried chicken and everything": it "makes me happy (...) because it speaks to me personally."

or audiences experience:

(vi) *Alienation* (distance themselves)

Skeptically assessing the chain of events they have constructed on screen, advertising's audiences can distance themselves from the narrative in a depth hermeneutics for cultural-political reasons. As the critical theorist Habermas reminds us, "every consensus in which interpretation terminates stands under the suspicion of having been pseudocommunicatively compelled" (1985: 314). In securing their stance apart from media marketing, consumers may represent themselves as citizens at odds with the civic implications of advertising's pre-scriptive definition of "success." Shopping now carries social anxieties over "eco-politics" and food pollution (Mort, 2000: 280).

Audiences can "voice out," distancing themselves from an advertisement because of ethical concerns appropriate to ethnic citizenship. Responding to phone network branding showing a Chinese family reunion dinner where all are using the global company's routes to call elsewhere, Chinese research participants occupied a "horizon of suspicion" critical of this media marketing:

> "it seems like the relationship between the family is not very close" (female Chinese); "(when) the whole family is taking the dinner, you're supposed … don't answer the phone"; "a bit offensive, it breaks the (Chinese) tradition. … You really have to focus on the dinner, not on the phone" (laughter) (male Chinese); it is "out of your culture" (male Eurasian); "you better go out to talk with your friends lah!" (female Chinese).

(vii) and *Analyze* (narrative)

Discovering their distance or alienation from screen branding, consumers reject the text's transparency or an apparently unproblematic accommodation. Instead, they turn to a diagnosing of its signs as symptoms. Reading more as critical citizens than as consenting consumers they "voice out" an emancipatory understanding which can be called (following Ricoeur) "depth hermeneutics."

Viewing a television marketing "infomercial" for the Malaysian identity card with a Malay civil servant lecturing at/to a studio audience an alienated male Indian member of a focus group argued that it is likely that those at home "don't see the connection" between the advertisement's initial images of state sub-versive terrorism, the resulting registration of citizens and the subsequent studio presentation on identity cards. The hermeneutic circle of understanding is in trouble.

What is the story being told here, one of forming a political or personal identity? Is it a narrative of developing citizenship (rights) or consumer cards (records): that "we" are thus now "recognized as a Malaysian citizen (…) we have the rights or (do) they want to show the importance of MyKad (…) you can put your data" (male Indian) on this digital technology? In this analytical reading an Indian Malaysian distances himself and resists immediate absorp-tion in the seamless flow of a Malay television presenter's audience address. The former's interrogation of this narrative can be characterized as engaging in a depth hermeneutics of disclosing the mediated ambivalence of this marketing: spoken at/ to by a Malay as a consumer, he speculates on his rights as Indian citizen.

## THE AGORA-BRANDSCAPES-CONSUMER CITIZENS (ABC) MODEL

Audiences aligning with advertising narrative agents in media marketing's more substantial stories enter agora on screen—the diegetic spaces and times of narratives in which people purchase products as consumers (with reasons) and citizens (with rights). Agora are often brandscapes—or branded landscapes where consumers are audio-visually equipped as "cultural engineers" (Csaba and Bengtsson, 2006: 123) to construct the corporate source of products as aesthetically rich, remarkable or merely reliable. Coca-Cola dissolves contradiction, enabling "impossible" action.

Advertising's agora, that is, frequently constitute branded space and time on screen media or shopping mall addressing and absorbing audiences in an immediately anticipatory moment. As prolonged narratives of place they succeed in accommodating consumer citizens who articulate an understanding of content to completion, subsequently appropriating scenarios on screen or in shopping mall to shape their sense of themselves. "Brand architectures" (Muzellec and Lambkin, 2009) delineate brandscape agora with their capacity to tell a tale and host consumer citizens.

Immersed in a brandscape we are absorbed in a profit oriented corporate discourse of space and time which supports us in constructing a screen mediated or shopping mall narrative of consumption. As the "principal concept of advertising" (Baudrillard, 2000: 236), brands create a "vital link" both in practice and theory between economy and culture (Ram, 2008: 430).

The necessary conditions of continuing immersion, we have noted, include both cultural contiguity (allowing identification *of* content) and consumer consensus (identification *with* views expressed). We are present not only as persons with reasons for being there (our being able to identify) but as persons with rights—as potentially critical citizens. And we appropriate or "connect to" these brandscapes, applying them to life beyond the agoric spheres of selling, both buying their practice and signaling dissent. "We define brand connection as the extent to which a consumer has incorporated a brand into his or her self-concept" (Rindfleisch et al., 2009: 1).

Consumers, then, appropriate brandscapes to shape and inform their lives, a relationship between screen and self which can be theorized as inter-personal (e.g. between a transnational telephone company's friendly "Yellow Fellow" icon and the individual subscribers): "brands can be conceptualized (as) entities with personality characteristics very similar to the human characteristics to which consumers can relate" (Veloutsou, 2009: 127). Brandscapes achieving a quasi-personal relationship with consumers (e.g. through evoking trust) can slice through a media marketing "sea of sameness" (De Chernatony, 2009: 102).

In the process of appropriating brandscapes, consumers "construct and perform identities and self-concepts, trying out new roles and creating their identity within, and in collaboration with, brand culture" (Schroeder, 2009: 123): "strong brands constantly develop prescriptive models" (ibid.: 124) for consumer appropriation in ideal life-styles. Hence, identification between consumers and (their constructions of) marketing's narrative agents may be in terms of the former's "actual identity or ideal 'aspirational' identity" (Smith and French, 2009: 217).

Brand communities of persons can form who identify with the use of a product and hence its appropriation in living. They may be people with their "own idiosyncratic backgrounds and reasons to join the community" (e.g. seeking quality reassurance or expressing their involvement with a product) (Ouwersloot and Odekerken-Schroder, 2008: 571). Communities need not be formal. Their primary focus can be in shared identification with the narrative agent(s) of media marketing (e.g. with the Yellow Fellow icon used by the transnational telecommunications company).

On the other hand, following our connection to a brand, it can, of course, disappoint with "brand misconduct": "brands do not always behave according to consumers' expectations" (Huber et al., 2009: 132). When pressed and critically analytical of media marketing, alienated consumers can remember they are citizens with duties and rights, turning to political brands to affirm positions. "Consumers can use political brands to affirm their civic duty" (Smith and French, 2009: 216).

Consumers may appropriate an aura (or self-image) of distinctiveness from a brand narrative. Brandscapes, in turn, "seek their aura of distinction (...) through allusions to time and place" (e.g. heritage) (Alexander, 2009: 551). Tourist destinations and universities which we discuss in this volume construct distinctive "aura of authenticity" (ibid.).

Places themselves are "increasingly conceptualized as brands" to be media marketed and locations within those defined spaces constructed as products to be consumed by tourists and travelers—the "commodification of selected attributes of the place" (Medway and Warnaby, 2008: 641). Place branding has developed as an "application of branding techniques to develop place images" (Iversen and Hem, 2008: 604). Such "destination branding" (Balakrishnan, 2009: 611) represents Malaysia as a tourist destination, an extended agoric brandscape of activities with which "real life" tourists can identify and subsequently appropriate to inform holiday and travel scenarios.

In place branding, "destination image" is said by Iversen and Hem to be "defined as an attitudinal concept consisting of the sum of beliefs, ideas, and impressions that a tourist holds about a destination" (2008: 609). Here "attitudes" are clearly beliefs, probably provided as a basis for rational purchase, not part of a causal chain presupposed by the logic of positivist methodology.

*Global Advertising* is a cognitive inquiry into the "brand to end customer link" (Glynn, 2009: 137)—the audience's processing of mediated product meaning. Constructing such a philosophical psychology of making sense from the screen furthers integration with political economy's focus on the semantic pursuit of profit in media marketing studies of guided consumption.

Brodie and De Chernatony argue that if brands exist as "cultural, ideological and political objects" (2009: 97–8), then brand researchers need appropriate theoretical tools for their study in addition to the customary armory of ideas in marketing management. Literary and philosophical models of consumer understanding and sometimes civic response are methodological requirements, for the "consumer perspective on brand architecture is significantly under-researched" (Devlin and McKechnie, 2008: 654). Drawing upon these models of making sense, we take an interpretive approach to the "miasma of meaning surrounding a brand" (Alexander, 2009: 552). From this research perspective, "brand image results from (cognitive) processing" (Burmann et al., 2009: 115).

Consumers, we shall see in subsequent chapters, not only project narrative content on screen, assembling their subjective story of events, but actually add information to Internet sites celebrating or criticizing marketing: "branding on the Internet exemplifies participation and co-creation of meaning" (Christo-doulides, 2009: 142) from cultures of consumption. Sequential stages of screen response are allied: confirmed projections support perceptions of closeness and ease identification. Audiences value finding familiarity on screen (Devlin and McKechnie, 2008: 660).

One can generalize and predict in marketing (e.g. where consumers identify with a narrative agent in media marketing they will appropriate or connect to the brand). However, the cognitive sequence between identifying and appro-priation is not ineluctably causal but informed by reason. "Belief and attitude formation" (Power and Whelan, 2008: 587) is a cognitive process in which giving reasons is appropriate rather than a matter of causation. Bringing a brand into our lives—sometimes selectively identifying (with) and appro-priating its scenario of success in consumption—manufactures a theatre of trust, at least until the doubting citizenry arrive.

Is the "brand belief-behavior relationship" (Winchester et al., 2008: 553) indeed a process in which reason-giving is appropriate? Further research, write Winchester and his colleagues, could "investigate what caused (a consumer) belief change, such as exposure to advertising, word-of-mouth or direct mail/sales activities" with each a "*possible cause* of the difference between negative and positive beliefs" (ibid.: 567) (emphasis added). In writing of "causation," researchers sensitive to methodological issues (and who is now not?) need to specify whether they are hard causalists or merely hermeneutically inaccurate interpretive theorists writing of reasons.

Causalists write curious prose in their bid to incorporate the human genesis of reasoning within a positivist framework. In a marketing study where methodology emphasizes effects from stimulus "priming" ["All partici-pants saw the target advertisement first in order to maximize the effect from the priming task" (Raju et al., 2009: 859)], the authors inform us that: "commitment researchers have assumed higher commitment to lead to more counter-argumentation without further examination of the mechanisms behind this effect" (Raju et al., 2009: 851). Perhaps where research was less obfuscated by the need to determine a cause and effect relationship between commitment and consequence (attitude!) the "mechanism" would be obvious: *reasoning.*

## MARKETING'S SEARCH FOR SELF-CONSCIOUSNESS

As a philosophical response to "marketing's search for self-consciousness" (Kocamaz, 2009: 86) hermeneutic phenomenology offers a spatial model of both the value of theory and visual communication between media or mall and self-immersing consumer which is particularly appropriate to global cross-cultural marketing. Tadajewski (2008), for instance, writes of how theory "sensitizes" or "restricts how we think" (465), a perspectival image of thought (or its absence in amnesia) captured by the metaphor "horizons of understanding" (Gadamer, 1975, 1976).

> The horizon is the range of vision that includes everything that can be seen from a particular vantage-point. Applying this to the thinking mind, we speak of narrowness of horizon, of the possible expansion of horizon, of the opening up of new horizons etc. (...) the working out of the hermeneutical situation means the achievement of the right horizon of enquiry for the questions evoked.
>
> (Gadamer, 1985: 269)

Hermeneutic marketing theory is not only a horizon of understanding consumers but can employ that spatial metaphor in analyses. For advertising builds in a brandscape (or agora) a profit-enhancing horizon of understanding products, a cultural space and time which it seeks to persuade consumers to occupy, to make it their own or "appropriate" (Gadamer, 1975) through a "proliferation of individualities, of the number of 'yous' on offer" (Mort, 2000: 278).

A marketing message moves to meet and be measured by the cultural horizons of its recipients. In our turn, spatially positioned on, and informed by our occupying the latter, we "project" (Gadamer, 1975) and articulate the former's narrative development in a "hermeneutic circle" (ibid.) of understanding. People proceed to interpret advertising's persuasive stories.

In this geography of understanding marketing, advertising strategies produce and tabulate sometimes all too familiar cultural horizons from which material acquisitions can be viewed. The significance of an object varies according to its "placement" (Hebdige, 2000: 131). But in the epistemological play of consumption and the creation of meaning, an audience's "transverse tactics" (De Certeau, 2000: 163) may refuse or reuse those horizons to see anew, to make a point.

Certain phone network branding was a "bit offensive, it breaks the (Chinese) tradition." Locating consumers within their cultural traditions or upon their horizons of anticipating understanding, is at the core of conceptualising audience response to marketing.

# 2 Beyond Attitudes: To the Audience Itself!

## Understanding Consumers: Interpretive Inductivism

### *With Khor Yoke Lim*

> The high context dependency of attitude judgments and weak attitude-behavior relationships (...) give rise to ever more sophisticated attempts to find people's "true" attitudes. In accounting for consumer behavior how can one be "highly sensitive to the specifics of the present," the "situated nature of human cognition."
>
> (Schwarz, 2006: 20)

*Global Advertising* focuses on readers forming consumer *attitudes*. We allow that term a richer meaning as denoting evaluative belief evident in the audience's aligning with (sharing) or alienation (separating) from their perception of prescriptive marketing narrative. We thereby transcend the reductionist treatment of the concept by inductivists who do not first recognize consumer interpretation of data as implicit in the process of audiences forming attitudes.

We also resist the inductivist presumption that establishing a positive statistical correlation is evidence of a cause and effect relationship, specifically between media advertising and attitude. "Consumer Responses to Advertising" (Olney et al., 1991), for example:

> examines the mediating roles of intervening variables along a hierarchical chain of effects in which advertising content influences emotions and attitude toward the ad, which, in turn, influence viewing time (...) we assume a forward recursive flow of effects from ad content through emotions and attitudinal responses to viewing behaviour.
>
> (Olney et al., 1991: 441)

Instead, we promote a meaningfully productive audience, far from passive in processing media.

Discussion of the subsequent relationship between attitude and action (e.g. purchase) remains with others in advertising research. Nonetheless, the account of consumers developing attitudes enabled by a hermeneutic phenomenology of their coming to understand branding emphasizes the interpretive structuring of all experience. The "constructive nature" (Allen, 2002: 519) of embodied practice, that is, characterizes gaining a purchase on meaning or a product as fitting either into pre-existing patterns of awareness. Audiences immerse in brandscapes, aligning with product use, knowing they can smoothly accommodate the narrative in understanding and the brand in life. Marketing which recognizes a consumer culture is easily made at home.

In positivist marketing studies, attitudes are "hypothetical constructs invented by researchers to explain phenomena of interest" (Schwarz, 2006: 19). Attitudes and their alteration are considered not only to be effected by advertising but as events to themselves cause action. Where explaining activities is said to be possible, that behavior is regarded as possessing a symmetrical predictability. But attitudes are beliefs, not causally potent events, often highly culturally specific in character.

Positivist "attitudes," alternatively, may be "defined as generalized predispositions to behave toward an object" (Park and MacInnis, 2006: 16). Thus, via one deductive route or another as "generalized predispositions" they permit consumer behavior to be analyzed, accounted for, and predicted in terms of constant, continuing or causal conjunctions of advertising, attitude and action.

Does this mean that attitudes are beliefs? If so, they may be consistent over time and hence states of mind announced in person-related evaluative propositions ("I believe that x is good"). But conceptually or logically as non-events they can possess no causal efficacy. Speaking about our attitudes tells others about our ethical or other preferences in the world around us.

Do these "attitudes," on the other hand, consist of recurring activity, general "predispositions" or tendencies to behave predictably towards brands or products (e.g. preferring to purchase them)? But then by "explaining" consumer behavior in terms of an attitude one is simply bringing that activity within a summative generalization. It occurs (or is predictable) as instantiating a pattern.

"One wonders whether *attitudes*, defined as generalized predispositions to behave toward an object, can or should be expected to predict stronger forms of behaviors" (e.g. "involvement in brand communities") (emphasis in original) (Park and MacInnis, 2006: 16). If favorable or unfavorable attitudes towards a product are general tendencies to (respectively) purchase or not to purchase that "object" then establishing these patterns may well have predictive power in regard to anticipating consumer "behaviors" (whether "stronger" or otherwise). But such deductive reference to attitudes lacks explanatory status. Why are they buying? Through what mental process have they travelled to arrive at such a purchasing decision?

Defining (mental) "attitudes" as modes of behavior is a characteristic feature of positivism. Agnostic as to that which we really need to investigate (the "black box" of mental processes before purchasing) this research methodology relates and reduces the "construct" (Schwarz, 2006: 19) to observable (quantifiably measurable) behavior. In this definitional deflation, personal attitudes become public tendencies to act. The result of such conceptual confusion has long been that:

> it is quite unclear what the attitude measurements mean, and how they are to be related to other phenomena. In the face of this self-generated problem, the (social) psychologist resorts further to "empirical" studies of the relation between attitude and behavior. But these in turn are difficult to interpret, in the absence of the conceptual analysis.
>
> (Harre and Secord, 1972: 302)

In *Global Advertising* screen user theory (emerging from an account of thinking about reader reception inspired by hermeneutic phenomenology) is drawn upon to conceptualize the cognitive process in which consumers appropriate (or are alienated from) marketing on media and in malls. We *interpret* their understanding as a conceptual foundation for *inductive* (generalizing) accounts.

## BEYOND THE ATTITUDE CONSTRUCT TO CONSUMER APPROPRIATION/ALIENATION

Is the cost of a rigorous ("scientific") research methodology the methodological (and methodical) suspension of believing that consumers have subjective thought processes? In focusing upon the advertising-attitude-action nexus, we hold that advertising does not cause audiences to form *attitudes* (whatever they are). For a more conceptually plausible view is that consumers *appropriate* meaning from marketing in their lives—or distance themselves in criticism.

Drawing on reader reception theory (grounded in earlier hermeneutic phenomenology), we wish to open up a "contestatory space" (Brownlie and Hewer, 2007: 44) to consider positivism's "opprobrious instrumentalism" (Bradshaw and Firat, 2007: 30). We argue for consumers actively immersing themselves in screen media (and shopping mall) as a seven-fold cognitive process. Aspects of this activity (e.g. refreshing a sense of self in shopping whether online or offline) are widely acknowledged to occur. But through interpreting consumption as a structured subjective process, unlike proponents of the attitude construct, we are able to coherently accommodate cultural *specifics of the present*. Media marketing reception theory integrates concrete empirical evidence with abstract considerations of analysis (whose authorial sources are much cited below).

In many positivist studies of branding culture, the connection between narrative content on screen and its consuming audience is considered reductively as stimulus and response. They are quantitatively compared as variables. Within this prevailing paradigm of consumer research, advertising "targets" audiences: its "effects" on them, their reactions, are causal consequences. Thus the title of a recently published research monograph: *Targeted Advertising Unintended Effects.*[1]

From an alternative perspective of screen reception theory on media use, advertising is said to "address" consumers with a "preferred reading": space is left for (relatively autonomous) actual audiences to respond to its narrative "actively." There is no closed causal chain between screen content and consumer subjectivity. For this model, rather, reactions are reading or interpretation.

Viewing, in the second paradigm, is a "constructive process" (Goffey, 2008: 15). It is shaped pre-cognitively (or prior to perception) by past audience experience in their continually anticipating and articulating meaningful content on screen: expecting particular events, our subsequent goal in understanding is placing them within a coherent narrative. Some consumers align, or identify with, while others are antagonistic to (their perceptions of) media marketing's prescriptive reading. "Behind any hard statistical data there are always the cognitive and social processes by which responses are constructed" (Ling and Haddon, 2003: 261). In the present chapter, we consider audiences constructively reading multiple narratives of food branding on screen.

Productively appropriating reception theory for consumer studies was initiated by Scott (1994a, 1994b). Reading advertisements should be shown to be a goal-directed "process" (Scott, 1994b: 461) in which the reader's "recognition of the genre of a given text frames and guides the reading experience" (ibid.: 464). We further articulate this psychology in our narrative of consumer response to malls and media marketing.[2] Here we "flesh out" consumer readings of "fast food" sites offline/online in our empirical study of eating (Brownlie et al., 2005: 8).

## MEDIA MARKETING RECEPTION THEORY: A PHILOSOPHICAL FRAMING OF CONSUMPTION

Consumer studies and communication theory have pursued separate accounts of media response or distinct intellectual trajectories in analyzing screen audiences. Scott has set out how reader reception theory [initiated by Iser (1978) and Jauss (1982)] can play a pivotal role in the former.[3] In advancing media marketing reception theory we agree that consumer and reception theory be integrated. Here we seek to show this to be a valuable rapprochement by analyzing within its conceptual framework discursive responses to transnational "fast food" branding in Malaysia.

Reader reception theory was developed by way of phenomenology and hermeneutics. From the former philosophical discipline [especially Heidegger (1962) and Husserl (1973)] its early authors drew their account of *perceiving as projection.* The cumulative process, that is, wherein readers come to understand texts, from the very first moment of its commencing, involves them in the continuing activity of interpretive anticipating—projecting meaning (later assessed for its accuracy) on the basis of their generically informed expectation. A Chinese female participant in earlier research, we noted, responded to a telecommunications branding narrative: "you won't know what happens next. So that you have to imagine first (...) you will think many things, 'Eh, what (are) they going to do?'" Advertising texts are read knowledgeably as following formats, instantiating types. Projection can be a response to managed uncertainty in media marketing.

Drawing on hermeneutics for further insight [principally Gadamer (1975)], reception theory presents readers as located on cultural *horizons of understanding*. Seeing is seeing *as*. We perceive everything around us as an instance of a known type (be it object or person) and expect (or project) our experience to take shape accordingly. In the process by which they produce meaning for texts, the interpretively active audience's anticipation of events is (in) formed or shaped by occupying this vantage point of wider awareness. Recognizing its corporate source (e.g. Starbucks), we view a branding narrative from a horizon of expectation regarding content: we read it as instantiating a type or genre (Starbucks marketing). Research participants can "misidentify" authorship or category of advertising they see leading to innovative interpretation or mistakes.

Gadamer argues that reading not only conforms to historical horizons of understanding content but that it is holistic or follows a hermeneutic circle of understanding through integrating perceived details of a text. Furthermore, the reader appropriates the resulting meaning, shaping the semantic horizon from which they view their lives. In a recent research interview (Wilson, 2009), a cellphone user talks of an SMS (short message service) message, "making her day" (female Chinese).

Reception theory's metaphorical construction of "understanding" as an activity spatially positioned within horizons is particularly apposite when investigating consumers' responses to transnational media marketing. For this process can be read as a fusion of cultural horizons enabled by audience comprehension and authorial management of branding crossing distance in a "passage across thresholds" (Fornäs, 2002). Here, "glocal" communication experienced by audiences as culturally close supports the latter as consumers in articulating narrative meaning.

Marketing theory, then, can productively mobilize not only substantial research insight into screens mediating the world through edited but none the less absorbing narrative or story telling but reader reception theory. Inclusion of the latter is particularly significant in the context of analyzing Asian responses to Western branding on screen of product space and time. Consumers read/view, reconciling their immediate expectations and emerging events, forming their coherent stories of screen content. As a cognitive activity, reading becomes especially interesting to study in cross-cultural contexts when issues of audiences comprehending narrative emerge for reflection.

Predicting events, for instance, may not be possible within the cultural formation (or limits) of an audience's horizon of understanding: for one of our research participants, speculating on developments in a story used to brand telecommunications is way "out of my imagination" (male Chinese). Recruiting reception theory we engage with such otherwise "aberrant" disruptive detail in consumer cultural responses and place it within a model of audience comprehension. We are able to understand the discourse of "understanding" with its minutiae of accomplishment and failure.

Developing the media marketing reception model further in consumer theory as a schematic account of the process through which people respond to online screen marketing (and, as we shall show, shopping malls) we can point to the following structuring aspects of audience perception:

> becoming *absorbed*$_{(1)}$ in narrative, always already informed consumers simultaneously *anticipate*$_{(2)}$ events which they coherently *articulate*$_{(3)}$ into an account of content; they *appropriate*$_{(4)}$ the latter by reason of *identification*$_{(5)}$, shaping conception of the self or reject the prescriptive narrative in an *alienated*$_{(6)}$ reading which invariably *analyzes*$_{(7)}$ mediated marketing (see also Wilson et al., 2006).

Following philosophical hermeneutics, reception theory considers understanding to be play-like. The consuming process of producing meaning is immersive, involving our focused attention in moving "to and fro" across the text, as well as being goal-oriented in achieving sense. It is thus appropriate to apply accounts of the ludic (Caillois, 1961; Hans, 1981; Huizinga, 1970) to analyzing our discursive response to media branding. In their social-economic role as citizen-consumers (Livingstone et al., 2007) people engage in game-like reading of "familiar foreign places," the recognizable but "set apart" agora (gathering places) of screen advertising.

Consumers bring cultural resources, shared perspectives, to interpreting media marketing or view branded space and time from horizons of understanding. Metaphorically "hanging out," we absorb ourselves actively in media marketing's gathering places for subjectivity on screen (as viewers elucidating narrative events). Becoming immersed in well stitched (edited) text, consumers simultaneously anticipate and subsequently articulate (assemble) accounts of content (invariably product stories of equilibrium, disequilibrium, and re-equilibrium). Relating expectation to event, we can linger as well as be ludic in branded space (whether *imaginatively* on screen media or *in fact* in shopping mall). When completed, these assembled narratives are consensually appropriated to inform our identities—or alienate potential purchasers into critical, sometimes political, analysis.

In summary, consumer research, guided by marketing reception theory, can move beyond the problematic positivist construct of "attitude" to phenomenology's account of viewers appropriating or becoming alienated from advertising meaning (which they themselves have actively articulated). We can then discuss the process of personal judgment involved in our structured achievement of understanding marketing. Engaging with familiar brands on screen media or in shopping malls we both absorb and anticipate their content, building likely stories of how we will experience them, put to the test in purchase. Within such horizons of confirmation or occasional collision we form selves.

## On Entering "Fast Food" Offline/Online Branded Landscapes: "Pull Open the Glass Door, Feel the Rush of Cool Air!"

City space and time is sliced and diced, curved and squared, shaped by profitable brands. These urban brandscapes[4] cajole customers multi-culturally to enter, to celebrate product-oriented lives. Coffee Bean calls us to drink, comfortably: McDonald's markets chicken porridge: Pizza Hut promotes a spicy haven of selectivity: Starbucks sells immersion in caffeine, cyberspace and settee.

Global brandscapes have been often Western in origin. Nonetheless, within such Occidental shaping of the world, Chinese meets Indian and Malay. Constructing accounts of its technology or tourism Asia promotes its own brandscapes for the world to visit. Whether as political marketing of a nation or as selling a suburban university campus, branding promotes stories of its inhabitants' identity forming immersion. Brandscapes are presented as beneficially extracting people from mundane everyday life, not infrequently to invest locally in the global. Branding icons are guarantees of customer comfort, support and distraction from dull circumstances. In advertising's (sometimes paedocratic) places activity becomes more purposefully play-like.

Media branding on Internet sites of so-called "fast food" restaurants is open to hermeneutic analysis. Our discussion positions these advertising narratives more widely, placing them first in a context of academic and corporate discourse about branded products and places followed by our reflecting upon customer experience of media and mall brandscapes as recounted in consumer web logs. In a final section, we more fully consider focus group responses to websites bearing branded constructions of fast food. For gaining insight into how people cognitively process an understanding of their consumption experience has become a "primary task" (Schembri and Sandberg, 2002: 195).

Our discussion has a philosophical (conceptual) rather than empirical (fact-establishing) focus. We are not undertaking a substantial survey with questionnaire either of brand building or of blogged consumer experience. Nor are we seeking to establish the quantitative dimensions of popular brand presence. Our purpose is to delineate the culturally shaped subjective process of consumers constructing and consuming fast food brandscapes on screen media and in shopping mall as reliable relief from tedium. For where marketing address succeeds, its consumers immerse themselves (imaginatively or in fact) in advertising agora, in corporate generated gathering places from Coffee Bean to Starbucks, McDonald's to Pizza Hut in a play-like producing of meaning.

Our starting point for a "cognitive reception theory" (Hamilton and Schneider, 2002) has been *seeing*. Fundamentally distinct from positivism, phenomenology argues that perception is from its first moment of inception *interpretive*: we view the world whether of fast food or slow scholarship from a culturally shaped horizon of expectations which we subsequently confirm or find falsified. Responses can celebrate successfully recognizing regularity, with consumers satisfying expectations based on knowing a brand genre and its narratives. Anticipation is actualized—or it fails to be achieved. Branding builds (globally, locally) familiar horizons of understanding a product which we put to the test in purchasing. Below, a blogger records that McDonald's globally predicable local life-worlds do not prevent irregular service in local Singapore. Brandscape blogging constructs space and duration as places and times of adoration or antipathy.

We posit research questions of fast food mediated and mall brandscapes and their reception which are addressed in considering consumer blogs (search engine evidence generated online) and offline focus group discussion. Both are sources of stories, narratives of eating, drinking and much more (albeit that we cannot determine blog authorship or intended audience with the bio-graphical precision that we can obtain from participants in face-to-face-discussion).

Can advertising be said to construct agora—absorbing and gathering con-sumer citizens who meet, achieving their varying intrinsic or extrinsic goals in reliably familiar landscapes (Grayson, 1999)? How do audiences (particular publics) interpret these global agora from their local horizons of expectation and understanding? We address such questions through developing a sequen-tial phenomenology of consumer perception and in doing so seek to advance methodological pluralism in marketing theory and its subsequently guided research (Tadajewski, 2008b).

Considering varieties of "hanging out", we cross horizons of understanding to hermeneutics—to briefly reflect upon moments or aspects of being in these accommodating fast food spaces and times as securely play-like (Knight and Weedon, 2008: 131). Below, our sliced and diced consumer discourse substantiates abstract analysis of experience.

## Consumer Immersion in Mediated and Materialized Brandscapes: From Absorbed Anticipation to Alienated Analysis

Passing consumers cross blurred borders into familiar life-worlds or forms of everyday life constructed around absorbing food and drink in malls. Such pleasure focused cultural geographies of production and purchasing support immersion in easy escape, in a slightly innovative brandscape of beverages and burgers, drinks and donuts, pepsi and pizza with a daily special. Here, enjoy-able "predictability" is a "basic principle" providing "much peace of mind" (Ritzer, 2008: xv, 97).

On cellphone, Internet and television screens, stories selling space and time as sites for consumption brand these culinary places. Media marketing narra-tives engage in materially oriented hegemonic address to consumer citizens, seeking to align and reconcile the interests of all (Thompson and Arsel, 2004: 632). Such spatiotemporal securing of life-worlds formed around food asserts "structural conditions" (Kirchberg, 2007: 116) of eating, enabling but encircling our human agency. Inscribed in practice, these brandscapes extend beyond screens to take concrete shape in city center malls—disturbing the "very idea of unbranded space" (Klein, 1999: 105).

Our immersing in brandscapes from Coffee Bean culture to Starbucks connoisseurship may be imagined (when viewing) or take place in practice (when shopping). "Pull open the glass door, feel the rush of cool air!" (Schlosser, 2001: 3). Consumption across these familiar forms of life does not so much require our engaging in the diversified "work of culture" (Bennett, 2007). Instead, perceiving or purchasing product prioritizes culturally shaped seeing on the part of convinced customers entering branded places. Crossing borders, they absorb and are absorbed by surroundings on screen or in shopping mall—a story of immersion we can conceptualize as cognitive play.

We are licensed by generic fast food marketing to be a little ludic in these life-worlds. Our everyday understanding is to be let off the leash, freed from the frenetic, permitted to play in the "brand cocoon" (Klein, 1999: 441). Recognizing McDonald's as an "oasis," a "small escape from the hectic world" (Ritzer, 2008: 217), people enter, turning away (as prescribed in media advertising) from the tiresome sidewalk. We are counseled that Starbucks is a "Comforting Third Place" (quoted in Klein, 1999: 135) between city and domestic space. Customers expect and engage with familiar (but fresh) food in goal oriented moments of pursuing a gustatory story—the good sense of good food "supposed to taste the same every day everywhere in the world" (Leidner, 1993: 45).

Consumers cross borders: they move cognitively, constructively and continually back and forth between their already informed horizons of understanding the world and the cultural frameworks within which mediated or mall content is always embedded. Drawing on such past experience we project likely events: in McDonald's we establish anticipated narratives of consumption by eating "predictable food at predictable pricing" (Stankevich, 1997). Thereby building meaning, imagining and involved, people inhabit profit oriented, popular brandscapes.

The "foundation categories" (Kirchberg, 2007: 121) used in accounting for these consumer responses to predictable parcels of space and time need to be appropriate. They must accommodate contributions in blogs, focus groups and interviews of those addressed by advertising, statements where "human understanding takes a narrative form" (Smith and Sparkes, 2008: 5).

The stories people tell of product appropriation or perturbed alienation are circumscribed by and creatively shape speech embedded cultural horizons of understanding. These are "conceptual frames" (Krotz, 2007) mapping out a person's "sphere of subjectivity" (Moreno, 2006: 302) often internationally (Mansell, 2007). Informed by happy meal concepts we consume our ludic narratives.

## Consumers Crossing Borders: Projections of Product Purchase—(E)Scaping in Discourses of Eating and Drinking

Audiences of mediated marketing cross borders—those of culture and screen—into often branded landscapes featuring stories about people with products. Transition is aided by a cognitive sense of "their" space and time as also our "homeland" (Strelitz, 2002), a perception of cultural proximity between subjective spheres of knowledgeable audience and narrative agent. Entering a brandscape, briefly and a little bravely renouncing ordinary routines (Watson, 1997: 36), intended audiences anticipate a slightly special story on screen will emerge in their visual field of play-like speculation. McDonald's latest will be—mildly—marvelous. Immersion in the latter continues with those viewing and those viewed aligned, building a coherent sequence of events.

Media use is always "interpretive cognition" (Feldman, 2001: 129)—invariably we look at content from informed horizons of understanding with the hermeneutic ambition of achieving complete narrative comprehension. We "check out" stories. Cognitively, we project meaning: yet our conjectures can be refuted by events on screen. Sometimes, as fans or focus group members, consumers analyze a narrative's shaping of local culture in supporting the play of meaning construction (e.g. readings of a KFC Malaysia chicken rice advertisement as "straight" or "parody").

On other occasions, audiences sight a cultural distance between viewer/viewed frameworks of understanding "facts" seen on screen (e.g. in judging acceptable family behavior). Situated as "alternative readers" (Rauch, 2007: 995) they engage in denying a "culture of proximity" (Volkmer, 2008) or closeness between their own and people's perceptions on screen. Consumers may voice alienated analytical readings of text as artifact: would-be persuasive advertising is deconstructed as thoroughly as an unhealthy product. The construction of brandscapes in media or mall can be indeed a vigorous "site of struggle" (Jackson, 2004: 166).

Consumers cross borders imaginatively into advertising brandscapes on screen. Depending on the class, ethnic, gender and generational horizons from which they consider and conceive the world they tell different tales of their immersion. Where some see harmony, others perceive chaos: they project and posit meaning on screen, appropriate or are alienated by narrative. Dealing with the real, enthusiasts effortlessly order product online (e.g. Food.com in Liddle, 2000).

Media marketing "models of the world" (Brockmeier and Harre, 2001: 54) are tested in consumption. People enjoy multiple fast (e)scapes in shopping malls and represent their experience in varying ways. These post-Fordist spaces have been regenerated as sites incorporating multiple "social distinctions" (Salcedo, 2003: 1084). Located therein, KFC and McDonald's are recurring "invariant" (Mintz, 1997: 191) life-worlds of instant fare whose "fun" and "familiarity" are predictable, reassuring but now made "multilocal" (Watson, 1997: 37, 14) or "place-specific" (Lyons, 2005: 14).

Consumer or corporate constructed difference denies a "supermall of sameness" (Hall, 2006: 347). Seen daily from consumers' horizons of interpretative understanding, "foreign cultural" (Yan, 1997: 40) brandscapes seem increasingly local landscapes. Seated customers or passing purchasers engage in culturally specific preferred readings of these places' "appropriateness, comfort and correctness" (Watson, 1997: 9). Wandering or watching, entered in fact or in fantasy, branded culinary spaces in actual shopping malls and advertising's screen media confirm or conflict with our ludic expectation of continual motion, eating at speed, slowing down (Brewis and Jack, 2005: 51).

Brandscapes can become the focus of buyers' intense imagining. Emphasizing her would-like-to-be immersive eating in ludic time elsewhere than the everyday, a contributor to this chapter enthused over the predictable pleasures of McDonald's chicken nuggets: "always in my dream, I can feel the taste, the chewy feeling, the smell, the just nice(ly) hot" sensations (female Chinese).

A brand makes particular subject positions or ways of being possible (Brownlie and Hewer, 2007: 229). We can inhabit and speak with an ethnic and generational identity in celebration or criticism as gendered consumers from its well-defined roles. Shopping malls are "woven" (Holt, 2006: 300) from branded life-worlds or brandscapes as a "locus of meaning" (Heisley and Cours, 2007: 425). Safely immersed and satisfied customers deliver their stories of comforting success.

Reflecting on the locally branded Kopitiam (polyglot Malay-Hakka for "coffee shop"), a female Chinese contributor wrote of its familiar h(e)aven, its "cosy environment" as a place apart. In marketing narratives, we eat easily and drink what we expect: shown in a media screen brandscape a server's pouring coffee enables our projection and production of a pleasurable self.

Variegated "webs of brands" (Klein, 1999: xiii) seen in mall shops and on media screens are visited or viewed from a diversity of consumer perspectives. Important cultural values ("face saving, reciprocity and *guanxi*") are implicit in celebrating "brand orientation" (Qian et al., 2007: 216) among gift giving buyers at Chinese New Year. Local customer accounts of a brandscape's global regularity are told from differing horizons of understanding, thus "typing" the experience of being served in alternative ways, as gendered "social equality" or "subordination" (Mintz, 1997: 195).

Beijing burger buyers have appropriated McDonald's for their particular culturally informed practices (e.g. children's birthday parties) (Yan, 1997: 40). Economic and efficient consumption can be less significant motives than in the United States: people linger, "taking the 'fast' out of fast food" (ibid.: 72) in these gathering places, challenging the global advancing of increased speed.

For some Shanghai consumers, McDonald's food practices and furniture positioning can be used to "uphold traditional thought patterns, values, and ways of interacting" whereas for others the restaurant is an appropriate site to "explore new beliefs and ways of acting" (Eckhardt and Houston, 2002: 69). Promoted politically and for profit the globally branded civic geographies encircling our everyday immersion are locally "domesticated" (Caldwell, 2004)—in productive moments of absorption, anticipation, articulating meaning, appropriation or alienated attention defining who we are. People engage in "coffee cultural discourses" (Kjeldgaard and Ostberg, 2007: 175) of escape and expectation, of celebratory identification and critical detachment from Coffee Bean to Pizza Hut.

## Building and Being in Western Branded Landscapes: Vacuum "Beans" and Hybrid "Huts"

"KFC Branding Campaign to Spice Up Image" (Sperber, 2001: 6). Brandscape narratives often bear prescriptive readings emphasizing an active consumer's distinctive choice—in the direction of corporate profit. "Do what you gotta do" (McDonald's tag line in Petrecca and McDowell, 1997).

Building branded spaces places products firmly on the menu: "(KFC's) not going to be afraid of fried (food) anymore" (Benezra, 1995). "Brand personality" (Burke, 1994) is developed in these product stories mapping out people's solutions to issues of consumption. Such marketing makeovers may also construct national identity "by weaving political events and ideological messages" (Holden, 2001: 287) into media place branding (Askegaard and Kjeldgaard, 2007).

Addressing a population of consumers who are also citizens, Malaysian marketing of personable pleasure is equally "chock full of secondary messages about who lives in Malaysia, how, with what values, tendencies and possibilities" (Holden, 2001: 282). But one must ask whether it is possible for governmental promotion of community values to be consistently maintained within the individualistic orientation and address of advertising? Can "relationship marketing" (Mohammad et al., 2005: 95) be focused on connecting harmoniously with people as well as with products?

Moreover, in the "identity management" or "development" (Burke, 1994) of a brand is its product "grooming" (Hare, 2004: 24) tailored to the nation? Or in its mode of address to customers does it divide such a "monolithic market" (Roberts and Rocks, 2005) into narrower categories of class, ethnic, gender or generational lifestyle? Are global company brandscapes able to culturally "custom(ar)ise" (Melewar et al., 2006: 407)—adapt successfully to locally "prevailing cultural and market conditions" (ibid.: 408) or "situate the global in the local" (Watson, 1997b: ix)? Or are there "commonalities transcending country and culture" (Khan, 2006) to be addressed in marketing?

Ritzer argues that global brandscapes do not congeal with (or accommodate) local custom: rather their widely predictable practices clash with the narrowly particular production of goods. Coffee Bean closes the corner barista. They are profitable enterprises for those who construct or "grow" them in a process which he refers to as "grobalization" (2008: 167). These global processes of "extreme standardization" enabling financial success challenge local variation: "Today's Special" meals suppress more culturally attuned specifics. "At McDonald's (...) local culture is invisible and irrelevant" (Leidner, 1993: 82, 47). But why must efficiency subvert the exotic?

From a political economy of meaning perspective, a basic condition of its profitability lies in a brandscape's predictability—its continuing to confirm paying customers' conjectures about content. In phenomenological terms, with this "routinization of interactive service" (Leidner, 1993: 179) at McDonald's and elsewhere customary events conform to consumers' horizons of expectation. Easy entry and immersion in brandscapes facilitates their comforting familiarity—whether the reassurance provided by embracing eudaemonic routine is globally or locally defined.

We consider here five Malaysian "fast food" brandscapes (familiar life-worlds to those Chinese, Indians and Malays who visit them frequently) from production and participant perspectives: Coffee Bean, Kentucky Fried Chicken, McDonald's, Pizza Hut and Starbucks. In accord with recruiting their mostly youthful clientele, substantial attention has been paid by companies to constructing these global brands on websites both in the USA and locally in Malaysia (sites visited 13th May 2008).[5] Consistent with their status as ludic life-worlds entertaining escapist expectation, the dominant motifs characterizing these brandscapes' online articulation (verbal and visual) are "fun" and "familiarity." As we suggested at the outset of this chapter, in corporate marketing, brands enhance everyday life, efficiently—as reliable relief from tedium.

Coffee Bean is (allegedly) "everyone's favorite 'time out' place." Denying the need to address specific groups of customers, apart from locations and pricing (and promoting the Actors' Studio, Kuala Lumpur), the website is largely impervious to local culture—linking instead the Malaysian home page to its "US Home." Perhaps because of its seeming corporate disdain for well established kopitiam (coffee houses), Coffee Bean's arrival subsequently prompted brand rivals promoting more Asian eateries and practices (such as Kopitiam and Old Town) to emerge. Immersed in locally brandscaped space as our female Chinese researcher said, "we can 'shout' loud." Cooking and cultural industries can "now defend their ways of life" (Jin, 2007: 755).

Like transnational "media giants," the four further "fast food" outlets which we discuss here think globally but act locally to "maintain and/or expand their dominance effectively" (Jin, 2007: 763). Using a panel insert featuring seven alternating Malaysian promotions, Kentucky Fried Chicken provides its website with a culturally specific address to visitors. But a playable TV commercial promises KFC's "Same Great Taste" is as much a feature of the local Malaysian brandscape as everywhere else: its theme music foregrounds ludic familiarity, good times with friends. "Something good, something great is just what we need (...) to brighten up our day. (...) Good times when we get together (...) everything's just right."

"We have shared some great moments, good food and fun times. You have been part of our many achievements. We have always been there together" (McDonald's Malaysia Website). Global McDonald's emphasizes a history of company and customers sharing a local ludic life-world (a space and time of serious fun and sustained familiarity), of "fun times" and "many achievements."

Pizza Hut's ("One Nation One Number") brandscape is equally a place characterized by being reassuringly personal and supportive of play: it "offers a cosy, friendly ambience in which to relax." The website's multi-ethnic Malaysian attuned video advertises "Hot and Oven Fresh" home delivery, spicy specials putting our taste buds "in play" but bearing a guarantee nonetheless of predictable processing, of meeting our expectations. Nutritional values (on a hyperlink) are in Malay (Pizza Hut Malaysia is owned by KFC Malaysia).

Starbucks is the only site with Malay on the home page: "'Selamat Datang' Starbucks Malaysia." "We are certified HALAL by JAKIM" (*halalenquiry @starbucks.com.my*). This global company addresses local issues through "contributing to local communities through local stores."

## Asian Blogging on Western Brandscapes: Cyberspace Immersing in Culinary Constructions

A web search was initiated (*www.technorati.com* on 15th and 16th May 2008) for blogs whose authors had immersed themselves (if briefly) in one or more of Malaysia's Coffee Bean, Kentucky Fried Chicken, McDonald's, Pizza Hut or Starbucks brandscapes. Hundreds were located—a rich field for discursive research—of which some are briefly explored in this chapter.

People position themselves within—or outside of—place branding. In casting an eye over blogging, we sought not to generalize from findings—a problem-attended process (Li and Walejko, 2008). Rather blogs are a source of rich narrative useful in testing our theory of (fast food) place branding as constructing life-worlds foregrounding familiarity of either global or local character. Do customers recognize known "moments" in immersing themselves on screen or in shopping mall?

As we have argued, Coffee Bean's brandscape resists an indigenous shape. Responding to this cultural indifference, locally branded spaces and times (e.g. Kopitiam, Old Town) have emerged wherein Malaysians continue to sip the "original, local brew" which "has always been wonderful"[6] and in doing so confirm and celebrate their horizons of expectation, serving their sense of identity. Customers distance themselves from culinary imperialism in city consumption.

Continuity is reassuring. At Kentucky Fried Chicken outlets, some take celebrating familiarity to the point of repeatedly returning (sometimes resolutely it seems) as a committed fan, "if you're one of the die-hard KFC fans like me."[7] But McDonald's globally predicable local life-worlds do not prevent irregular service in Singapore: "The geog(raphy) people went (to) macs to eat breakfast and I did have a shock of my life. (...) She charged me $3.50 for the free mcmuffin! I voiced out my displeasure immediately and she said 'alamak!

sorry!'" Among those immersed in this brandscape, appropriating their narrative of events can shock and subvert self-image: we "kept talking about how skinny the group people were (...). Then the arrival of YY in LOOSE skinny jeans made me feel like puking out the mcgriddles. See how bad McDonalds is" (capitals in original).[8]

Absorbed by/in brandscapes, people may regard the available "personalities" associated with products mapped out by menus for those eating or drinking as a list of lifestyles. Picking out an item from this sheet of selves, we select an identity, a passing or more permanent personality. We construct a short story of ourselves as cafe latte or expresso types. In choosing a vegetarian pizza a customer may be articulating and appropriating for herself or himself an ethical identity—a morally manageable meal. Semiotically as well as materially, we are what we eat, making ourselves from features of a familiar life-world. We become a brand. Safely self-defined as enthusiasts for spicy or vegetarian varieties of topping, people assume Pizza Hut personae. "Most people are other people. Their thoughts are someone else's opinions, their lives a mimicry (...) out of a Pizza Hut menu."[9]

Over time, we shape our horizons of viewing cities to acknowledge frequently confirmed expectation. Regularly visited global landscapes are eventually seen as local. "Cafes mushroomed everywhere in KL's trendiest spots, and big names such as Coffee Bean and Tea Leaf and Starbucks made their presence felt. With these cafes, KLites often lepaked (hung out) way into the wee hours and now it has become a part of our pop culture."[10]

Global and locally resourced brandscapes enable consumers to construct competing narratives of "coffee culture," maintaining a "diversify culture"[11] for audiences to appropriate. After "Starbucks and Coffee Bean setting up shop in Malaysia" "not to be outdone, the kopitiams are also streaming steadily into the main markets to attract city-dwellers."[12]

For some, branded spaces are a place for play: I "slack at KFC playing PSP"[13] exemplifying the expected entertainment of sustained fun. Others put anticipation to the test, aiming at "checking out" comments doubting predictable practice: "I've always hear [sic] comments that KFC in the UK doesn't taste as good as the ones in Malaysia. (...) Sounds strange to me given that it's an international chain and the food should be standardized."[14]

Anticipation can be actualized in song, appropriating an identity from McDonald's: "Big Mac Chant Grace isn't a little prayer you chant before receiving a meal. It's a way to live."[15] The fast food brandscape's global predictability is a topic for praise in meeting horizons of e-expectation. "Say what you will about McDonaldization of the world, it provides free wi-fi and enables this blogger to blog in an air-conditioned place (outside temperature 34C and very humid)."[16]

Personality as a culturally specified self can be equally appropriated from narratives of Pizza Hut eating. "Whenever we travel, we get very excited when we discover Korean influences in the simplest form. For example, we were so excited to discover that Pizza Hut in Bali, Indonesia served bulgogi-flavoured pizza."[17] Pizza Hut pluralism is celebrated. In the hut's hybrid menu, they "implant the Indian curry in the Italian spaghetti" (female Chinese contributor). Brandscapes, above all, profit from predictably enabling pleasurably comfortable construction of "who I am": in the widest possible way, they ease eating, "me making my all-time favorite hot drink at Starbucks."[18]

## Regarding Western Forms of Familiarity from the East: Culinary Construction in Focus Groups

Phenomenology explores the cognitive structures of familiar experience—structures themselves not always immediately evident. Watching television, for example, by its very nature involves audiences in anticipating the resolution to enigmas or uncertainties in drama and news stories. Consciousness is continually future-oriented, always already extending across time.

Everyday expectation is underwritten, supported by a platform of constantly recurring phenomena defining family, university, or work. We are located or "thrown" amidst such familiarity marking out the forms of life or life-worlds in which we move and have our being. Branding by media on television or website markets product-enhanced life-worlds as three-dimensional brandscapes (safe but special immersive places) in whose reliability you can assuredly believe.

Facilitated by female Chinese coordinators (with occasional questions from the book's male Caucasian author), four focus groups with mostly Chinese, Indian and Malay student participants met at two public and two private universities in Penang and Kuala Lumpur between 7th and 14th June 2008.[19] Their responses articulated dimensions or "moments" of experiencing the five fast food branded life-worlds under discussion: respondents grew absorbed in or were alienated by places for profitably predictable cognitive and consumerist play.

We considered the following media artifacts (Internet home pages and television advertising) constructing brandscapes for always already partly Westernized, often urban consumers to inhabit with pleasure, anticipating and articulating narratives of self realization:

Coffee Bean Website: *http://coffeebean.com.my/* (home page, May 2008)
Pizza Hut Website: *http://www.pizzahut.com.my/* (home page, May 2008)
Starbucks Website: *http://starbucks.com.my/en-US/* (home page, May 2008)
Kentucky Fried Chicken Advertising Video (Malaysian TV, early 2008)—chicken rice
McDonald's Advertising Video (TV) (Malaysian TV, early 2008)—breakfast specials
Pizza Hut Advertising Video (TV) (Malaysian TV, early 2008)—"original" pizza, not "pirated."

Students at all the higher education institutions where we conducted focus groups referred to fast food restaurants as spaces in which they could "hang out." These brandscapes were confirmed as ludic life-worlds (detached from duty), regular places for the intrinsic pleasures of recreation or familiar fun with friends which could take nonetheless an instrumental direction (e.g. in study).

Conveying these establishments' intrinsic status as supportive sanctuaries from stress, a contributor told us how she withdrew immersively from the daily grind to "treat myself after maybe a very horrible week then (...) one cup of coffee from Coffee Bean 'cos it's pricey" (female Malay). On the other hand, increasing demands from everyday duties meant that because of "time constraints (...) when there's not enough time to have a proper meal" (female Malay), McDonald's (to whom participants would also phone in an order) became a place of regular consumption compressed by limited available time for meals. Extrinsic interests or tasks could be thereby addressed.

Eating in this way as a consequence of "time constraints" emphasizes the "fast" in fast food, a shortening of serving time in making the product available achieved by a restaurant's familiar or established routines. However, drinking a cup of coffee for a "treat" draws attention instead to the comforting quality of the ludic escape space constituted by a place like Coffee Bean, defined by its supportive sofas. Brandscape regularity and release are appropriated differently.

The "Old Town (local coffee shop) is like, I eat, I drink, I go, that kind of feeling" (female Chinese). Using a more expensive Coffee Bean or Starbucks, people "want to stay there longer, to meet up with their friends, gathering" information and intimacy: these branded places are advertised agora "comfortable for gathering purposes" (female Indian), separate and supportive of their consumer citizens. Coffee Bean and Starbucks stay open in the evening much longer than local kopitiams which close at 6 p.m. Featuring a "lot of sofas" (female Indian) the cafes are more comfortable than McDonald's with its "plastic chairs" (male Chinese)—although McDonald's hard seating can be reminiscent of a rural cafe, reminding new urbanites of earlier recognized regularity.

Additionally, a chorus of female voices at one of the two institutions we visited in Penang (corroborated by an Indian female contributor at the other establishment) informed us that local McDonald's are frequented by a younger generation as "study zones." In this role, fast food outlets (notably with an Internet wi-fi connection) support their instrumental use by students as a liminally ludic space. The restaurant experience has been articulated by these consumers as conceptually located on the slightly subversive edge between behavioral categories (or as a hybrid time of "immersive escape" curbed by "interactive education"). With an eye on tomorrow's college, the students are not quite absorbed today: they engage in a seriously functional but still play-like generation of (what they hope will be) tomorrow's correct and creative assignments. Talking and thinking interactively to-and-fro, they articulate and aim at a narrative of scoring high, thereby stretching their ambition from screen to school. Students have found McDonald's to be a comfortably air-conditioned relatively inexpensive zone permitting prolonged and functional serious fun. Their pleasure is intrinsic—extrapolated by addressing the wider purpose of the next day.

As audiences, gazing or glancing at the mall and media brandscapes of Coffee Bean or Pizza Hut from the horizons of our understanding, we interpret content. We share with people their focus on food. Drawing on experience, our capacity to project meaning on to what we see (establish mall or media content) is our measure of experiencing cultural proximity to the "world" on screen/ in shops. As gazing or glancing audiences (citizens, consumers) we identify with their inhabitants' goal of narrative intelligibility. But do we do so in their terms (sharing their sense of significance)—or do we discover a more distancing "troubled closeness" (Couldry and Markham, 2008: 17)?

Unlike the monocultural Malaysian home page for the "bean," "I can relate" to (appropriate) the culinary hybrid Pizza Hut website "because I do like curried chicken and everything"; it "makes me happy (…) because it speaks to me personally" (female Indian); "I do find it culturally close because as Malaysians we love rice" (male Chinese); the food has "local delicacy kinda flavoring" (female Chinese); "very localized, not just the flavors of the delicacies that they offer but also stuff like the Sensasi Delight" (female Malay); "they adapt their menus to Malaysian styles" (female Indonesian).

On the other hand, in our research, the Coffee Bean website is culturally distancing: even the "price (of the cake) is too painful to look at" (female Indian); "it doesn't work like any kind of Malaysian culture" (female Indian); the content "is like really common everywhere, so not much of a Malaysian kinda thing" (female Chinese); consistent with these responses, "culturally I don't find it close because I'm a Chinese" (male); it "doesn't welcome me," it "looks very generic" (female Malay); "it doesn't build that relationship you would want to build with your company" (female Indian).

Between the single cultures and multi-cultures (respectively) of "bean" and "hut," the Starbucks Malaysia website bears a sketch of "cool" Western coffee drinkers, an indeterminacy of content enabling consumer involvement and identification. For it "kind of connects you to the person from another land" (female Malay), perhaps because Malaysian "people who actually go to Starbucks are working class people and from the picture you can see that those people are actually from the working class (albeit European)" (male Eurasian). A vignette of coffee drinkers clad in Malaysian national costume would seem constructed. Yet the home page carries (as noted) a localizing halal certificate. "I like the way they actually put the halal sign. Yes, that's very helpful because some of us are very strict with our, um, things that we take in" (female Malay).

Audiences whether enjoying "lean-back" traditional media or "lean-forward" Internet (the "ultra handbook") immerse themselves in short narrative or cyberspace constructions of brandscapes (Schoenbach, 2007: 346, 344). Articulating and aligning herself with the television advertisement we screened, a female Indian participant exclaimed: "McDonald's (...) that could be me!" On these screens, the places where we consume are branded as culturally indifferent or inflected, as locally disassociated self contained vacuum "beans" or as varying cross-culturally responsive diverse "huts."

The Pizza Hut television advertisement marketing multiple Italian flavors was a "little unexpected. That really turned off the mood of buying" (female Chinese). In marketing, product difference must be carefully delineated to the measure of the consumer. Familiar television narratives of pleasant places-to-be—beamed down beans and hybrid huts—absorb assumed audiences in safe "tamed" (ibid.: 347) surprises. This is the limited indeterminacy characterizing rule-governed playful escape. Cyberspace travel can be more challenging.

Engaging with brands may be extra-ordinarily enthusiastic. An immersive response to a media constructed and mall embodied brandscape can move from absorbed articulation of a narrative to appropriation of its content in perceiving the self. One Chinese female contributor to a focus group embraced the Starbucks brand as defining the territory in which she travels and arrives, as marking her own space and time with a "special" "design": "every day, almost one week, I got three cups of Starbucks just to collect (their) diary. (...) In the office, I'm using a Starbucks mug, at home I have a Starbucks glass, my water bottle, I'm using Starbucks. (...) I'm totally Starbucks" (female Chinese). The Starbucks bottles may be made in China, with different monthly colors.

In this narrative of appropriation to inform identity, the enabling cultural closeness is age related. A coffee blend like caramel macchiato "gives me a feeling of generation" (female Chinese), of associating with a younger group and identifying with their cultural practice in consumption.

This Chinese participant (a part-time student working as public relations event organizer) informed us that she was "seriously addicted to fast food," a "coffee lover." She arranged Pizza Hut deliveries for her grandparents rather than taking them to hawker food because it's much more "convenient": although they prefer traditional fare, "recently I am trying to brainwash them."


## FROM POSITIVISM'S "ATTITUDE" TO PHENOMENOLOGY'S "APPROPRIATION/ALIENATION"

In our account of consumer responses to branding and their subsequent behavior we have attempted to replace positivism's *attitudes* with phenomenology's *appropriation/alienation*. On the positivist model, reference to an attitude explains only by invoking a behavioral generalization or a "black box" of cognitive unknowables. Our work urges gaining a purchase on phenomenology. This proposed hermeneutics of consumption would *not* exclude quantitative study but rather constitutes its subject experientially as audiences appropriating media and mall marketing. Through the concepts of consumers projecting and positioning meaning we wish to introduce a culturally and historically located approach to studies of branding reception by media and mall audiences which will recognize the often complex "trajectory of brand meaning" (Hatch and Rubin, 2006: 41).

We have considered corporate and consumer constructions of "fast food," their stories of culinary substance. Painting a portrait of such branded experience (or being in a "brandscape") we hope contributes to the philosophical dimension of marketing theory. For branding (and its study) emphasizes aspects of life or moments in human existence with which European phenomenology has long been concerned. How is familiarity constructed (or even guaranteed) and experienced? What is the ontological structure of human security? Epistemologically, how do we experience the different but not *too* different? Or, more straightforwardly, what is a *happy meal*?

Brandscapes offer to enhance everyday life, efficiently: they enable moderate escape from the mundane, safely. Convinced consumers immersed in these play-like places find a life-world made lighter, eudaemonic eating, happy meals: experience of a culinary familiar "other" is comfortable (or comforting). Such (dare we say) is the essence of branded eating in fast food cafes, albeit inflected and complicated by cultural difference and dissent.

From Coffee Bean to Starbucks, McDonald's to Pizza Hut carefully manufactured and media marketed places absorb intended consumers in familiar facilities. Hearing the corporate call to be "part of our many achievements" (McDonald's) we who trust and enter do so within a "horizon of expectations" (Gadamer, 1975) that we will be able to continue lives refreshed around consumption. After all, sharing with us "great moments, good food and fun times," such well known (swiftly recognizable) life-worlds should underwrite our welfare. Sometimes, as customers, we presume these "moments" to be globally occurring as in our experience of Coffee Bean's continuity across cultures, its constancy or invariance. On other occasions our assumption is that such "moments" of enjoyment are glocally particular, or inflected by local culture as at hybrid Pizza Hut.

Governed by the predictability of a McDonald's production line, the immersive safety of these supportive spaces is sold as having always met our anticipation of realizing therein (along with others) a sustained and satisfied sense of reviving our selves. "We have always been there together" in these well established, set apart, routinized spaces. Populated places of this known character are constructed in screen media and city malls as long term ludic life-worlds or (in less "heavy" terms) seriously fun in securely familiar circumstances (brandscapes). Being in such assertively benevolent "beans" or "huts" with their cultural constants or pluralism for pleasurable consumption is leading a life less—or more—local. Brandscapes surround us with horizons of understanding food for thought.

Brandscaped life-worlds foreground their familiarity for actual and anticipated participants. Marketing emphasizes the regularity and reliability of their
practices for inhabitants when it addresses consumers on screen media and in
shopping malls urging immersion. Branding the landscape is "two-way"
(Couldry, 2008: 380): it mediates between exhibited product and the experience of consumption, both shaping and being shaped by the worldly. McDonald's
equally processes and is prevailed upon by portions of the city—perhaps in
responses to public relations pressure. Audiences have authority, consumers
complain. Branding addresses—and is addressed.

The concept of *brandscaping* enables a rapprochement between audience
and consumer studies, on the one hand, and, on the other, a political economy
of space and time (Jenkins and Deuze, 2008: 5). Constructed for corporate
profit on screen media, brandscapes take material shape in shopping
malls. They are quintessentially ludic life-worlds, designed for familiar fun,
secure and serious play. Generically global and glocal practices of place
branding (here characterized as coffee bean universality and pizza hut hybrid-
ity) extend beyond media and malls to be manifestly present everywhere,
instantiated in marketing nations, from educational institution to tourist
destination.

The "electronic promotional apparatus" (Scherer, 2007: 476) of media
marketing wherein "fast food" is branded on screen operates as a semiotic
resource of signifiers. Archetypal golden arches in the sky or avuncular KFC
figures (often written into television's narratives) are used materially in "mul-
timodal" (Machin and Thornborrow, 2003: 453) discourses to generate a
labeled corporate space and time in shopping malls for their products' designated consumption. These places function, that is, as familiar or "regular"
points of self-confirmation which in their default role support consumers'
play-like release, allowing them to idle or be indifferent inside to sometimes
"very horrible" (female Malay) external daily demands. As well as underwriting this wholly immersive enjoyment, such spaces can be used more
instrumentally (e.g. as playfully productive "study zones").

The routinization of interactive service in such a culinary brandscape (deli-
vering food and drink to customers) supports a reliable collective memory for
participants as well as compliant producers of goods. Beneath the golden
arches of McDonald's well recognized material displays, servers facilitate
near automated arrival of closely regulated "happy meals." We all know what
we are doing. People eat—subjectively surrounded by dependable horizons of
anticipation enabling them to articulate and substantiate stories of familiar
purchases on regular "shiny, happy surfaces" (Schlosser, 2001: 10) of enjoyable
consumption, emerging as McDonald's "regulars."

Cafes support deliberative chatting as sometimes sites of "semiotic democracy" (Karppinen, 2007: 495, 502), agora for the public sphere pursuit of social
issues as well as private controversies. Further research could be conducted on
the *cognitive play* between places branded for profit and the personal responses of those who inhabit them, between agora and appropriation. Studying the

"play of power over meaning" (Corner, 2007: 676) may well show "beans" and "huts" of plural politics.

Branding success depends on customers realizing intrinsic and instrumental, "cognitive and utilitarian" (Smith et al., 2007: 78) aspects of product use. In celebrating the first, these spaces and times confirm guarantees of both reliable activity and affirming assumptions, of supporting culinary cutting and the "way we cut up the world in our mind" (ibid.: 81): meals will be found to be warm *and* welcoming. We enjoy happy meals within secure horizons, the "interpretive frameworks" (Holt, 1995: 3) of brandscapes built from "breaking" "reality into (reliable) groupings of meanings" (Smith et al., 2007: 82). But a coffee orientated branded space can underwrite both escape *and* efficiency. "I hang out at, kind of, Starbucks. It's more efficient" (male Chinese contributor). To be instrumentally stretched by sending local e-mails while immersed in sipping global brew is to be liminally ludic.

# 3  Interpreting Place Branding
## Absorbing or Alienating?

*With Azizah Hamzah*

A "horrible pseudo-scientific normative psychological analysis" is "still the dominant mode of analysis (...) in consumer research."

(Wilk, 2009: 301)

How do active audiences respond to advertised agora, these gathering places for consumer citizens viewed in screen media and shopping malls? What can we say about the consensual or critical relationship between these located "commercial rationalities" and people's "individual subjectivities" (Du Gay, 2004a: 99)? How does media branding "fit" buyers' banal experience?

Drawing upon media reception theory's narrative of understanding as a structured process, the "thick" talk of everyday life can be treated theoretically. Analysis moves "out of the misleading rhetoric of causes and effects into the more transparent terminology of meanings and rules" (Harre, 2004: 1451).[1] We are able to explore in people's actual or imagined stories their immersively experiencing an extended consumption(e)scape on media screen or in shopping mall. Some are actively absorbed in the flow of narrative, others sip globally marketed coffee in cafes. People appropriate branded meaning, bringing agora (in)to life.

Place branding narratives present the space and time of city or nation (Sinclair, 2008) for reliable consumption. Malaysia's One Golden Celebration video invites its audience to visit: "it's the place for us to be, it's the time to feel so free." Here we consider consumer citizen responses to the marketing presentation of nation on screen.

## MAKING SENSE:
## MEDIA MARKETING RECEPTION THEORY

In writing about consumers from the perspective adopted in media reception studies or seeking to understand the process of people understanding advertising we are positioning ourselves with critical marketing theory. Pursuing such a focus on consumption as interpretation, we distance ourselves from an "inductive-statistical" positivism in research method (Brian Jones and

Monieson, 2008: 59). For by dogmatically asserting the "supremacy of quantitative measurement" without first considering how accounts of what is being counted are established we "shut out most of marketing reality" (Gummesson, 2001: 28). There is no theory-neutral observation language, presupposition-free mode of describing facts (Tadajewski, 2006). So what does the consumer say?

All seeing is seeing-as, a perspectival looking at the world from culturally constructed horizons of understanding. In our recruitment of post-positivist methodology (Brown et al., 2001) to avoid the cognitive bias (Tadajewski, 2008b) of philosophically indefensible research (Tadajewski, 2004) we align here with "marketing critterati" as we think our way through critical hermeneutic phenomenology to consider analytically how audiences variously and vigorously interpret advertising (Brownlie and Hewer, 2007).

Europeanizing earlier English audience studies, Silverstone (1999) outlined for the new century a hermeneutic phenomenology of reception which asserted a homology between engaging in games and media users generating meaning. We argue that perceiving would-be persuasive visual sketches by marketing on screen media or in shopping malls can be modeled as such a process of mental play, a goal-directed moving to and fro absorbed in a "playscape" (Daliot-Bul, 2007: 955), in a "transcendence beyond the ordinary" (Iacobucci, 2001: 109). Ludic, we become immersed in an "ongoing knowledge project" of articulating advertising agora (Zwick and Dholakia, 2006: 30), "the place for us to be" (a One Golden Celebration chorus marketing Malaysia).

Thompson's "Interpreting Consumers: A Hermeneutical Framework" (1997) secured hermeneutics within marketing's consumer response studies (see also Thompson et al., 1994). Drawing on such a philosophically rooted psychology, "key patterns of meaning" characterizing the "narrative structuring of cognition and understanding" can be discerned embedded in focus group participant reactions to media advertising (Thompson, 1997: 438). The subjective space and time of readerly understanding, wherein the consumer's processing of marketed meaning occurs, is opened to being theorized as constructively "ludic"—as enabling the mind to be "in play."

Immersed in a continuing mental play of meaning formation, audiences attempt to articulate a coherent screen content from branding: their goal is understanding. The consumer's "response to an advertisement depends first on the cognitive activity of reading text" (Scott, 1994b). Absorption is equally a time of anticipating sense. Consciousness of the present is perpetually future-oriented. People's view of the marketed meaning which they anticipate (at which they often arrive) clearly underwrites their spoken contribution in discussion. Where audience expectation based on their knowledge of format or genre is not met by emerging event, puzzlement arises, producing consumers' analytical if not alienated attention to content.

We return below to our argument that the structured process of making sense has seven fundamental aspects (phenomenological "moments") which we outline (using alternative terms) and illustrate in relation to consumers' responses to advertising's agora (branded landscapes or ludic life-worlds of would-be reliable release). Audience readings of media from cellphone to cinema have a similar seven-fold dimension discussed elsewhere (see Wilson, 2009).

Interested in internationalizing media studies (Preston, 2006), we reflect on inflections of this singular cognitive route wherein real consumers arrive at specific multi-cultural readings of television's marketing a nation—Malaysia— an anglophone gateway to S.E. Asia. Conversely, we equally explore the implications of this national marketing and the "less-apparent" "coming into being" (Hill and Cromartie, 2004: 70, 72) of consumer citizen responses for a greater scholarly context—rendering global (mostly) Malaysian readings (Kjeldgaard and Ostberg, 2007: 176).

## Consumers Understanding Media Marketing:
## How We Project Meaning on Product Narrative

Audience theory emphasizes the role viewers play in constructing a meaning for screen content. A text's interpretation cannot be left anchored with a long departed author. What is the route followed in making sense of marketing's sometimes rich aesthetics of branding products on television? Are there cross-cultural processes wherein consumers come to understand content or is audience interpretation simply culturally relative? Do they view marketing primarily as consumers or as politically aware citizens, as new purchasers or as nationally positioned with a particular ethnicity and gender? Consumers give life meanings (Peñaloza and Venkatesh, 2006: 305).

We attempt answers to such questions here by discussing advertising and audience thought at a focused moment in Malaysia's remembering (as a much mediated nation) fifty years of merdeka (freedom or independence). Our consumer citizens construct and view this "golden celebration" from disparate horizons of understanding. Exemplifying such productive activity, our groups of marketing viewers bearing varying ethnicity (Chinese, Indian, Malay) and nationhood (China, Indonesia and Malaysia) are shown to relate (consensually, critically) to screened branding.

Always already informed, from the first immersive moment of identifying narrative content, audiences implicitly infer its future. In focus group or interview discourse, we find they do so explicitly, drawing on a personal history of culturally entangled interpretation inflected towards the self. Far from perceiving positivism's atomic sense-data, we construct molecular chains of meaning.

Media users (i) perceive screen events from perspectives shaped by memory. Involved long term or intermittently looking, in viewing television we immediately interpret that which we see from inter-subjective horizons of understanding (in)formed by an awareness of types (genera) such as textual formats. As a female Chinese participant in our research (see below) informed us, information perceived as presented in a lecture-like format on screen "looks like very true."

Always culturally located, viewers draw upon their knowledge of the generally occurring to anticipate specific content or (ii) project narrative on screen. "We have a mindset before we watch the advert(isement)" (male Chinese). Such expectation is an "individuated expression" (Cook, 2003: 117)—an application to the text before one—of shared if not stated knowledge about advertising as a genre drawing upon traditions and conventions of visual culture (Schroeder and Zwick, 2004: 21). Faced with a "space" (an indeterminacy or absence of information) one projects possible content:

> "you can just imagine yourself" in the space and time of the advertisement: "they didn't show the very detailed thing exactly," "they leave a space for you so that to continue (...) you have to think yourself"; "you won't know what happens next. So that you have to imagine first (...) you will think many things, 'Eh, what (are) they going to do?' You will imagine it, what they're going to do." (female Chinese cited earlier)

Looking at screens, media users (iii) posit or articulate meaning thereon. They exercise a cognitive (or intrinsic) interest in "checking out" conjectures, ascertaining the accuracy of their anticipation. The female Chinese respondent (above) continues: "'Eh, what happened?' You will just watch it out. 'Eh, actually, what's going (to) happen?'" "(I) wait, wait and then to see what happens next." Circling cognitively, moving from expectation to noting eventuality, one's aim is articulating coherent stories which represent and complete understanding. "I guessed out what they are trying to say" (female Chinese). Viewing is "narrative inquiry" (Friend and Thompson, 2003: 23).

Subsequently (iv) positioning themselves and thereby (v) producing their "consumer and social personhood" (Cook, 2003: 118) in the light of such perceived communication, audiences engage in "identity negotiation" with texts they have constructed (Shelton and Peters, 2006: 207). In response to Malaysian place branding, we begin perhaps to plan our own "golden celebration," extrapolating a narrative identity as exotic explorers. Consumers appropriate both products bought and brand persona to inform their sense of the everyday enhanced. Having carefully produced a media advertised "other," whether fabula or food, we incorporate its content into our lives, as a quasi-magical lightening of the mundane, therapeutic release from the tedious (Martin, 2005: 27). Screens inform the very relationship of self to time (Brewis and Jack, 2005: 51).

Advertising their cellphone network access, telecommunications television branding speaks to consumers' desire to be close despite distance. Subscribe "because distance should bring you closer"! Aligning themselves with the enabling if paradoxical logic of this product promotion, potential consumers revise their social circumstances, inflect their identity. "Because of (the telco), the family is getting closer" (male Indian). "I could really connect me with my mum, me and my dad" (male Chinese) (in Wilson, 2009). When family membership is important or one belongs to a culturally central or important familial life-world stretched across "dispersed sites," watching such media branding narrative can inform and guide one through inhabiting that world's evolving roles (Hogg et al., 2004: 255). The "self" is rarely metaphorically settled in stone with an inflexible identity.

In "self-making," media users appropriate, or, as we noted earlier, are (vi) alienated, distancing themselves in (vii) analyzing accounts of reality on screen read as prescriptive (Cherrier and Murray, 2007: 1). In politic cultural responses to branding across ethnic horizons, where harmony can be "teeth grinding," scarcely concealed irritated indifference may be presented aloud as incomprehension. Implicitly emphasizing her separate ethnic identity as critical citizen, a female Chinese Malaysian research participant responded with a vigorous discourse of alienated self-distancing to a Malay television presenter's lecture (see below) defining the history and use of identity cards for a studio audience and (an implied) national gathering of domestic viewers:

> I am not interested to know what that (Malay) guy is talking about so that is the problem. (...) From (the) start until the end I don't know what he is talking about. (...) I will just close my ear(s), I don't want to listen to it, the feeling is like *that* (emphasis in original).

When it does take place, our play-like immersion in screen content or "escape" can be cathartic "enlightenment" associated with media use, perhaps through empathy with narrative agents (Henry and Caldwell, 2007: 169, 159). Absorbed in the screen's separate space and time, we purposefully project and produce a story's meaning, positioning ourselves accordingly. Continuously immersed, I will "want to watch the advertisement until (it is) finished" (female Chinese).

Media branding constructs (would-be) persuasive narrative sketches in which (persuaded) consumers building and buying meaning pursue their being. Gathered safely in advertising's ludic agora ("It's the place for us to be"), we gain a purchase on success. Such brandscaping maps out in visual detail on private domestic and public screens (e.g. in malls) both the "retailed and the retold" (Small, 2006: 317). These repeated accounts of happy acquisition (from Coffee Bean to university degrees) are primed to (in)form consumer horizons of understanding marketed goods. Audiences articulate their indeterminacy into prescriptive narrative, appropriating persuasion.

Prescribing alternative possibilities for consumer lives through product stories sketched out on screen, brandscapes support our "sense of (separate) order that removes us, briefly, from the larger disorders of everyday life" (Small, 2006: 318). Their narrative territory offers redemption. Nevertheless projecting their sense from widely differing horizons of cultural understanding we interpret their meaning as a "swirl of signifiers we inhabit yet never settle" (ibid.: 322). In disparate if involved ways consumers fill out the format of elliptical advertising sketches whose creative writers or "cultural intermediaries" themselves draw on wide horizons of cultural packaging, the extended "terrain of popular culture" (Cronin, 2004: 349, 354). [See Kawashima (2006) and Kelly et al. (2005) on advertising as commercial-in-cultural practice with consequent conflict and contradiction.]

Brandscapes and their performance on media (or extended in malls) define spaces and times for audience occupancy, consumption zones produced by authorial "aesthetic labor" on scripts in pursuit of economic success (Pettinger, 2004: 165, 180). As argued, our intrinsic immersive interest in branding or other media narrative "for its own sake" (Charters, 2006: 246) draws upon a shared, wider "structural framework" of generic awareness to establish an often pleasurable content (Stern and Russell. 2004: 371). Nonetheless we can concurrently exercise an instrumental interest in using that knowledge for a material world where the demands of our professional duty or "other-centered behavior" extract us intermittently or irrevocably from our screen involvement (Bajde, 2006: 305).

Drawing on the philosophical psychology of phenomenology (above), our consumer citizens' responses to screen narratives structuring a national brandscape as a story can be given a "more nuanced understanding" (Lindridge et al., 2004: 211). Sometimes, for instance, we can see that where advertising travels across cultural distance readers question which is the correct perspective from which to assess its narrative and normative propositions. Responding to one instance of the television marketing we screened, a male research participant from mainland China asked: is the Malaysian narrative civic or commercial, "is it related to the (national) celebrations or it is just a commercial?" Uncertain as to which interpretative horizon of understanding to occupy in viewing events, his perception, projection of meaning and positioning of self are rendered diffuse.

As active audiences, potential purchasers immerse themselves in advertising's self-acclaiming "lived meanings" (Smith et al., 2007: 77). Motivated by travel desires, we explore the marketing of a nation online (two-dimensionally) or on buses (three-dimensionally) (Shepherd, 2003: 133). If the former path is chosen, our focus of interest can be stretched between being immediate and intrinsic (centered on digital text) and being instrumental in employing narrative to achieve real world results. Audience absorption in meaningful content found persuasive leads to its extrinsic application.

As a cultural resource for the "interpretive repertoires" of advertising's addressees (or potential purchasers) evocations of escape such as Malaysia's One Golden Celebration (see below) prescribe products not simply to orchestrate but to transcend the "little rituals and practices of everyday life" (Moisander and Eriksson, 2006: 257, 259). In imagination or in reality we proceed to explore them, "bestowing meaning on experience" (Du Gay, 2004b: 150). A brandscape's stories can encourage enthusiastic audience immersion and prolonged identification with not just playful but "carnivalesque" narrative agents forging on holiday a gathered meaning for an advertised agora (Beyes and Steyaert, 2006: 101).

## SCREEN MEDIATED MARKETING OF
## ADVERTISING AGORA

Branding colonizes a broad environment from flat screen media to three-dimensional shopping malls with narratives of seemingly safe inhabitable landscapes. These spatio-temporal constructions by marketing we noted have been called "brandscapes" (Sherry, 1998). Branded space and time on screen we have denoted advertising's diegetic agora or gathering places, subsequently "written" by corporate bodies from bookshops to tourist agencies into three-dimensional practice with more or less ability and accuracy. Here, present day occupants continue to be consumer citizens. For the Ancient Greek agora was a place of assembly, of coming together, peopled by citizens and subsequently a market or purchasing place for consumers. Occupying this conjoint role, immersed in media screen advertising or articulated shopping mall, we still inhabit agora—from Borders bookshops to Singapore Airlines and Starbucks coffee houses. In these spaces and beyond, people express their "citizen interest primarily through their active role as consumer" (Livingstone et al., 2007: 107). Global environmentalism has emerged within the horizons of guilty materialism.

Brands become product related "platforms" for human activity. Their marketing management lies in commending profitable programs or narratives of customization by consumers. Malaysian Boh teas are promoted as "bringing people together." Advertised agora address audiences of potential customers supporting their immersion—their absorbed anticipation, articulating of their own product stories and subsequent shaping of personal identity. The paradox in branding episodes of real life (e.g. Christmas or Muslim Hari Raya) as product focused "special time" lies in offering people an opportunity to escape to a space where consumers are "free to play" (Moor, 2003: 55).

Branded space and time is safe and special, a product-enhanced place featuring consistent predictability supporting our cognitive and corporeal play-like experience. Secure brandscapes can evoke nostalgia as retroscapes, reminding occupants of earlier time. In marketing's agora from McDonald's to Pizza Hut, familiarity of practice and personnel is foregrounded, marking out these corporate forms as life-worlds, places of separate, supported and sometimes imaginative play.

Celebrating fifty years of being an independent nation in 2007, Malaysia's Tourism Board produced a video with a theme song for Visit Malaysia Year: Malaysia One Golden Celebration.

> Malaysia
> There's a place not far away
> Different faces yet all the same
> With a million dreams
> In one golden celebration
> Malaysia

It's the place for us to be
It's the time to feel so free
With a million smiles
In one golden celebration
Malaysia
Come and spread your wings
There's so much to see
There's a million colors
Right before your eyes
It's one golden celebration.

> [The complete version of the One Golden Celebration song can be located at: *http://malaysiahotelnews.blogspot.com/2006/11/vmy2007-theme-song.html* (15th Sept. 2008)]

Within this invitation narrative, the Malaysian nation is branded for its potential visitors as ludic life-world, a place not only of recognizable practices but of play. It becomes a space and "time to feel so free" ("come and spread your wings"): yet it is secure and somehow familiar, a "place not far away" with "different faces yet all the same." In this advertised agora, consumer citizens can gather together congenially for "one golden celebration" as the "place for us to be" with "a million smiles." In this chapter we reflect on the reception process wherein such branding of place and product is read—placed within conceptual horizons of understanding and furnished with meaning.

## Producing and Perceiving Place: Consumer Citizens Constructing Stories, Construing Selves

At the University of Malaya, Kuala Lumpur, Malaysia, in February 2008 we recorded the responses (or cognitive activity discursively displayed) in two focus groups of Chinese, Indian and Malays talking about place branding. Participants viewed the televised media marketing (below) of the nation and closely associated products, branding on screens celebrating national independence.

The cultural context of reading image and text is important. Sensitive to the need to reflect on diverse responses from education and industry, talking with these graduate students of both genders and multiple ethnicities was preceded by considering the material outside an academic environment in discussion with a public relations professional [female Chinese event organizer (CEO)].

The University of Malaya focus groups were held on 12th February, facilitated by the two authors of this chapter. Before the discussion, we showed fifteen minutes of mediated marketing, the "hard sale of Malaysia" (CEO) or the nation's branding on screen (the constituent videos are listed below). Participants viewed the advertisements (several times) seated around a wide screen laptop in a computer room. Some had seen this media marketing in domestic circumstances.

Each focus group lasted approximately thirty minutes, with both involving four contributors. There were five female and three male student participants, of mixed ethnicity (one from China, one Indian Malaysian, and six Malays) and three nationalities (Chinese, Indonesian, Malaysian) present. Each author facilitated a group: paid a small fee for expenses, these volunteer participants from a graduate publishing class were "innocent" (as far as we are aware) of prior knowledge about media reception theory. They were informed that we were interested in their responses to media marketing of Malaysia and its products during the year in which the nation celebrated fifty years of post-colonial independence from Britain. Hence our selected prescriptive narratives of place branding were conjointly preoccupied with corporate sponsored civic persuasion of consumer citizens.

With the exception of the Malaysian Tourist Board production, the marketing narratives we showed to contributors were recorded during 2007 from Malaysian television. The following questions loosely structured our discussion focused on these branding stories for television:

(1) Are they involving?
(2) Do they meet your expectations?
(3) What's happening?
(4) Do they influence you?

The narratives picturing national persona and products were:

Golden Celebrations—media marketing of the nation for tourists in a video produced by the Malaysian Tourist Board to celebrate fifty years of independence

Media Prima—a brief audio-visual history showing Malaysian progress since separation from Britain, marketing this independent media company as informing the nation it represents.

New Straits Times—an account of the newspaper focusing on its coverage of independence day, marketing both the artifact and the nation as prime product for emotional and financial investing

MyKad—an illustrated history and explanation (in lecture format) of the Malaysian identity card (IC), selling a civic understanding of national and personal "selfhood" (e.g. as anti-communist)

Petronas (*The Boat*)—the story of an ill-constructed sinking sampan shows the wider necessity for national development to be securely based

Petronas (*The Red Shoes*)—in a story urging civic pride in the nation, a couple's acknowledging that they both own locally produced shoes initiates a Malay romance

Both Petronas videos market the nation and its oil company as purchasable products.
(The last Petronas Oil narrative was viewed in two versions, with Malay and English voiceover.)

These advertisements could be said to belong to a television mini-genre of "docu-marketing" which here celebrates Malaysian merdeka (free nationhood or independence) for its consumer citizens. Showing a segment of national history or as naturalistic narrative (emphasizing participant cultural environment) they conclude by briefly featuring the sponsoring corporate body (e.g. Petronas—the national oil company). One of our contributors (CEO) raised the question of whether advertisements are an appropriate vehicle for the celebratory construction of national identity: in the presence of such television focused on selling, audience attention (ironically) may be spasmodic.

Our respondents show both intrinsic and instrumental interest in screen advertising content, enjoying it for what it is (e.g. as "fun to watch") and for what acquiescence may attain (Yoon and Ok, 2007). Listening to accounts of either in research reveals the audience's hermeneutic project of securing narrative intelligibility, the "narratological nature of human understanding" (Thompson, 1997). This goal of making sense of events is fundamental to the consumer's identification with characters likewise engaged in comprehending their circumstances in stories on screen. Alignment may be pleasurable (e.g. where we participate in narrative agents' enjoyable expectations of generosity—emotions are epistemological, ways of seeing the world). We can call such sharing of intrinsic interest in developing coherent accounts identification with a narrative project.

In the "hermeneutic/ narratological model of understanding," as reading takes place "perceptual information is assimilated to preexisting schematic knowledge" (Thompson, 1997: 440, 441). Our memories can conflate similar narratives, abstracting a story schemata or type to which particular accounts often subsequently conform: "I will mix up my memory because (it's) all the same thing they're talking about" (CEO). In knowing a narrative schema for media marketing, consumers "pre-understand" or presume being able to construct (or project) and confirm a series of consecutive connections between cause and effect on screen to constitute an advertisement. As we have suggested, awareness of story genre forms a subjective horizon of expecting characteristic events.

We argued above that audiences articulate parts to form a narrative: a "desire for completeness and closure is a prominent consumer motivation" (Thompson, 1997: 444). The point at which it is considered complete depends on perception of the story's generic membership: advertisements are thought to need less detail than a product information guide. Reading as the "cognitive generation of meaning" (Morris, 2005: 697) thereby serves two functions, a "chronological function" or "narrative movement" and a "holism-creating function" or "narrative framing" (Thompson, 1997: 443). We fit the story together fully. Identifying a marketing narrative as meaningful (ascertaining "what happened next") precedes identification with its advised action—or prescribed purchase ("message").

> You will want to know what happened next (in the story). And then what message they're going to tell us. (...) I will guess, "eh, what happened next?" And what they're going to tell, I will actually find out the answer, I try to find out the answer. (CEO)

Identification of narrative content (as the precursor of alignment or identification with its message) is enabled, then, by a consumer's "personalized cultural frame of reference." Where marketing is meaningful, respondents can "relate to" actions on screen, locating and interpreting them within a "broader cultural system of meanings," a horizon of understanding such as their awareness of genre (Thompson, 1997). The Caucasian tourist gaze seen as "consummating" a relationship with the "natives" marketing and massaging throughout One Golden Celebration is appropriately read as signaling a narrative on the pay and play of exotic travel. "Cues" for classifying advertising are recognized by its intended audience: as such they are culturally close (Scott, 1994b).

Petronas Oil company advertising (of the kind we screened) is "always near to people (...) close to people" (female Malays). Already acquainted with their type, audiences appropriately equipped with such Malaysian cultural capital are able to anticipate and actualize stories, supporting alignment with narrative agents. Consumer "recognition of the genre of a given text frames and guides the reading experience" (Scott, 1994b: 464). We expect—project—a Coke advertisement to tell a story celebrating consumption and articulate its narrative meaning accordingly—along with those imbibing the drink. On the other hand, a respondent (male) from mainland China with limited local cultural knowledge ("background") expressed himself "lost" when viewing our Malaysian advertising: "I didn't understand the meaning of the commercial."

Continuing involvement or identification with constructing a narrative may be inhibited where texts inappropriately address audiences. "I want to know the story of ... but at the end I feel like 'boring'" (CEO). A youthful viewer can distance herself or himself from history on screen, albeit that for older others those events (such as the Petronas video of small boat building we screened) may be the focus of nostalgia for a once familiar life-world of regularity, safety and trust.

Responding to this account of 1950s kampung (countryside) Malaysia, our public relations and marketing contributor (in her twenties) commented: "the generation (shown) is the old generation, not now." Marketing may fail to meet consumer expectations of how advertising ought to promote products, "because not interesting." "I expect like this, this, this, this, this. The story must go through like this. But at the end, sorry, disappointed" (CEO).

When we do articulate content adequately, as suggested above, we appropriate (Arnold and Fischer, 1994: 59: Money, 2007: 355) advertising, drawing upon its events to inform a "coherent narrative of self" (Thompson, 1997: 447). Consumers act as cajoled—sometimes. We can refer to this response as identifying with a normative proposition (or preferred reading). Audiences align with people on screen they have established as achieving instrumental interests. They may be convinced that phone calls further family propinquity and incorporate that tag line into life. Watching its television brandscaping, a female Malay student concludes that the "messages from Petronas (oil) clips is [*sic*] very ... related to our life everyday." Carrying appropriative moments of viewing further, consumers ascribe to themselves a product-using social identity (Eckhardt and Houston, 2002: 69). During situations of such "self-construal," we realize selves over time as we buy (Swaminathan et al., 2007: 248). Following phenomenology, Fournier classifies subjective "lived experiences" with brands as extended "process phenomena" (1998: 347, 344).

Addressing the "salient conditions of their lives," advertising constructs "goods" as means of achieving consumer goals (Thompson, 1997). Some appropriate Apple computers for art. Through narratives on screen, branding invites potential users to align with product purchasers already shown attaining our objectives. We are persuaded to "'need' more things" (Bauman, 2007: 28). Marketing seeks to align consumers who will build then "buy" its stories focused on featured goods: "Quite touching you know!" (CEO). Skeptics with their "countervailing market responses" (Thompson and Coskuner-Balli, 2007: 135) resist recruitment: a "very negative message there" (male Indian).

Listening to participants in focus groups, the ludic universal process of understanding which we have suggested be employed as heuristic account of consumer response to branding can be heard being enriched by contributors' particular narratives of comprehending the marketing screen in a "hermeneutic process of assimilation and accommodation" (Thompson, 1997). Academic theory and interviewee talk, integrated in mutual illumination, allow researchers to generate from the former "nuanced conceptualizations of market segments" and from the latter a "richly textured understanding of the consumption meanings that arise from these constructions of self identity" (ibid.: 439, 448). Marketing insight is gained through realizing local consumer response to mall and media is a process instantiating a global structure of anticipating and actualizing narrative rather than by arguing that what is said in focus groups "parallels everyday situations" (Holt, 1997: 329).

## Getting a Marketing Message: The Audience's Absorbed Alignment or Analytical Alienation

Media marketing responses are structured processes exemplified in consumer understanding of product branding. In our seeing a story, culture and cognition interact: they "shape consumer behavior" (Fischer et al., 2007: 425). We absorb ourselves in/become absorbed by brandscapes on screen media: within these spaces and times enabling immersive identification we share people's "human" interests and consequently pursue the goal of rendering their narratives coherent:

> "you want to see from the beginning to the end because there is human interest inside (...) to make you listen and hear what they say" (female Malay). Later this contributor adds: "they put the human interest inside the advertisement, that makes us really feel inside. You can feel like you're watching (a) short film. You want to know from the beginning to the end of the story" (female Malay).

On other occasions, audiences dip into these discourses less than productively, viewing perhaps from inappropriate horizons of interpretation. Readings can range from "those people who really concentrate and listen, they can get the message" to consumers who with transient attention to screens, "go through in a few seconds, just like that, maybe they can't get the concept" (male Indian).

People "getting a message" read interpretatively to identify meaning on screen and (as we have suggested) consequently share positioning and goal-directed cognitive play with narrative agents themselves engaged in making diegetic sense (an intelligible story). All manufacture meaning. Thompson writes of the "apt description of interpretation as a playful endeavor" and goes on to discuss how "hermeneutic interpretation exhibits this player-in-a-game quality" (1997: 452).

More specifically, the cognitive process informing consumer response to mediated marketing is mental activity [our absorbed "play of interpretation" (ibid.)] aligning viewers with narrative characters making meaning out of the world through purchasing product on television. Immersed, we share meaning building and buying. In one S.E. Asian research group our contributors identified with Coca-Cola purchasers at play both semantically and in the street (Wilson et al., 2006).

Consumers exercise a cognitive interest in establishing coherent (advertising) narrative, and as a consequence position themselves with those making sense on screen. Immersed, readers identify a type of content and thereafter engage in "checking out" expectation in a (sometimes) continually confirmed process of recognition: "this exactly show the Malaysian scenery" (CEO). But from time to time narrative anticipation is not met: "the things that I expect they're going to show to others they didn't" (CEO). Involvement can be question-begging: "they still wear like that?" (CEO).

Identification (coining a name for content) fails when a story seems like a "stranger" (CEO). Finding "elements" impossible to identify as generic (of a type), audiences distance themselves from the unfamiliar or are alienated. "I just like (very?) wonder actually what's going on. Suddenly, this (MyKad) one (does) not look like (an) advertisement. (...) So sorry I can't accept it" (CEO).

Where projection of likely content is impossible because a narrative cannot be framed as familiar or generically identified as instantiating a type an audience's response is likely to be one of analytical attention to screen discourse. Cultural distance as well as citizenship can elicit critical alienation. Postmodern marketing, on the other hand, draws attention to the process of reading with intensely familiar images foregrounding or emphasizing that which is well known to intended consumers: we not only project but become aware that we are projecting. Using focus groups and interviews, of course, one is able to explore these discourses of cognitive revolt and recognition.

People's untroubled perception of narrative content (apparently instant access) can give way to their critically analytical reading both of event and encouragement on screen as entirely ("totally") enigmatic. Projection of particular occurrence on the basis of their prior knowledge becomes profoundly problematic: "I don't know what I can expect (for?) it"; "I don't understand why the ending (is) like that" (CEO). Claiming to be "blur" (unclear) as to meaning or "message" where two Malays meet romantically through shared admiration for red shoes made in Malaysia, our Chinese Malaysian public relations respondent conveys her analytical alienation,

> "I don't know what I can expect (for?) it." "I (am) also quite blur, I don't know what message they're going to tell me. (…) I don't know what happened. (…) I totally don't understand, no matter how many times I already watch the story." (CEO)

Petronas' *The Boat* is a story of Malay camaraderie marred by a shared but flawed sinking sampan. The final shot bears the caption: "Can what we build today take us into tomorrow?" Like the respondent to *Red Shoes*, an Indian Malaysian discussant finds attaining *The Boat*'s prescriptive reading (discerning a "message") difficult: "we cannot grab it easily." Abstractly analyzing narrative comprehension with its "linking" of anticipation and actual occurrence on screen to establish (posit) a coherent story ("conclusion") our participant summarized prolonged peer group readings. He emphasizes their repeated viewing "again and again" only (for some) to arrive at incomprehension—they cannot secure a meaning or the "message cannot reach them":

> "we have to watch it again and again and again (…) the message there, we cannot grab it easily. We have to think and then we have to do the link, you know. And then we have to do our own conclusion, and finally we also think 'Why, suddenly, the boat sinks?' I think, for (the) audience, maybe certain groups can understand, for others the 'message cannot reach them.'" (male Indian)

Question-begging branding (ambivalent advertising) is much less than easily involving with our apathy or analytical attention as likely as appropriation. It's "not touching nothing" (male Indian). Distanced from (perceiving) uncertain discourses of mediated marketing, consumers deconstruct potential prescriptive readings, debating their purpose, deciding a differing interpretation. These texts "ask us to do our own message, so maybe our message is out of the topic" (male Indian).

Absorbed in a story on screen, unless fan or philosopher we do not often turn to reflect upon its construction (Jenkins, 1992: 65). However, when far from transparently accessible content of immersing proportions, we attend to modes of enigmatic narrative building on television and our uncertainty in understanding. "I feel I grab the message but I don't know whether the content that I predict or maybe the conclusion that I can make, my own, is correct or not" (male Indian).

Viewing television advertising for the Malaysian identity card with its history of MyKad by a Malay civil servant lecturing at/to a studio audience this male Indian respondent claimed "even the people in the ad(vertisement)" are not caught up in following its story: they're "just sitting, there's no involvement, only one person is talking there." A domestic audience's immersion is implausible.

Moreover, our Malaysian Indian contributor continues, it is likely that those at home intent on holistic understanding of brandscape content "don't see the connection" between the advertisement's initial images of state subversive terrorism, the resulting registration of citizens and the subsequent studio presentation on identity cards. What is the story being told here, one of political or personal identity? Is it a narrative of developing citizenship (rights) or merely data cards (records): that we are now "recognized as a Malaysian citizen (…) we have the rights or (do) they want to show the importance of MyKad (…) you can put your data" (male Indian) on this digital technology?

## Citizens Contesting Consumption:
## Resisting Media Marketing's Preferred Readings

Our "consumption entanglements" (Chin, 2007: 335) are complex, sometimes a subtle site of cultural politics in progress (Schrøder and Phillips, 2007: 891). Consumers can engage in the process of constructing a brandscape agora yet evade its advertising. We are absorbed but resist.

Contesting the narration of nation in One Golden Celebration the Chinese female public relations professional commented: this is "actually not the real image of Malaysia" (female Chinese). Challenging (his perception of) an advertisement's call to collectivist conformity with others, a male Indian participant urged belief in one's own judgment: individually, one "must feel comfortable without caring, don't bother about other people, not to compare."

Audiences in the process of understanding a "consumptionscape" may identify with its narrative agents as producers of meaning and purchasers of marketed goods (Kjeldgaard and Ostberg, 2007: 176). They similarly pursue shared intrinsic and instrumental interests. Gazing at innovative basketball players in Coca-Cola television advertising, as we noted, one of our research participants commented: watching "makes me feel like I'm one of them" (female Indian). Thereby "buying into a particular image" (Connolly and Prothero, 2003: 275), some purchasers will emerge "fanatical consumers" (Smith et al., 2007: 77) with "cultic" enthusiasm (Belk and Tumbat, 2005: 205). Others dismiss the narrative of purchase as a recipe for success or "self-service" (Du Gay, 2004b).

Subaltern consumers (Varman and Vikas, 2007: 117) contesting power can critically perceive place branding as Orientalism, as representing cultural imperialism (Roach, 1997). They may protest against advertising's easy acquiescence in hegemonic positioning (Roy, 2007: 570). One Golden Celebration's marketing to Western travelers presents a Malaysian agora of "a million smiles" as a "not developed country" the female Chinese public relations respondent complained. Her nation is "not really like that" (laughs): showing it as exotic and pre-industrial is "cheating."

The Malaysian Ministry of Information asks advertising agencies to "project a balanced proportion of Malaysia's main ethnic groups" in their work for television (Kemper, 2001: 53). Consistent with this policy, an Indian (male) argued that marketing addressing and advocating a (cross-) culturally cooperating Malaysia is at fault if its narrative shows only one ethnicity. Many Indians consider themselves an unrepresented minority. Petronas' *The Boat* "refer(s) to one race, especially like, the Malays but when you're talking about the nation, our harmonies, OK, and then how we can maintain independence it must involve other races (…) the unity there."

Decidedly alienated rather than apathetic, consumers may speak out, engaging in analytical discourses we have referred to as depth hermeneutics to distance themselves from a brandscape. Here they can be heard as rule-governed citizens evoking an ethnic cultural identity. Responding to a phone network branding narrative of a Chinese family reunion dinner where those present are using the global company's routes to call friends elsewhere, Chinese, we noted, were critical: "a bit offensive, it breaks the (Chinese) tradition. … You really have to focus on the dinner, not on the phone" (laughter) (male Chinese); "you better go out to talk with your friends lah!" (female Chinese).

Resisting consumption in these explicit ways maintains an ethical-political position (Belk et al., 2005: 275; Jubas, 2007: 247) or remembers group boundaries (Lindridge et al., 2004: 214). But such vigorous viewer "heterogenization" (Kjeldgaard and Ostberg, 2007: 175) or their discursive distancing in analytical antipathetic response to advertising can be coded as (apparent) apathy. "I already feel (it's) boring: then I won't care actually what they're talking about" (female Chinese).

Our nation branding research analyzed consumer responses to the six stories (above) of merdeka (freedom) for all on screen. The Chinese public relations professional who spoke to us commented more as distanced political citizen than as anticipating delighted purchasing consumers in

Malaysia's holiday marketing of a "time to feel so free." In noting the limits of ludicity, neither her narrative construction nor perception of its content feature "harmony":

> "we are not really that (characterized by) harmony," "they just try to present a good side to foreigners but actually we are Malaysian, we know that it's not like that": "actually, for me, that's not the truth." Marketing can be too much "like a movie": "the content must be the real one," they make the nation "nicer, beautiful to cover the truth." (CEO)

## Meaning Making as a Ludic Process: Media Marketing Consumption as Immersed Interpretation

Consumer culture is said to be a "set of practices" (Miller, 2009: 421), those of an often anonymous author producer (or implied institutional writer) meeting the reader's response within the latter's cultural horizons of understanding. Audiences of immersed consumer citizens articulate storied meaning for the agora of advertising, appropriating it further to define themselves. In contributing to "post-positivistic" (Foxall, 2001: 182) media marketing reception theory, we argue that the culturally situated responses heard in our focus groups illustrate successive stages in the ludic structure of understanding text claimed by hermeneutic phenomenology to be universal. Listening to them, we are able to get an epistemological grip on this cognitive process.

Marginalizing positivism we are making a case for phenomenology, for interpretive scholarship rather than the former's "impositional" (Brown et al., 2001: 50) discarding of local cultural meaning. Hermeneutics accounts for our making sense of surroundings as a process informed by particular pasts: but in actualizing such meaning we draw on the abstract. In always seeing phenomena as instantiating an already experienced type (from advertising to universities) or classifying perceptual content we thereby can simultaneously project or anticipate their future. Relating expectation to emerging event we shape—processually—marketing's narratives.

Such an inter-subjective model of consumers producing their own sense on screen (or in mall) is fundamental to analyzing contributions in focus groups and interviews. Otherwise, lacking awareness of the mediated cognitive route audiences have followed in constructing meaning, marketing's consumer culture paradigm joins much communication theory in viewing citizens reductively as immediately (already) arriving at their conclusions about branded landscapes.

Immersed and identifying, audiences position themselves with narrative agents in building and buying meaning. Consumers articulating a national brandscape may find difficulty as citizens in aligning with its values because they perceive them to be contradictory—or they may feel excluded. Understanding branding requires research on the time-taking process of our assembling agora.

# 4 From Productive Consumer to Reflective Citizen

## A Reception Study of Advertising Academia Online

*With Kiranjit Kaur*

Where is the consumer citizen? In audience reception theory, s/he is using a screen. When merchandise is marketed on cellphone, television or Internet, he or she is absorbed in watching the persuasive story unfold, immersed in the media-branded agora[1] of advertising. Drawing on her or his memory of marketing, the viewer anticipates and articulates events s/he sees on screen into an intelligible narrative of people pursuing the use of purchases. Consumers appropriate these stories, defining themselves as acquiring audiences, or distance themselves into alienation as the analytical citizens of depth hermeneutics.[2] Addressed by the tag lines of marketing media, we buy or deny.

In political theory, consumer citizens are *ipso facto* positioned in agora: the space and time we inhabit as purchasers is also a discursive public sphere. Tourists and other travelers necessarily take a place in environmental debate, especially if they stay silent on the subject. Addressed online by university branding, students are located as consumer citizens in advertised agora.

Communication theory with its close understanding of screen narrative as spatio-temporal sequence having political import for citizens, we argue, now needs to take on board marketing theory and its metaphorical model of consumer as reader producing meaning ("prosumer"). For then media users can be conceptualized and considered in research as consumer citizens "gaining a purchase" on sense, producing (projecting) meaning for the screen perceived from their own particular perspectives or culturally shaped horizons of understanding agora amidst life. Producerly consumers are able to reflect as citizens on the very conditions of their manufacturing meaning.

In this chapter, we think theoretically from the perspective of reader reception theory about an instance of Islamic student focus group responses to online academic brandscapes or branded campus agora.[3] To do so, we draw from marketing and media studies research on Internet use, in particular the concepts of "citizen-consumer" (Livingstone et al., 2007) and "prosumer" (Toffler, 1980). We seek to show that prosumers' or producerly consumers' readings of the screen involve a process of forming meaning open to analysis, localized cognitive activity allowing them also as reflective consumer citizens to consider the cultural conditions of successful communication. Sometimes, as we have seen, they will do so from a hermeneutic distance, alienated from agora.

## RESPONDING TO BRANDED AGORA:
## COMMUNICATION + CONSUMER THEORY

Branding shapes space and time for profitable pleasurable consumption. Kentucky Fried Chicken is marketed on city trains not as fast food instrumentally organized to speed us through life but as offering the intrinsic enjoyment of "breakfast food far too good to rush." Brandscapes like Coffee Bean are distinguished as places set apart for comfortable gathering purposes: they provide familiar reliable encouragement to their inhabitants in supporting social or study activities. Goals can be various in such ludic, separate yet easily recognizable spaces.

Brandscapes, like molecules of marketing, are concretized in long chains linked together as malls. We are present in these constant life-worlds like Starbucks as consumers of immediate pleasure and sometimes also as citizens aware of the mediated political implications of our being materially satisfied. More instrumentally inclined, some rush through, "downing" fast food or quick caffeine, declining screen advertising's call to set a special time apart from the mundane.

Modern media brandscapes in malls are akin to agora of Ancient Greece. Located at the heart of the city, we have noted, the agora was a safe and separate place for citizen assembly and consumers subsequently to gather. The consumer citizen's imagination could be set in play by grand public buildings, then in later times, by merchant promoted goods in the agora made market. The agora became a life-world whose familiarity simultaneously featured ludic inventiveness on the part of architects, audiences and artisans alike projecting and realizing their narratives. Modern shopping malls in city or suburbia can likewise address civic pride and imaginative calculation.

Universities are equally advertised agora, branded as a strategy for survival (Stensaker, 2005), and sold on screen as separate and supportive spaces for gathering friends and knowledge. Higher education is marketed as international destination for personal discovery, multiple brandscaping for the brain. Consumer citizens are offered an immersive experience of study (mental play) and sport (physical play) on campus, a safe space to develop their hybrid identity for elaboration in extrinsic employment. Advertising's narrative sketches invite our fulfilling completion of their story by "projections of an ideal servicescape" (McGrath, 1998: 439) on screen from their virtual materials for consumption (Watson, 2008). So how do we consume?

Communication and consumer studies, we observed, have followed distinct paths in their accounts of screen audiences. Largely absent from the first, reader reception theory [associated initially with Iser (1978) and Jauss (1982)] has played a core role in the latter's development as qualitative discipline. We suggest that the intellectual nexus between communication and consumer theory be furthered in media marketing narrative reception theory: here we draw on the latter by using the theory to interpret significant moments in which students as prosumers "voice out" responses to university websites with international aspirations.

Reader reception theory, we observed, was the prodigy of phenomenology and hermeneutics. From the first philosophical discipline its early academic authors drew their account of perceiving as projection already pre-cognitively shaped by generic awareness. The cumulative process whereby readers or viewers come to understand texts essentially involves them in the continuing activity of interpretive anticipating—adding meaning (later assessed for accuracy) on the basis of their generically informed expectation. Advertising texts, to take an appropriate instance, are read as following formats, instantiating types from narratives marketing academia to soap powder.

Drawing on hermeneutics to substantiate this processual account of perception, reception theory presents readers as located on cultural horizons of understanding. We see all around us as an instance of already known phenomena (be it object or person) and expect (or project) our future experience to take shape accordingly. In the process by which they produce a meaningful world, the always interpretively active audience's anticipation of specific events is (in)formed or shaped by an enhanced awareness of greater generality. Recognizing the corporate source of marketing (e.g. Starbucks), we view its branding narratives from a horizon of expectation regarding content: as prosumers generating meaning we read them as instantiating a type or genre (Starbucks marketing).

Communication theory, then, can productively mobilize not only substantial research insight into screens mediating the world through narrative or story telling but reader reception theory, particularly in the context of analyzing Asian responses to Western branding of product space and time. Consumers read, reconciling expectations and events, forming their coherent stories of screen content. As a cognitive activity traversing horizons, reading becomes especially interesting to study in cross-cultural contexts when issues of audiences comprehending narrative emerge for thought.

Following philosophical hermeneutics, as we have seen, reception theory considers audience understanding to be play-like. The actively consuming process of producing meaning is immersive, involving our focused attention in moving "to and fro" across the text, as well as being goal-oriented in achieving sense. It is thus appropriate to apply a theoretical disclosing of the ludic to analyzing our discursive response to branding. As consumer citizens, people engage in game-like mode with branded space and time, the recognizable but distinctive agora of screen advertising, as places for conjoining minds and materialism. We play productively understanding the meaning of marketing.

## ACADEMIC AGORA AS LUDIC LIFE-WORLDS

Here we discuss audience appropriation of—and alienation from—education branding on Internet site and TV advertisement. We consider a wide range of higher education brandscapes on websites and responses from actual or potential participants in Malaysia for whom such institutions would be possible places for studying locally or overseas: Leicester University, UK; Limkokwing University of Creative Technology, Malaysia; Monash University, Australia; Ohio University, USA; University Technology MARA, Malaysia; University of Malaya, Malaysia. A television "infomercial" for Open University Malaysia was also viewed in the focus groups.[4]

Seen from the perspective of phenomenology, universities are branded on Internet and television screens as ludic life-worlds of learning. Activity in these brandscapes, in other words, is characterized as fundamentally if flexibly play-like (creatively structured by skilled achieving) but taking place with familiar student-friendly predictability (or comfortably and consistently supported). In these shared life-worlds, participants are surrounded and sustained by drawing on education's defining of the world (its interpretative perspectives or horizons of understanding).

Absorbed by/in these academic agora, the consumer citizens we see in advertising's narratives continually (always already) anticipate, articulate and appropriate text from particular articles to world wide web—in a more or less creative pursuit (Hargittai and Walejko, 2008) of sense. Guided to books, these brandscaped beings assemble ideas in safe reflective spaces.

First, as skilled "players," these students are immersed and interactive, collaboratively and competitively in "Fun. Hard work. And great team chemistry" (Ohio University). "Everyday you will interact and study with students around the world" (Limkokwing). "Monash is fully engaged in the communities in which it is located." "UiTM's research—multidisciplinary, record-breaking."

The participants implied by these brandscape narratives have intrinsic (academic) and extrinsic (instrumental) goals: institutions "mould" or integrate these "innovative" and industry-related ambitions. Limkokwing University of Creative Technology's "multi-cultural exposure and the highly creative and innovative experience will mould you into the most international, most confident and most accomplished in-demand graduate in the region."

Second, university brandscapes are supportive scholarly spheres separate from secular life. As ludic life-worlds, they offer continuing (predictable) reassuring familiarity to inhabitants or "players." University of Malaya's "core value" of "teamwork" "nurtures a caring and warm" space and time. Twelfth in the UK *Independent* newspaper's football-style "Main League Table 2009," "Leicester's compact and friendly campus is an ideal place to be a student" in an institution here branded as a competitively collegial, very ludic life-world indeed.

Perceived from a political economy perspective, tension can arise across higher education's human moulding of youthful consumers and citizens. University life is shaped instrumentally as an economically sustainable purchase for gain but it is also organized around the presumption of open debate as of intrinsic value. Conflicts thus occur between academic brandscapes being considered rational public spheres (of "creative and innovative experience")

they responded to the
cted on a large screen.
g(s) participants give to
ting public and private
l is exclusively Malay
ll Muslims, allowing us
to branding academic
occasion) by a Chinese
Caucasian male author
duates addressed three


place (if anything)?
it "culturally close"?
buying the product?


focus groups on media
ience of using the Inter-
, 2008) nature of much
sites). Internet pages can
, "not (that) much inter-
has moving graphics or
elevision infomercial for
ebsite address—to which


dents as a one-off image,
what they were seeing
teenagers to *surf* more to
riginal). In other words,
of media users or prosu-
volving and establishing
f hypertext links for them


counter with their wider
in a full picture of where
ter University provides a
constitute a dependable
u") where ludic intrinsic
d "planning your future
basics of all universities"
consumers are offered a
fety:

and reliable sources of products (an "in-demand graduate"). Financiers and philosophers look from distinct horizons of understanding.

## Consumer Citizens in Advertised Agora: Monetized Ordering of the Information Order

Corporate brandscaping for profit of places in narratives of space and time does not determine meaning in people's lives. Instead, we are selective. As if at ease and play, some passers-by will immerse themselves within but others will equally easily persuade themselves to resist Kentucky Fried Chicken's familiar focused life-world of "breakfast food far too good to rush." Commuters convinced of this measured pleasure are no doubt able indeed to anticipate and articulate (more or less fully formed) accounts of an early morning graced by "good" eating.

Branding articulates a counterfactual hypothetical focus on product—promoting a narrative of how we would personally profit if we bought into its story of success. "Staging time, space, and the market" for consumer specula-tion is a "corporate priority" (Brown, 2003: 3). In gazing at such a marketed world of purchasable artifact on screen, we can become absorbed by the agoric space and time of advertising (lively Starbucks, library spaces), articu-lating our elongated stories of succulent burgers and stimulating study. Immersed therein, viewers "feel involved, absorbed, engaged and experience intensity and excitement" (Lee, 2005: 50).

Consumer culture theory (Arnould and Thompson, 2005) conceptualizes how drawing on narratives of brand immersion informs a buyer's identity. In this "exchange-nexus" (Sandikci and Holt, 1998: 309) between product and person, sellers' stories surround the self. Appropriating an absorbed/absorbing item, constructing ourselves as customers, we are what we eat or how we educate ourselves in a community of brand users, a life-world of "ludic sociality" (ibid.: 331). Some wear all-embracing academic gowns to pronounce to others their "emotional ownership" (Balmer, 2004), their near tribal identification with a university's branded architecture and audience.

From screen media to shopping malls, advertised agora of coffee quaffing or campus questioning are absorbed, with content anticipated, articulated and appropriated to (in)form the self. People can be actively discursive citizens albeit addressed instead as passively dependent customers immersed in "breakfast food far too good to rush." As the latter, mouthing "brand mantras" (Balmer, 2004) establishing corporate-preferred horizons of understanding people's consumption, we easily become purchasers of books or burgers in these ludic landscapes of focused intrinsic pleasure. Both "brand marshalls" (ibid.) and buyers celebrate (with an "I'm lovin' it!") the topology of a well defined life-world wherein we escape to safely rejoice in products with reduced risk.

In persuasively produced places, we purchase. Rather than be disturbed by enigma, the model brandscape customer expects engaged enjoyment. Here participants engage efficiently as a smooth enhancing of activity not so much regarded as fast convenience but rather as a flow of familiar comfort.

Reconciled somehow with such predictability, ludic exploration is rendered possible for us in dependably serviced (e)scapes of eating and education, coffee at Starbucks and creative study.

Screen marketing brands not only fast food and philosophical education but being a media audience itself. In self-reflexive discourses of on-screen advertising, BBC World and CNN Television prescribe how and when we should watch news (e.g. in CNN "partner hotels"). Thus immersed in passively placating comfort as well as actively playful creativity, the longer people stay in consumption settings, the more likely they are to let loose of their dollar (Ryan, 2005).

Online media interfaces (such as the web pages shown to students in our research) present university brandscapes "imbued with stories" (Holt, 2004: where material and virtual connect (as My Monash! or Ohio online) campus lives continuing the global process of the Internet's being localized (Postill, 2008: 414). Reflecting on Internet access in universities or universal discerns two narratives, one of our responding instrumentally to cyberspace financing corporate profit and the other, our intrinsic interest in serious absenteeism (cognitive play) online.

In the first account, "marketing tries to colonize cyberspace" and we thus addressed as consumers. The second narrative presents citizens "trying use cyberspace as a place to exercise their freedoms and establish their identities, and to use cyberspace as a 'life-world'" (Venkatesh, 1998: 343). ( blogging can be a hybrid response, using a commercial site as an instrument establish "selves" in cyberspace. Groups are also "co-opting Internet technology from commercial interests to amplify various cooperative process (Pickard, 2008: 625), developing thereby a cyberspace "platform of engagement" (Kobayashi et al., 2006: 583).

In a university's brandscaping at its website of campus and cyberspace connectivity (e.g. Limkokwing University of Creative Technology Home Page), both speculative pre-enrolled and subscribed post-enrolled students addressed as a "citizen with civic identity and a consumer with desires needs" (Venkatesh, 1998: 346). Enjoying the complexity of such personal the intended audience of consumer citizen scholar surfers exercises the intrinsic interest of cognitive inquiry [guiding the "heterogeneous" "performance active citizenship" (Elovaara and Mortberg, 2007: 404–5)] alongside seeking satisfy a paying customer's instrumental expectation of later gainful employment Model recipients of media marketing indeed may be busy people.

Surfers scarcely stand still. While immersing themselves in the brands institution of a university, prosumers [or "users and consumers" (St 2007: 548)] of Internet facilities anticipate and articulate narratives of creating identity as "digital citizens" (ibid.: 564) through innovative end and support networks. "While radio and television disseminate, the In the reasoning goes, is about dialogue" (Moe, 2008: 319). "Online civic sion" can function as an enabling "lubricant for democracy" (Kobayash 2006: 582). Somehow in harmony with this intrinsic interest, implied

...ns, 2008: 200) as
"multiplicity...Internet sites proje
visual mate...explore the meanin
Focus group...e, 2008: 258). Mix
ideas and t...nt?) entry to UiTM
categories, ...contributors were
(Roudakov...an Islamic response
to explore ...ctured (on the first
agora. In d...ond occasion) by the
female rese...d five male undergr
of this cha...
questions:

(i)   describ...website—what's takin
(ii)  can you...you see—do you find
(iii) do you...ives you reason(s) for

Screening si...pages for discussion i
branding ab...oving interactive exper
net and th...r "transmedia" (Evans
brandscape...television as well as web
appear (err...cipants as being isolate
active" (ma...adays, every web page
videos in it...Likewise, we showed a
Open Univ...hich concluded with a w
we did not...focus groups.

Showing...ely) a website to these st
that is, ine...e to repeated claims tha
should be r...for instance, to attract
get more i...ale Malay) (emphasis in
the likeliho...nitive activity on the part
mers—their...g in the mental play of
ideas—is c...d by the ready availability o
to gather f...tion.

Website...ys support an articulated e
institution...oint, allowing students to g
they may ...ll. On its home page, Leice
menu of i...atures which may be said
("guarante...ld ("taking good care of y
and instru...s ("teaching that inspires"
career") ca...d. This lists familiar core
(male Mala...pus and online. Web surfin
space struc...eatively skilled achieving in s

"A frie...us"
"A pla...—guaranteed"

and reliable sources of products (an "in-demand graduate"). Financiers and philosophers look from distinct horizons of understanding.

## Consumer Citizens in Advertised Agora: Monetized Ordering of the Information Order

Corporate brandscaping for profit of places in narratives of space and time does not determine meaning in people's lives. Instead, we are selective. As if at ease and play, some passers-by will immerse themselves within but others will equally easily persuade themselves to resist Kentucky Fried Chicken's familiar focused life-world of "breakfast food far too good to rush." Commuters convinced of this measured pleasure are no doubt able indeed to anticipate and articulate (more or less fully formed) accounts of an early morning graced by "good" eating.

Branding articulates a counterfactual hypothetical focus on product— promoting a narrative of how we would personally profit if we bought into its story of success. "Staging time, space, and the market" for consumer speculation is a "corporate priority" (Brown, 2003: 3). In gazing at such a marketed world of purchasable artifact on screen, we can become absorbed by the agoric space and time of advertising (lively Starbucks, library spaces), articulating our elongated stories of succulent burgers and stimulating study. Immersed therein, viewers "feel involved, absorbed, engaged and experience intensity and excitement" (Lee, 2005: 50).

Consumer culture theory (Arnould and Thompson, 2005) conceptualizes how drawing on narratives of brand immersion informs a buyer's identity. In this "exchange-nexus" (Sandikci and Holt, 1998: 309) between product and person, sellers' stories surround the self. Appropriating an absorbed/absorbing item, constructing ourselves as customers, we are what we eat or how we educate ourselves in a community of brand users, a life-world of "ludic sociality" (ibid.: 331). Some wear all-embracing academic gowns to pronounce to others their "emotional ownership" (Balmer, 2004), their near tribal identification with a university's branded architecture and audience.

From screen media to shopping malls, advertised agora of coffee quaffing or campus questioning are absorbed, with content anticipated, articulated and appropriated to (in)form the self. People can be actively discursive citizens albeit addressed instead as passively dependent customers immersed in "breakfast food far too good to rush." As the latter, mouthing "brand mantras" (Balmer, 2004) establishing corporate-preferred horizons of understanding people's consumption, we easily become purchasers of books or burgers in these ludic landscapes of focused intrinsic pleasure. Both "brand marshalls" (ibid.) and buyers celebrate (with an "I'm lovin' it!") the topology of a well defined life-world wherein we escape to safely rejoice in products with reduced risk.

In persuasively produced places, we purchase. Rather than be disturbed by enigma, the model brandscape customer expects engaged enjoyment. Here participants engage efficiently as a smooth enhancing of activity not so much regarded as fast convenience but rather as a flow of familiar comfort.

Reconciled somehow with such predictability, ludic exploration is rendered possible for us in dependably serviced (e)scapes of eating and education, coffee at Starbucks and creative study.

Screen marketing brands not only fast food and philosophical education but being a media audience itself. In self-reflexive discourses of on-screen advertising, BBC World and CNN Television prescribe how and when we should watch news (e.g. in CNN "partner hotels"). Thus immersed in passively placating comfort as well as actively playful creativity, the longer people stay in consumption settings, the more likely they are to let loose of their dollars (Ryan, 2005).

Online media interfaces (such as the web pages shown to students in our research) present university brandscapes "imbued with stories" (Holt, 2004: 3) where material and virtual connect (as My Monash! or Ohio online) in campus lives continuing the global process of the Internet's being localized (Postill, 2008: 414). Reflecting on Internet access in universities or universally discerns two narratives, one of our responding instrumentally to cyberspace financing corporate profit and the other, our intrinsic interest in serious absenteeism (cognitive play) online.

In the first account, "marketing tries to colonize cyberspace" and we are thus addressed as consumers. The second narrative presents citizens "trying to use cyberspace as a place to exercise their freedoms and establish their identities, and to use cyberspace as a 'life-world'" (Venkatesh, 1998: 343). (We) blogging can be a hybrid response, using a commercial site as an instrument to establish "selves" in cyberspace. Groups are also "co-opting Internet technology from commercial interests to amplify various cooperative processes" (Pickard, 2008: 625), developing thereby a cyberspace "platform of civic engagement" (Kobayashi et al., 2006: 583).

In a university's brandscaping at its website of campus and cyberspace connectivity (e.g. Limkokwing University of Creative Technology Home Page), both speculative pre-enrolled and subscribed post-enrolled student is addressed as a "citizen with civic identity and a consumer with desires and needs" (Venkatesh, 1998: 346). Enjoying the complexity of such personhood, the intended audience of consumer citizen scholar surfers exercises the intrinsic interest of cognitive inquiry [guiding the "heterogeneous" "performance of active citizenship" (Elovaara and Mortberg, 2007: 404–5)] alongside seeking to satisfy a paying customer's instrumental expectation of later gainful employment.[5] Model recipients of media marketing indeed may be busy people.

Surfers scarcely stand still. While immersing themselves in the brandscaped institution of a university, prosumers [or "users and consumers" (Stewart, 2007: 548)] of Internet facilities anticipate and articulate narratives of self-creating identity as "digital citizens" (ibid.: 564) through innovative endeavor and support networks. "While radio and television disseminate, the Internet, the reasoning goes, is about dialogue" (Moe, 2008: 319). "Online civic discussion" can function as an enabling "lubricant for democracy" (Kobayashi et al., 2006: 582). Somehow in harmony with this intrinsic interest, implied student media readers and reasoners also entertain as important, industry focused goals for achievement beyond their academic life-world.

More widely, the "online world" is a "new arena for meaningful social relationships which is increasingly intertwined with the offline world" (Di Gennaro and Dutton, 2007: 594). Internet friendships are enjoyed for their own sake in universities as well as stretched—extrinsically "intertwined" with the "offline world" on campus. As such, they continue to sustain immersion in the advertised agora of academia. Equally, students engage in the intrinsic pleasure (sometimes pain) of "reconfiguring friendships" (ibid.) with cyber-citizen peers online while cultivating or networking with Internet others to achieve the doubly extrinsic goal of material advancement elsewhere and outside scholarly space and time. Here, indeed, prosumer "use of the Internet is instrumental, motivated by a need established offline" (Livingstone and Helsper, 2007: 633).

In a summative political economy of how virtual space and time (Laguerre, 2004: 225) are made concrete, advertising's agoras can be understood as representing off-screen life-worldly comfort for creative ludic citizenship which cyber-cafes and the cultural spaces of nations extend to "political debates on the Internet" (Albrecht, 2006: 62). In places where we go online, entrants may "strive to develop the Internet as a democratic tool" enhancing "non-commercial civil society" (Salter, 2004: 185). Mediated brandscapes such as Leicester and Limkokwing are often eloquently shown on screen as supportive places wherein students of life engage in the processes of cognitive play (absorbing, anticipating, articulating, appropriating text) through extended personalized exploration (Kennedy, 2008: 311) with multiple purpose. Nonetheless, such ludic learning is silently shaped by "balancing the books." Our dialectic with citizenship can be structured by another's selling donuts.

## Cloistered Quadrangles in Cyberspace? Visitors with Viewpoints

In early July 2008, at the Universiti Teknologi MARA Malaysia (UiTM) campus (Kuala Lumpur) ten Malaysians (the female Indian co-author of this chapter and nine Malay public relations students) contributed to focus groups (two) of mixed gender considering the university websites and television infomercial discussed as the immediate subject of our research:

> Leicester University Undergraduate Prospectus Home Page
> Limkokwing University of Creative Technology Home Page
> Monash University My Monash Student Portal
> Ohio University Home Page
> University Technology MARA Undergraduate Home Page
> University of Malaya Undergraduate Home Page
> Malaysian Open University Television "Infomercial."

We were interested in our prosumers' cognitive activity, their constructively "moving minds" (Universiti Teknologi MARA Malaysia tag line), a "multiplicity of interactivity" (Evans, 2008: 200) as they responded to the visual material contained in these Internet sites projected on a large screen. Focus groups allow researchers to "explore the meaning(s) participants give to ideas and terms" (Kazmer and Xie, 2008: 258). Mixing public and private categories, consumer citizen (client?) entry to UiTM is exclusively Malay (Roudakova, 2008: 42). Hence our contributors were all Muslims, allowing us to explore (albeit superficially) an Islamic response to branding academic agora. In discussions loosely structured (on the first occasion) by a Chinese female researcher[6] and (on the second occasion) by the Caucasian male author of this chapter, four female and five male undergraduates addressed three questions:

(i)   describe the content of the website—what's taking place (if anything)?
(ii)  can you identify with what you see—do you find it "culturally close"?
(iii) do you think the website gives you reason(s) for buying the product?

Screening single static Internet pages for discussion in focus groups on media branding abstracts from the moving interactive experience of using the Internet and the cross-platform or "transmedia" (Evans, 2008) nature of much brandscape construction (on television as well as websites). Internet pages can appear (erroneously) to participants as being isolated, "not (that) much interactive" (male Malay). "Nowadays, every web page has moving graphics or videos in it" (male Malay). Likewise, we showed a television infomercial for Open University Malaysia which concluded with a website address—to which we did not travel during the focus groups.

Showing (rather reductively) a website to these students as a one-off image, that is, inevitably gave rise to repeated claims that what they were seeing should be more interactive, for instance, to attract "teenagers to *surf* more to get more information" (male Malay) (emphasis in original). In other words, the likelihood of ludic cognitive activity on the part of media users or prosumers—their easy engaging in the mental play of evolving and establishing ideas—is clearly enhanced by the ready availability of hypertext links for them to gather further information.

Websites do not always support an articulated encounter with their wider institutional reference point, allowing students to gain a full picture of where they may wish to enroll. On its home page, Leicester University provides a menu of institutional features which may be said to constitute a dependable ("guaranteed") life-world ("taking good care of you") where ludic intrinsic and instrumental goals ("teaching that inspires" and "planning your future career") can be secured. This lists familiar core "basics of all universities" (male Malay) on campus and online. Web surfing consumers are offered a space structured by creatively skilled achieving in safety:

"A friendly campus"
"A place to live—guaranteed"

"Teaching that inspires"
"Planning your future career"
"Taking good care of you."

But the image prevailing on the Leicester University home page of a sole Caucasian female—disassociated from the detailed "life of the campus" (male Malay)—inhibits viewers from articulating a "full picture" (male Malay) of the university (particularly and importantly for potential Asian students, from learning of the climatic conditions under which people live). The website doesn't show the "whole picture" (male Malay). Likewise, developing a coherent view of its institutional activity is said to be prevented by the complexity of website/sighted signifiers, there being "too many words" (male Malay) present on this "introduction page" (female Malay).

Prosumers can find inconsistencies and inhibiting circumstances as they travel across website brandscapes constraining production of coherent meaning. "Producing Leaders Since 1905," University of Malaya's life-world is familiar and well established even though the youthful students shown on the website hardly "suit" this "headline," being some distance from leadership (male Malay). In the eyes of another contributor, the American Ohio website was culturally distant, lacking images to "attract the *Asian* to study there" (male Malay) (emphasis in original).

The Monash University student portal with its reference to "my future" invites visitors to immediately project anticipated meaning, to produce from items therein a likely narrative of their university life within and beyond the academic agora. But its content is not "centralized," "there's a word here, a word there," "you can't focus" on "one point" from which other items can be integrated (male Malay). Cognitive play in the construction of future meaning is scattered.

People "move minds," bringing knowledge to bear upon the world. We look from horizons of understanding: media users identify and involve themselves in selected web pages, turning away from others. All our seeing is seeing *as*, placing the sighted in categories, generating expectations. Presuming particular further features will be found (projection) is part of perceiving websites to be of a certain character. We become absorbed in national news online, simultaneously seeing items as instantiating types of information, anticipating their development. In (expressly) catching sight of and (implicitly) classifying reports, we immediately (always already) consider they are likely to contain a certain content, a narrative of news.

As with marketing communication more widely, prior knowledge of a university's branding establishes our anticipation of what will be found once its website has been identified. We approach from a horizon of expectations. In regard to one home page our participants viewed, visitors already know that this is associated with "maybe a world-wide university, maybe international university, so they expect much more information" (male Malay).

Our prior classification of a university brandscape as being of a certain character, generating on that basis expectations of particular content, can clash with what is found there, producing a mystifying media experience. The consumer enters as prosumer of meaning and emerges as critically reflective reader. A male contributor exclaimed that "totally, I'm lost!" in the process of seeking to provide the Malaysian Open University television text with intelligibility ("I cannot get much from this video to actually understand what it's all about"). He is unable to accommodate (fit) content within his generic assumptions about the purpose of media advertising. "I don't understand the reason why they come out with this TVC."

This inability to comprehend why particular content is present results from his misreading its electronic televisual "liveness" (Levine, 2008) leading to his misidentifying the text on screen as a current commercial rather than a past celebration. It was made during Malaysia's fiftieth year of independence (2007) to inform citizens about the national contribution of the Open University (with information about careers achieved, "the scope of work" after graduation)—not to market the brand to student consumers by focusing upon the "exact courses" provided. Eclipsing time, our confused prosumer makes a category mistake in allocating the televisual message to a genre, interpreting the narrative from the wrong horizons of understanding.

In media use, we producerly consumers "move (our) minds" across the screen, continually projecting and positioning (confirming) meaningful content. Somewhat paradoxically, the locally global Limkokwing University website asks viewers and potential consumers of its vocational education to exercise their minds in imaginative play around "optimistic" images of "how work as an architect will be": "you can achieve your goals by study there" (male Malay).

In doing so, even "first time viewers" can identify with people already enrolled, "quite interesting" students of "different ethnicity (...) black people, Caucasians and Asians" shown "focusing" upon drawings on site, "really doing their job" (male Malays). Here, as audiences understanding content we align with architectural undergraduates in making sense of visual sketches. We look with the latter, all of us engaged in the pursuit of intelligibility—whether upon a screen or upon a studio drawing board. In this fusion of perceptual horizons, we share a focus.

Limkokwing's brandscape with its intensely engaged multi-ethnic students sets out to establish for consumers their close cultural connection to activity which this intended audience of international citizens "will do as well" (Indian female co-author). But the prosumer being able to generate integrated online meaning for this site is inhibited again by the page being "cluttered," "so *packed* with (...) advertising" (Malay male reflective citizens) (emphasis in original).

Minds engaging with inconsistent meaning may move slowly. Resisting an integrated reading, University Technology MARA Malaysia's undergraduate web page conveyed cultural contradiction ("the picture does not suit the words") with its "Moving Minds (motif), but showing the students only walking there" (female Malay). In offering undergraduates such a distancing focus for their (self-critical) hermeneutic cognitive play in producing understanding of civic self identity, web authors "assume that our minds will move slowly!" (male Malay reflective citizen).

Nonetheless with its "Arabic words" and tudung (head scarf) wearing students the site is culturally close not only to Malaysians but to an international Islamic community (male Malay). Reading everywhere involves absorbed anticipation and articulation of content by identity forming media users. Often but not always we construct our interpretation from horizons of understanding already shared with the text: in this way culture shapes similar cognitive styles for screen content and speculative consumer (Faiola and MacDorman, 2008: 349).

Apparent proximity in horizon of understanding may rest on choice of color for a website. "We Malays (...) we are much into the Islamic looks and the color itself (on the Leicester University site) is not much of what Malays use in their everyday life. We Malays we like to use very *soft* colors" (male Malay, emphasis in original). However, the Ohio University brandscape is said to be culturally close to the world of Islamic Malay consumer citizens as it emphasizes green: "it doesn't use striking colors, it uses soft colors" (male Malay). Color matters materially.

Like website marketing, television advertising promotes identification by consumers with people using products in a brandscape. A citizenry able to recognize an instant vignette on screen is important in aligning audience and purchaser. For identifying an instance of a character type is clearly the necessary first step in identification with that person. Where television's characters are recognizable and familiar they "orient the audience within the narrative" (Evans, 2008: 203).

The Open University Malaysia infomercial sought to establish cultural closeness with audiences through its claim to be the "University for *All*" (emphasis in original), although its presence on local television rather than a global website meant that this welcome was addressed to students in Malaysia, "not for foreign students" (male Malay). However, images of motherhood in this brief marketing narrative "really suit" (male Malay) the claim to universal education: "if you are a mother, you also can study." Pictures were coherent with prose.

We have argued that the branded landscape of universities bears a preferred reading as a life-world to be experienced as regular reassuring familiarity. Given that students spend much time in cyberspace, does this comfort and conviviality extend online? Can such a promise of dependability continue to institutionally underwriting "cyber-trust" for student consumer citizens as "confident expectation" (Dutton and Shepherd, 2006: 433) of securely accessing and achieving a presence on the Internet? Do academia agora advertised online as supportive themselves extend to embrace a caring cyber-space given the latter's "complex interaction between trust, intimacy, disclosure and time as complex relationships develop" (Carter, 2005: 149)?

## Blogging on University Brandscapes: Ludic Life-Worlds Online

We have argued that university brandscapes form a comfortable world of aspirational security focused on pursuing intrinsic and instrumental goals albeit in not always evident harmony. While their authorship is relatively anonymous compared with focus groups, student blogging attaches similar characteristics to academic agora. To read that the University of Leicester has undertaken a survey of world happiness is to be informed of appropriate activity, consistent with branding. Likewise, we read online that the "dark side of Limkokwing University is all covered up" (18th June, 2008),[7] in conformity with its construction as supportive life-world.

Citizens and consumers blog upon brandscapes: people engage with their values politically and as sites of valuable products. The academic agora can be the focus of scholarship or selling. Many such narratives on brandscaped "transformations of public space" (Mackenzie, 2006: 784) concern maintaining (or the withering away therein of) social equilibrium. At the conclusion of this anecdote by a concerned citizen, student life-world security is restored with "exhilaration."[8]

> My first encounter with racism came one night while slightly inebriated after a night at a student hang-out of the campus of Ohio University in Athens, Ohio. A white male student, obviously drunk also, called me a nigger. I was taken aback because I was never called that in all my life. I ran up to him and asked him to repeat what he had just said. He, obviously realizing that he was grossly outnumbered, started saying that he was from Queens, New York and had a lot of black friends. One of my male friends slapped him up a little and we left feeling that exhilarated, in some way.

When evaluating a product, consumers can structure their familiar university life-world of immersive play (whether physically engaged at the "swimming center" or as more cognitively focused in quality) by fore-grounding distinctions between ability, age or gender:[9]

> Finally, I went swimming today. Thank God it's open. UiTM Shah Alam swimming center by far is the best pool! Bersih. Jernih. (Clean. Pure.) And the best part is they separate the opening hours between ladies and men.

In assessing academic agora, we can occupy a hybrid ground of political-product evaluation as citizen consumers, moving from philosophical considerations to points about purchase. The familiar dependability of a brandscape may be doubted with its trusted status called into question, made problematic in an online narrative evincing a negative assessment of its space and time as a safe place to engage in creative play. Here an author seeks readers' alignment in alienation:[10]

> Sunday, May 11, 2008 UM, The Trusted University No More University Malaya (UM) was branded as "Trusted Brand 2007" but this is the year 2008 and I guess I will stop trusting UM. How about you guys out there? Are you guys going to trust UM anymore?

University bloggers were listened to more widely (in August, 2008) during our research by setting up a weekly Google Alert (Blogs) for writers using the words "university life" as well as entering the phrase in the search engine on the blogging Internet content format website: *www.technorati.com*. The ludic consumer citizen "voices" which were thereby located took as their reflective focus events and surrounding circumstances intrinsic to university life-worlds locally or world-wide, albeit sometimes speaking from an instrumental perspective.

In so searching for accounts of life in the academic agora of East and West, the research method followed here was not one of inductive generalizing from instances which could be aberrant. The perils of thereby arriving at conclusions about "bloggers and their blogs" are on record: "developing a probability sampling strategy that produces generalizable results about bloggers and their blogs remains difficult" (Li and Walejko, 2008: 279). Rather the aim in the present scientific (or more specifically hypothetico-deductive) pursuit of a valid conclusion is to test a theory-based perception (or hypothesis) of branded places as ludic life-worlds against found narratives online of lived experience (discovered data). Accessing blogs allows a diverse range of global accounts to be considered in addition to information from talking in local focus groups.

University brandscapes for the brain are marketed as safe and supportive locations (life-worlds) for realizing narratives of living: in this serious play of mental production people focus creatively on present study and future proposition. Advertised academic agora and actuality can coincide in an undergraduate's ludic life-world which (as in Indonesia) is "friendly and fun":[11]

> "I've been surrounded with friends who never fail to give me a helping hand, accompany me to lecture, tutorials and library. Friends who I bump into gave me a smile making me feel so at home. I've thought university life is full of fake people who are selfish and snobbish. But, they prove me wrong."
>
> "Life always has its way—Indonesia. That's where I am now! University life has begun. Yipee? Sobs? Yay? Mixed feelings. Friends are wonderful. Lucky me, I have a wonderful roommate and the dentistry students are the best. Friendly and Fun [*sic*] to be with."

The academic agora should be not only supportive but is anticipated as a space and time to engage in the play of ideas amidst ethnic and social diversity:[12] "I always assumed that one of the main pillars surrounding university life was the pursuit of scholarship in the midst of diversity, not just in terms of ideas but also amidst people of different ethnic groups, income levels, etc."

But behavioral regularities defining and sustaining expectations of the university student brandscape can be encountered as repetitive tedium, "humdrum":[13] I "have had some tiring days, settling into the humdrum of being a university student, of having to get to know people, again and again and again and again." Actualizing anticipation may be tedious ("tiring").

Play can be casual or competitive, a practice defined by "slacking around" or "striving" with "so many things to be done," whether physically on the games field or cognitively dispersed across academic agora.[14] Intrinsic delight postpones instrumental duty. "Omg (oh my god). i [*sic*] realize there are so many things to be done. homework [*sic*], assignments and projects … never ending stuff and yet im [*sic*] still slacking around. anyhow, tomorrow's business law lesson is postponed and i don't have school on tuesday, which means that i have a super long weekend."

Resisting an intrinsic focus on the academic agora by which one finds oneself totally immersed (which "never ever wants to give you a break") to gaze instead instrumentally on the future can be "desperately" difficult. An articulately branded (or "lucid dream" of a) supportive life-world ("sweet, problem-free and rather laidback university life") can be the "exact opposite" of the "real world" beyond academic space and time:[15]

> Just like what I've expected, university life, once kicking in action, never ever wants to give you a break. Suddenly that dreadful 24 hours just whizzes past you without you even battering [*sic*] an eyelid—time flies just way too quickly for you to hang on to the best moments of it. Desperately trying to strike a harmonious balance between upholding the lucid dream of a sweet, problem-free and rather laidback university life and pushing myself to accept the truth that the real world is the exact opposite.

But the familiar friendly life-world of immersive, intensive "buzz and chatter" signaling the characteristic cognitive play of voices and views associated with an absorbing academic agora is interpreted more traumatically by others as psychologically subversive, alienating, "sealing your friendless doom." Heard from a distinctively "other" horizon of understanding:[16]

> "The buzz and chatter that go on around you press in on your ears like a surgical probe, taunting you, mocking your loneliness and sealing your friendless doom with vicious delight and raucous laughter."

## Categorial Types, Hypes and Hermeneutics:
## Experiencing Education's "Emplaced Practices" (Cook, 2008)

"Brandscapes" are places "designed by marketers and experienced by consumers" (Sherry, 1998b: 1). Emplaced therein, practices such as modes of dependable education or food delivery are further articulated through our narratives and activity of "being-in-the-marketplace" (Sherry, 1998c: 113). There is no simple opposition between constructed branding spectacle and consumer everyday speech and substantiation of the brandscape. We make meals meaningful.

In these pages we have outlined aspects or moments in a phenomenology of perceiving as gaining a purchase on a promoted life-world, arguing that it is a cognitive process occurring within people's widely varying cultural horizons of understanding production. Prosumers actively and independently interpret advertising representing them as passively dependent. "Comfortable" consumption for some as a focus of intrinsic enjoyment is rushed through more instrumentally as a matter of "convenience" by others. Simply equating cultural stereotypes of consumption with countries (Dubois, 2000: 217) limits our insights into *who* is convinced of *what* narrative meaning.

We can conclude that given their intrinsic focus on developing the creative play of the mind academic agora as advertised are prosumer oriented to the point of producing reflective citizens. The immersed campus-located consumer citizens implied participate in articulating their conjoint selves through activity which can be modeled as cognitive play having extrinsic consequence. Some will even visit "civic/political" (Livingstone et al., 2005: 287) websites. Our producerly consumers conspicuously generate meaning from these media marketed brandscapes (or cyber-cultural architectures of education). Where cognitive play in a cultural context is constrained or confusing, these prosumers emerge as citizens reflective on identity.

Screen media and super-malls shape human contact: we nonetheless guide what we do. Immersed in acclaimed and advertised agora we can be modeled metaphorically, placed in theory, as "purposive players in a variety of games, following an established set of traditions, rules and disciplines" (Parvez and Ahmed, 2006: 617). But we are producerly consumers.

Culinary and cultural global brandscapes built around products from food to philosophy are "hybrid spaces" (Viseu et al., 2006: 633) of comforting familiarity and creative play, places which consumer citizens enter with ambition. We are constrained but enabled by our self-submersion in surroundings with structured constancy. Focus groups offer consumers a discursive route to recognizing and reflecting upon representations of these life-worlds as citizens.

# 5 Cellphone Connections
## Audiences Activating Agora

*With Norsita Lin Binti Ahmad*

Cellphone connections can be competitively marketed by telecommunication companies as saving cash for consumers. High speed links between handphones may also be sold as supporting extended families and furthering friendship. The structured convenience of their use has generated a world of more or less continuing contact (in activated agora)[1] upon which people depend as both cultural citizens and consenting or critical consumers to belong, bond and do business.

Commercial branding of a handphone heaven of quick connection denying separation in space and time may involve substantial narratives on traditional media (particularly television). Consumer reactions to both cellphone connections and their branding can involve significant stories (as in diverse interviews or digital blogging). New media are richly represented in these accounts.

We have argued that inductivist studies of media branding and its cultural consequences for consumers reduce the interpretive (and arguably ethical) importance of respecting and realizing the intricacies of that culture. Instead, the rich complexity of consumer "attitudes" discerned during focus groups or interviews needs to be read by academic researchers within alternative horizons of analytical understanding. From the latter perspective these detailed evaluative beliefs or discourses can be seen as expressions of alignment with or being alienated by wider cultural narratives, not the least of which is the mediated marketing of branding. Engaging in a frequently analytical discourse (which can be deemed one of self-distancing depth hermeneutics) the Chinese event organizer we interviewed distanced herself from the promotional place branding of Malaysia in the video Golden Celebrations: "they just try to present a good side to foreigners but actually we are Malaysian, we know that it's not like that"; "actually, for me, that's not the truth."

Far from the causalist discourse of regarding "targeted" audience attitudes as effects of screen events, consumer appropriation of corporate branding is rational or a cognitive activity for which reasons can be given (albeit perhaps retrospectively).[2] In this immersive process audiences align with marketing's prescriptive narrative, buying its meaning, bringing its story into their life-world, amending everyday familiarity. Reducing this complex cognitive activity to the merely caused consequence of advertising is indeed an effect of administering audience silencing questionnaires as an instrument of measurement. But collecting data begins with culturally saturated discourse.

From the interpretive perspective on consumer audiences forming attitudes from branding it is important that the latter is seen as edited, segmented and sometimes subverting expectations. For elliptical accounts on Internet or television screen bearing information about the perfect paradoxes of multicultural nations or the perfecting qualities of much travelled products (such as Coca-Cola) require a reader to complete their prescriptive narrative, to shape them into a coherent story.[3]

Responding to Petronas oil company branding, not with an attitude, but by recognizing the cognitive necessity of articulating "our own" prescriptive story therein, an Indian male member of our research audience (we noted) concluded: "We have to think and then we have to do the link, you know. And then we have to do our own conclusion." Drawing on the information implicit in their long formed generic horizons of understanding narrative, readers "link" the edited elements of a story together with a "conclusion." Here we shall rely on reception theory to systematically analyze discursive cultural responses to transnational telecommunications cellphone branding in Malaysia.

We have been arguing that hermeneutic phenomenology in marketing theory claims the process of understanding phenomena or our surroundings fundamentally structures our perceiving content: all seeing is seeing *as*. Guiding perception in projecting meaning on our very being, such interpretative activity draws upon our cultural circumstances or horizons of understanding. As a cognitive process for which we are able to provide reasons concurrently or subsequently, it cannot be considered passively caused by a screen. We actualize meaning in response to textual detail.

Phenomenology studies the ready to hand or always available "implicit conscious structures of understanding" (Deetz, 1977: 58). We read or negotiate our way amidst media content, engaging with narrative through our past-informed but future oriented projection of meaning in/on to the text. Our anticipating appropriate content is put to the test of accuracy. Success substantiates our articulating its sense. Surprise at outcomes signals our earlier implicitly expecting events on screen.

Seeing is conceptualized not caused: it is "filtered by, through, and for culture" (Tharp and Scott, 1990: 47). Generating meaning across a marketing text, relating expectations to emerging evidence, we arrive holistically at a moment of ideational understanding for reasons. "Not one among many theories of the cause of human behavior, (a hermeneutic phenomenology of perception) rejects the very causal questions" (Levin, 1991: 62). Events on screen and mental occurrence—or text and thought—are not related as a "series of mechanistic starts and stops" (Gallagher, 2004) but as perceived content and completed comprehension.

According to Hunt (1989: 4), drawing on earlier incursions by others, "'positivistic social science' implies the search for order in the social world, that is, law-like generalizations." However, he later continues (1991b: 34), "positivists rejected causality because they viewed 'cause' as an unobservable, metaphysical concept." More precisely, for positivists committed to science as the study of what could be seen, referring to "cause" and "effect" denotes only the constant conjoining of evidential events. The same observable evidence is sufficient to both explain and predict data.

Statistical "generalization" is "in order." But attempting to account for perceived constant conjunctions of data involving media marketing and consumer as cause and effect connections (whether observable or not) is conceptually inappropriate. Particularly problematic is the reifying of a quasi-technical concept of audience "attitudes" as mental events brought about by branding. Instead, consumers articulate media marketing, rendering its much segmented stories into coherent accounts. If successful, audiences align with these prescriptive narratives bearing *prima facie* reasons for their appropriating presentations of branded space, time and produce use to shape lives.

After watching telecommunications screen branding showing a Chinese New Year reunion dinner where all are phoning friends elsewhere, Malay research respondents aligned in shared identity, appropriating the very favorable meaning they had constructed for this narrative. When the latter celebrate festivals, "we (also) invite our friends ... our family, sit together and eat together." In typifying the dinner as communitarian "getting together" the Malays clearly read and responded to this marketing story from a different cultural horizon of understanding to that occupied by its Chinese viewers whom we noted placed the narrative within the genre of "offensive behaviour." Appropriating a brandscape's prescriptive stories, consumers incorporate its vision for everyday life to illuminate a moment in (or aspect of) their own "narrative identity" (Borgerson, 2005: 439).

Audiences align or identify with brand narrative characters (actants) more or less explicitly in the subjective process of making sense from product-centered screen events: viewers may also be alienated by or appropriate (because they identify with) the latter's significance set out in tag lines.

> "Because distance should bring you closer (connect!)" (telecommunications branding advertisement)
> "Because of (the telco), the family is getting closer." (male Indian research participant)

In short, *Global Advertising* rejects the ever-returning "neological positivism of logical empiricism" (O'Shaughnessy and O'Shaughnessy, 2002: 110). Instead of the spurious "scientific" concept of audience attitude, acknowledging cultural diversity, we argue that consumers located on multiple horizons of understanding the world project meaning on media marketing and position themselves in respect of the resulting prescriptive narrative. Articulating the perspectives of brandscape space and time, audiences align and appropriate their evaluative dimensions or distance themselves in the alienated analysis we have termed depth hermeneutics. Sensitive to situated concepts in text or context of reception, hermeneutics "brings meaning to the center to understand lived experience rather than to posit universal laws and categories" (Turner and Krizek, 2006: 124).

Consumers' ludic cognitive investment in screen responses producing meaning for media marketing narrative can underwrite their subsequent investment in the material product advertised. Audience alignment with aspirational advertising may indeed not result in action: there can be "wanting without buying" (O'Shaughnessy, 1987). But otherwise, if paradoxically, immersion in comprehending a branding story can initiate its appropriation in subsequent real world buying.

A suitably attuned reception theory allows fine-grained accounting for audience discourse focused on their reading and absorbing themselves in screen media and shopping mall. Equally, consumer talk can be seen as testing our model of audiences responding to advertising [following the logic of potentially falsifying or refuting hypothetical conjectures as described in Popper's (1963) now classical statement of scientific method]. The conceptual and more concrete connect.

"Data" from local focus groups is able to put flesh on a global skeletal model of consumer reception. "You can just imagine yourself" immersively in the space of the narrative advertisement we screened, our Chinese female event organizer responded: "they didn't show the very detailed thing exactly," "they leave a space for you so that to continue (...) you have to think yourself." More abstractly, seeking determinate meaning, this consumer "in (cognitive) play" "wants something to 'go,' 'to come off'; he [sic] wants to 'succeed' by his own exertions" (Huizinga, 1970: 29).

By drawing on media theory and a hermeneutic account of reading as cultural projection the relationship between digital stories of products and their purchasing can be disclosed. We seek conceptual connections between cellphone branding on screen and embodied consumers, between these "promotional messages" and their reception in a "produced symbolic world" (Wernick, 2000: 301). Our empirical approach (Krotz, 2006: 303) is guided by an interest in forms of cellphone life.

"Cellphone Connections" considers conceptual hypotheses—speculative digital definitions:

> (H1) that media marketing or screen branding of cellphone connections addresses an intended audience with a familiar world (a linked life-world) of safe/saving digitally supported relationships.
>
> (H2) immersed in branding narrative, people absorb, articulate (actualize) and align or are alienated by screen meaning as consumer citizens active in constructive cognitive play (as ludic).[4]

Our research method is not inductive [the "Achilles heel" (Hoijer, 2008: 275) of qualitative research] but *abductive*. Establishing support for (H1) we analyze several brief branding stories to abstract their common core of narrative practice, a similar linking of screen story to intended subject (or audience). Advertising accounts of a would-be (perhaps actual) world provide envisaged viewers with culturally close reassuring content.

Screen use is constantly interpretative. Through considering discussions with television viewers of diverse ethnic background we arrive at shared themes in what they say which can be used to test (or attempt to falsify) the second hypothesis (H2).

Our approach does not exclude research aimed at quantifying relationships between (say) ethnicity, gender and cellphone feature preferences. However, we are interested in establishing a subjective narrative of discursive or qualitative response (as cognitive play) to cellphone branding stories on screen. Remembering comparable advertising and hence continually anticipating content, people read with attaining coherence as a goal. Audiences articulate the narrative sketches they see into stories of a virtual "gathering place" of saving, supportive protection for consumer citizens in continuing digital contact. Drawing on philosophical concepts from agora to life-world, a qualitative account of reactions to branding can support others making quantified research connections.

"Cellphone Connections" discusses its findings in the context of wider research on the cellphone's "marketing representations" (Lillie, 2005: 41). On the one hand, we here seek not confrontation but rather to display within those other investigations an implicit or tacit conception of responses to branding as play-like perception of promised protection. Mobile phones are "bound to a sense of place and community" (Hjorth, 2008: 93). On the other hand, in studies of media use the "full range" of "intricate processes" involved is "oversimplified" and "homogenized" if research is conducted within a positivistic paradigm's "narrow epistemological assumptions" (Ringberg and Reihlen, 2008: 173). As we have seen, these reductive axioms assert that viewing is constituted by quantifiable cause and effect relationships between observable variables—screen content and audience behavior, with communication studies blind to reading's connecting subjective process.

## ADVERTISING—ARTICULATING AGORA—ABSORBING AUDIENCES

Branding is a narrative palette of image and text which persuades intended consumers to immerse themselves in its product-centered places—to become part of its possible counterfactual culture or share its subjunctive sense. They identify with occupants, imagine enjoying the latter's product-focused lives, purchasing coffee or cellphone connection: passing through, they "challenge grinding everyday routines" (Daliot-Bul, 2007: 955). Like media marketed fast food fantasy spaces, advertising's screen brandscapes are extended places of extra-playful otherness (permitted excess) yet simultaneously identifiable.

Through understanding inhabitants' stories, as "co-creators of meaning" (Thompson and Tian, 2008: 596) we come to share a sense of circumstances and occasion, their potent cultural awareness of product.

In the process of identifying with these people's product-emphasizing comprehension of life, we re-shape our own conceptual horizons of interpreting the world, re-reading our categorizing of education, eating and edifying nationhood. Moving to a new vantage point, perhaps, we see universities as not only information but income generating. Through this sequence, our perception emerges as a result of reaching immersive consensus with students already occupying their advertised academic agora as communities of citizens actively realizing purchased consumption.

A brand's consumer address strives to structure our perspectives, the commodified "way we see things, places, and people" (Cayla and Eckhardt, 2008: 217). Ringtones are purchasable cultural icons. Yet branding space into often urban product-centered place may be accompanied by media constructions of "moral responsibility" holding within a "community" of purchasers (ibid.: 216). Convinced consumers develop a relationship as ethical citizens, a sense of moral interconnection or "mutual belonging" (ibid.: 217) and "mediated sociality" (ibid.: 225). Branded telecommunications marketing can remind us to purchase "because so much needs to be said" between friends.

Displacing specific geographical locations, advertised agora on screen may offer space for a "virtual plebiscite" (Thompson and Tian, 2008: 611) of discussion to citizens as well as dining to consumers: like brands these populated places can be transnational. With its extended cultural identity, McDonald's presents as corporate citizen of moral standing, with an ethical purchase, bonding with buyers in happy meals.

Digital agora are spaces for consumer citizens to collect and connect through "intermediated togetherness" (Bell, 2005: 72), perhaps as close companions in "primary social relationships over distance" (Katz, 2005: 173). Yet critically distanced and disingenuous, we can also appropriately ask of advertised "mobilities" (Larsen et al., 2008): "what are we to be connected to—each other, systems of regulation and surveillance, or a marketplace of commodities?" (Lillie, 2005: 47).

Cellphones replaced "location-based with person-based communicative systems" (Geser, 2005: 25), purchasable digital agora of caller involvement through casual, anytime, anywhere linking. "In this way, the mobile can function as a 'pacifier for adults' that reduces feelings of loneliness and vulnerability in any place and any time" (ibid.: 26). We are always in potential contact albeit within a temporal horizon of constraint by work and other duties when one switches off or resorts to "silent" mode. Otherwise, we can celebrate with cellphones in extended episodes an increasingly pervasive, "naturalized" (Bell, 2005: 69) immersive ludic life-world of on-screen supportive connection or "convivial proximity" (De Gournay and Smoreda, 2003: 58).

"Cellphone Connections" uses an interpretative approach in bringing to the fore consciousness and citizenship in consumer studies. People are actively-passively absorbed in cellular brandscapes, enriching the latter's edited narrative "architectures of (audience) participation" (Wilson, 2006: 229). Our interviewees engaged in "actualizing" (Zhao and Belk, 2008: 234) marketing stories on screen. Viewers appropriate content through "self-branding" (Hearn, 2008: 198) as users, even forming a reflexive "post-traditional self" (Lüders, 2008: 683) supported by smart phones. Tacit (or implicit) knowledge of these responses emerges in "consumer narratives" (Kozinets, 2008: 866).

Developing and downloading stories from advertising, of course, can be to imbibe the power of corporations over consumers (and subscribe to their ideology). But with the inventive resistance characteristic of culture jamming, responding to branding is able to be equally creative of a certain independence from capitalism. Cognitive play may be plural to the point of protest: "divergent interpretive processes" (Ringberg and Reihlen, 2008: 176) are heard to occur where consumers view from varying horizons of understanding. A nation's "subaltern population" (Varman and Belk, 2008: 228) can detach itself from the media discourse of a colonial power, rescuing itself from global cultural recruitment, remembering local citizenship.

Immersing ourselves in brandscaped accounts of screen technology, enjoyment is not invariably politically liberating. However, reflecting on the concluding years of the last century, Kozinets argues that such "technology had become ineluctably interconnected to realms of playful pleasure," to psychologically "escaping into dramatically altered digital realities" (2008: 871). Nonetheless (not least because an exclusive focus on the latter attracts moral censure as Internet "addiction"), one can adopt a more instrumentalist version of absorbing technology where the consumer experience is said to be that of "practical calls" (Licoppe, 2003: 174) stretching its facilities to serve external "real world" goals. Mobile phones, for instance, are said to be important in (spatially) opening up the range of social possibilities for their youthful users (Tutt, 2005: 60). Agoric access to peers through these "coordination technologies" (Larsen et al., 2008: 640) can allow "micro-coordination of activities" (Ling and Haddon, 2003: 245) by cellphone.

## THEORIZING THE LIVED EXPERIENCE OF CELLPHONES AS LUDIC AND LINKED

Play can be used as a metaphor of media involvement—as a model of the audience's coming to understand narrative with the goal of constructing screen content. Appealing to multiple aspects of ludic experience allows us to consider and conceptualize (to recognize culturally) both shared cognitive processes and separating differences in the many forms of media reception and response at leisure or work. In our understanding cellphone use as a "platform of play" (Daliot-Bul, 2007: 966), there is a "synergy" between "mobile communication and gaming" (Hjorth, 2007: 369).

Cellphones deliver a "technological enframing of the world" (Arnold, 2003: 237). Owning and operating a handphone one cultivates a co-presence [or "simultaneous presence" (Lasen, 2006: 227)] as contactable in both (geographically) determinate place and (potentially) always on digital agora. People switch attention, glancing or gazing around, at least minimally monitoring their surroundings while concurrently more or less immersed in the ludic co-operative construction of sense on their cellphones. In their abbreviated or absolute focus on scrutiny of the screen, they manage the "autonomy/connectedness dialectic" (Aakhus, 2003: 40).

Immersive games and media use may be evaluated aesthetically: they can be judged as constructing personality, distributing power, evoking well-being. These electronic forms of digital departure from daily immediacy may be profoundly absorbing, although they can yield also to a more instrumental off-screen interest in using "data" which limits one's ludic escape. In this experiential tension between the immersive and the instrumental, "cultural borders between play and non-play blur" (Daliot-Bul, 2007: 955) thereby "furthering the collapse between work and leisure distinctions" (Hjorth, 2005: 53). Absorption may be abbreviated. Reading emails or sms relaying worldly obligation is frequently laborious work.

Cellphones allow their consumer citizen users to become continually absorbed in agora or digitally gathered connections which are "multiplexed" (Sooryamoorthy et al., 2008: 729) or related to multiple media. Personal use of mobile phone technology can provide long distant linkage and an alternative record by citizen journalists of "critical (public) situations" (Gordon, 2007: 308) such as the real life drama of natural disasters. Nonetheless, this telephoning to connect others to major events may not significantly subvert or even call into question "primary definitions" (ibid.: 316) of those situations in reporting media (such as newspapers) with established editorial processes.

Our absorbed immersion in the diegetic (story-constructed) agora or spaces and times of televised drama is also possible (sometimes with difficulty) on these comparatively diminutive screens. During their "perambulatory public leisure" (Dawson, 2007: 233), consumer citizens link through a slender cellphone signal to enjoy or become infuriated with the often short, segmented "new modes of storytelling, distribution, and reception" cellphones "inaugurate" (ibid.: 232).

## CONCEPTUALIZING THE DISCOURSE OF BRANDING AND CONSUMER CITIZEN RESPONSE

Branding aims to "colonize the lived experience of consumers in the interests of capital accumulation" (Hearn, 2008: 200). As "culture bearers" (Kozinets, 2008: 871) reading within our informed horizons of understanding we have an interpretative choice or hermeneutic liberty to follow interests intrinsic or extrinsic to screen narratives when actualizing their advertised agora. Should we share or subvert perspectives on screen?

To further our own investigation of how to philosophically conceptualize corporate branding and its discursive audience "reading," we conducted a series of interviews involving eight very different Malaysian everyday users of cellphones. These discussions took place in a customer service walk-in centre operated by a transnational telecommunications provider at Berjaya Times Square mega-mall (claimed to have a floor area greater than the Pentagon) in central Kuala Lumpur. We showed four of their brief television branding advertisements to self-selected local Chinese of both genders, an Indian couple who negotiated a shared account of their content and Malay male interviewees. The longest screened commercial was thirty-eight seconds and the shortest twenty-six seconds. Our discussion allowed us to explore local reception of a marketed and mediated experiential logic of continuing contact for consumers, citizens and more or less close companions participating in digital agora or global "personal networks" (Boase, 2008: 490).

Emphasizing the company's support for roaming (or overseas use of cellphones), three of these marketing narratives were (ostensibly) set in Beijing during the 2008 Chinese Olympics and featured the company's Yellow (Coverage) Fellow [a "cute" (Hjorth, 2007) character in a bulky yellow costume]. He is a frequently sighted iconic corporate "icebreaker" or "mascot" (Chinese male) visually conveying its omnipresent invisible digital signal, song and tag line: "I Will Follow You" (adapted from the 1963 Rick Nelson song with the same name). "The Yellow Man (...) changed the market (...) so they really move up" (male Malay—formerly a civil servant in the Malaysian government's telecommunications division, responding here to our questions as a retired person or, as he said, a member of a "particular public").

In the first advertisement, the Yellow Fellow dives alongside a competitor, reaches the water first, and guides him with his hands safely and skillfully to effect a "perfect dive" (male Chinese). The second features the Fellow accompanying a gymnast in a routine (as elegantly as possible given the Yellow Man's bulk!) flourishing ceremoniously a long white ribbon which they weave around their bodies and then pass between them in a stylish display. In the third, he assists a weight lifter, wiping the sweat from the competitor's brow, and hoists the latter's dumb bells higher.

The fourth branding narrative we showed our interviewees before discussing them was a short compilation of Malaysian everyday scenes from bus stop to supermarket, predominantly with a romantic focus and multiple ambient floating yellow hearts: the concluding tag line here was "Everybody <Yellow Heart> Savings" (or everybody loves savings). Unlike the Beijing trilogy, it featured "localized practices of mobile multimedia" (Hjorth, 2008: 91) supporting connections substantiating the everyday practices of one nation.

Each of these corporate tales of collaboration and success was screened to our three Chinese, two Indian and two Malay participants (two females and five males). [One female participant provided a Chinese name but refused to confirm this as her ethnicity.] As occasional translator, our female Chinese researcher was an eighth contributor to the interviews (as indicated).

The questions we directed at our interviewees to prompt discussion explored responses to screen events often reductively regarded as the "emotional" aspect of branding. Reference to their contributions enabled a "grounded approach in building analytic concepts" (Aakhus, 2003: 32) for use in telecommunications analysis (such as "agora"). These structuring queries were:

(i) Please describe the content of the advertisement—what's taking place? Does it involve you?
Did it surprise you? Could you make sense of it?
(ii) Can you identify with what you see? Do you find it "culturally close"?
(iii) Do you think the advertising gives you reason(s) for buying a (brand name) connection?

The longest discussion was twenty-five minutes and the shortest twelve minutes.

## INTERPRETING BRANDING AWARENESS: RESEARCH AND RESULTS

### Conceptual Hypothesis (H1): Branding Conceptualizes Cellphone Connections as Supportive Links Across Life-Worlds

Narrative analysis of each television advertisement suggests a predominant authorial concern to enable audiences to believe in a secure world of cellphone support—to brand on purchasers of products a storied awareness of "cellphone savings." All three of the Beijing Games commercials emphasized emblematically the capacity of the Yellow Fellow (or a cellphone connection) to support swimmer, gymnast and weight lifter (us) in their (our) striving for success: the bulky fellow becomes a benign and familiar presence regularly active in their (our) life-world. His intensely playful activity on screen can be read as physical correlative of consumer cognitive play when interpreting the telecommunication company's narrative sketch to form a fully fledged story. Both competitive agora and cognitive appropriation of meaning are instantiated as ludic.

The final advertisement we screened likewise inscribed a familiar, friendly Malaysian life-world ("lovely day") of playful (ludic) relationships on screen. In each everyday sequence forming this brief compilation increasingly close friends (or partners already intimate) are connected, linked together, supported and strengthened by an omnipresent floating and flourishing iconic Yellow Heart [brand(ish)ing benevolence on those below]. "When I wake up in the morning light. ... "

Each of the Beijing stories concludes with a positive image of continuing reassurance (a narrative equilibrium). Safely restored to dry land from the swimming pool, signaling a "V for Victory" sign to Olympic audiences, smiling across distance in direct address to the brand's consumer citizens seated at home in Malaysia, the Yellow Fellow is "Always With You." In the final sequence of the fourth advertisement, a driver's fractured Yellow Heart (caused by the cost of car petrol?) is restored to unity when cyclists pass the filling station. "Lovely day, lovely day. ... "

## Conceptual Hypothesis (H2): Consumer Citizens Align and Appropriate/Analytically Assert Alienation from Brandscapes

Interviewees enriched these short narrative sketches (with an average length of thirty seconds), developing both the latter's denotative (descriptive) and connotative dimensions as carefully crafted meaningful messages bearing transnational telecommunications branding. Skillful diving into the pool supported by the Yellow Man (or strong cellphone connection) "showed how smooth the line should be" "no matter what happens" (male Indian). There is "no distraction of noise" in either pool or phone but rather "perfect (...) connectivity" (male Indian).

The corporate branding narrative shows that "any place that you are, (the company) is there to help you, to assist you": "that's why (the Yellow Fellow) dives into the pool and saves or helps (the competitor) to dive smoothly." "At any place, when you have difficulties (the Yellow Man or cellphone connection) will be there to assist you," always reliably "being with you": "they're always there for you" "able to respond at *any* length (distance)," continually "there to help you in whatever situation" (female Indian) (emphasis in original) providing ontological security.

In the third example of Beijing branding (as noted) the Yellow Fellow wipes the sweat from the weightlifter's brow during a "more emotionally inclined" scenario. "In times of difficulty (as a cellphone connection) he's there to help (...) wiping off the sweat" (female Indian). This narrative could signify a family separated by distance, with its members struggling to succeed, but eventually "happy talking" (male Indian) supported by cellphone connection and the Yellow Man.

Consumers perceive in the three short stories of far away Beijing support a cellphone brandscape being effectively claimed as articulated "around the world" (female Chinese) wherein people should feel themselves secure—or indeed "saved" (firmly and perhaps financially) from "difficulties." In this advertised agora, "wherever I go, everywhere, even down under the sea (...) (the coverage) is around me," "always around us" connecting or gathering us. It "supports you," "helps you" even "in the wrong position" or "having problems," it is "*always* there for you" (female Chinese) (emphasis in original with laughter). It "helps us always" (tr. male Malay).

Repeated marketing and regular media use render this corporate screen entered immersive agora (signaled appropriately by the Beijing Olympics swimming pool) an increasingly familiar supportive structure purporting to characterize and link everyone's everyday life-world. Branding renders the invisible visible. Coverage—a virtual space and time of connecting—becomes thereby "part of our system" (male Chinese). We "have seen a number of (these) advertisements" (female Indian). Viewing them, audiences build a tacit awareness of claimed-to-be supportive digital agora.

Branding is narrative "social shaping of mobile interactivity" (Goggin and Spurgeon, 2007: 755). Completed by viewers these screen sketches shape the "mindset of the people" (male Malay) reflectively remembered during interviews. A Chinese (male) contributor swiftly recognizes such cellphone connectedness "from the advertisements I see *every* day" (emphasis in original).

Some of our interviewees celebrate these frequently screen presented horizons from which to understand the company's service as being "culturally close" (tr. male Malay). But others talk critically of being unable to comprehend the branding, its "concept." Reception of these texts is incomplete: "I don't *get* what (they're) trying to tell me" (male Malay) (emphasis in original). It "(doesn't) really come to me. (...) It doesn't make sense to me, you know" (female Chinese).

Audiences also respond to uplifting screen scenarios branding worldly agora of product acquisition as people aware of citizen defining culture and ethnicity (particularly in Malaysia). The "Yellow Man (...) blends very well into culture no matter what race you are ... whether you are Chinese, Indian, Malay or 'others.'" This iconic signifier of certain connection functions as a "'tag line' to other cultures (...) it carries very well" being culturally close to "everybody." "It doesn't matter what you are, you're still able to use (it)." The ribbon in the Beijing gymnast advertisement "indicates the line (...) when it tangles around it shows it supports *any* culture," it is both culturally and digitally "close to anybody" (emphasis in original). After viewing this media marketing "the Yellow Man actually stays in everyone('s mind) whether it's (the) young or the old" (male Indian).

The final video featured scenes from multi-cultural Malaysian everyday life rendered romantically euphoric by the glowing presence of a Yellow Heart. Not surprisingly content was "culturally close, yes!" (female Indian), "more involving," "more connected" (male Chinese). It "keeps people closer, connects them" (male Chinese). Music unfolding with the message ("Everybody <Yellow Heart> Savings") "we always hear during my younger days" (male Malay).

But the advertisement's iconic address to audiences signaling the availability of the cellphone "close link" was global as well as local. This story "explains everything that we said! (...) It just blends very well with your culture (...) in any part of the world" (male Indian): "it does not matter what race you are, what color you are" (female Indian). The two Indian interviewees clearly considered these brandscaping narratives de-distance or de-spatialize, bringing people together.

Likewise, a Chinese (female) contributor emphasized to us the significance of this televised telecommunications branding as digitally shaping an agora bringing its citizens and consumers together: allowing "all your relationships, your friends, your relatives, your loved ones, everyone that (would be?) close to reach (one) another": "anytime, anywhere, that you can call them you'll feel closer to each other. (Whether) they're young or old (it) brings all together." Other respondents reflecting on the last advertisement we screened distanced themselves in hermeneutic suspicion. They conceded critically: "I can't see the connection" (male Malay) between its several tales of the heart and tag line. Are these images of caring and inventive capitalism to be connected: "I can't understand it. (...) You want to show the love or what? Or the discount?" (male Chinese).

We recorded in these interviews subjective stories from respondents differing in ethnicity, gender and generation (one was receiving government superannuation payments). They are research participants' perceptions of ways in which immersive branding content could plausibly be read (some of those we talked to claimed interpretative skill).

Conveyed to us in public linguistically mediated thought processes, these audience accounts of their productive goal-directed cognitive play constitute subjectively real (not merely observable) data. Our contributors aimed at forming advertising narratives and attained coherently articulated conceptual constructions of cellphone linked and supported life-worlds to which they respond as culturally oriented citizens as well as product consumers. Branding shaped their understanding.

Responding to a television advertisement by the same company, an interviewee in earlier research we noted spoke of being faced with a "space" (an absence of information) in screen marketing: "you won't know what happens next. So that you have to imagine first (...) you will think many things, 'Eh, what (are) they going to do?' You will imagine it, what they're going to do" (Chinese female). As in a game, always forward looking, one plunges into the detail of reaching a successful narrative ending (goal) by completing a preceding chain of events.

Like diving, watching successful corporate branding on screen is often but not always passively immersive. ["It grabs me!" (female Indian). It "pulls you, attracts you!" (male Malay). It "(doesn't) attract me!" (female Chinese).] We simultaneously anticipate actively realizing a story of corporate support: after seeing the Yellow Fellow icon, "it doesn't surprise me" (male Malay). Involvement is then a function of whether one can successfully infer narrative and one's capacity to identify with those seen in play: "It's out of my prediction. (...) Does it involve me? Of course not, lah, because I'm (...) not athletic. (...) I only play games for table tennis!" (male Chinese).

Media marketing may be "interestingly different" (male Malay) in its reception, "quite unusual, I mean 'funny'" (male Chinese). Tacking to and fro across a swimming pool or story, from expecting to establishing success or sense, one can strive to reach a goal and so substantiate a personal identity as performing or producing meaning. But narrative implausibility may intrude: "this one cannot be happen(ing)" (male Chinese), it is a "shock" (tr. male Malay).

Our research participant accounts of insight and immersion in media marketing's linked and ludic life-worlds corroborate (or fail to falsify) our two hypotheses (H1) and (H2). Branding emphasizes the cellphone's specially supportive status (far from the banal) as a small screen saving us from stress. Consumer citizens conceptualize its frequently advertised agora as familiar (or even familial) gathering places, generating a holistic meaning in understanding them from elliptical narrative sketches on screen. Occasionally, hermeneutic anticipation is halted, our deliberation is dumbfounded, predicting events is not within an audience's horizons of understanding: speculating on the story's development is "out of my imagination" (male Chinese). But otherwise, in providing extended narratives of marketing's subjective reception, these interviewees experientially enriched our abstract academic speculation in research.

## CONSUMER CITIZENS BLOGGING

In order to further analyze varying perspectives on the lived experience of cellphones, we turned from thoughts about branding to accounts of communicating using the technology itself. We moved to different horizons of understanding screen media and their intricate support for everyday life. Deploying Technorati.com as a search engine yielded recent web logs or personal Internet narratives of response to the transnational telecommunications provider whose services we were exploring as well as experiential accounts of "my cellphone."

Assessing these stories was not inductive but abductive, a search again for themes related to those of linkage, protection and support we had already discovered operated in branding and in how consumers perceptually constructed this genre of screen marketing. Does handphone use wrap one safely within an extended life-world of familiar, familial connection, perhaps even of "mobile parenting" (Rizzo, 2008: 140)? Does everyday cellphone access position people culturally as consumer citizens within digital agora, gathering them together in extended contact? What does blogging say about our ludic small screen immersion? Anon (2008), for instance, tells us of the anguished "'Disconnect Anxiety' That Affects 68 Percent of (the) U.S. Population."

For a Malaysian couple (JesuLalaine, 2008), phone contact brought emerging if not immediate confirmation of their extended familial life-world: a relative was "playing tricks." Their excited anticipation of winning a nice "3,000 RM lucky draw" was not actualized: despite initial "seriousness" of expectation a successful self did not eventuate. Nonetheless in this safely connected familiar space they were not victims of a "sort of a scam or something." The blogging narrative sets actual and possible disequilibria (disappointments or disasters) against the story's final equilibrium of "linking" to a "lady on the other side" (the call recipient wife's "sister-in-law"). People are brought together here in a storied digital agora of continuing contact as law-abiding consuming citizens.

There was once we received a call when we were in Malaysia. My Hubby answered it and it was from a lady who spoke in Malay. I just overheard my Hubby saying, "Yes ... yes ... yes." With seriousness on his face. The lady seemed to be telling my Hubby that he won a 3,000 RM lucky draw from (the telco) and he must go to their office to claim their prize. When he asked the address of their office, the address sounded so familiar. It was our house address in Taiping and the lady on the other side was already laughing "Anna, it's me! Susan!" It was my sister-in-law all the while playing tricks on him! Whew! I thought that it was sort of a scam or something. Since, there's a scam that is going now that tells you that you win something and they get all your account details and stuff. And at the end they steal money from you.

(JesuLalaine, 2008)

On other occasions, cellphone contact varied from short to surprisingly substantial. Suseela (2008) who sought a housing loan with the support of "Sham" and paid the latter a cash fee suddenly found she "is not answering my calls or SMS's." Far from a story of branded support, readers who articulate her prescriptive narrative can appropriate a hermeneutic of distancing suspicion towards cellphone "cheats." "As long as there are people like me who, in spite of life's incessant lessons, continue to trust so easily, there will be cheats like Sham. Please people be aware. Don't get cheated like me!!" A cellphone's connectivity can be abruptly cut.

Akin to gargantuan assistance from the Yellow Fellow, cellphone support for another user of the company's service consisted of her winning the "Grand Prize," an absorbing link to rapture or "dumbstruck" appropriation of success beyond a brandscaped agora. "After I got off the line, I was still sitting down and staring at my phone in my hand. I was dumbstruck ... and I'm still pretty dumbstruck. Well now, I'm happy and dumbstruck" (WMW, 2008).

But cellphone linking can be too constant, producing a rash not rapture. Admin (2008) comments on the Web image of a heavy handphone user: "He's upset for other reasons. Do you suffer from 'mobile phone dermatitis'? It's a rash that develops on your ears and cheeks that's the result of prolonged cellphone use." Immersion may lead to irritation not only on the skin but with the service provider. Being connected can function for the imprecise as a repeated reminder of turpitude. The service provider "never failed to call me every time I'm late a day or two on the payment. (Err ... not that I know the exact date to pay, anyway)" (Cinderella Jane, 2008).

## Cellphone Agora of Activated Contact: Connecting to Future Considerations

Branding places ideal consumer citizens of its products in a linked familiar life-world, an agora or market meeting place. Such mediated selling constructs through edited ellipsis a supportive "playscape" (Daliot-Bul, 2007) for the mind: convinced viewers immersively enter a caring "ludic experiential commodity" (ibid.: 965) such as campus, coffee house or cellphone connection represented (as by the Yellow Coverage Fellow) on screen. Subsequently, remembering this virtually promised land/life-world we aim to reproduce its circumstances materially. "Consumers recognize, use, and live through the brand" (Hearn, 2008: 200)—not always convinced of quality.

"Cellphone Connections" explored two processes at the core of marketing and consumption. First, what does television branding say about a "new media" product—in this case a Malaysian cellphone network—to intended customers? What horizon of understanding (perspective on) products does it seek to construct or shape? Do consumers perceive and acquiesce in this branding statement? Secondly, media use is "constitutive" of "meaning-making processes" (Hartmann, 2006: 278). How do audiences make sense of the elliptical and sometimes enigmatic segmented narrative which characterizes television branding? How do consumers assemble a coherent meaning?

In regard to the first process, we argued that branding builds an agora (or gathering place), a linked and ludic life-world (familiar space and time) of support for its consumer citizens. Of course, immersing in one group (of friends) can separate from another (one's family). In our interviews with telecommunications customers, we heard them discursively celebrate this digital embrace.

In respect of consumers interpreting the stories of branding, we claim that they do so in play-like mode: immersed within horizons of understanding which inform or shape comprehension, they engage in game-like, goal-directed, to-and-fro processes of constructing meaning. Recognizing content on screen, audiences become absorbed and immediately anticipate narrative development, articulating the latter into accounts of events, which they appropriate as self-regarding stories.

Branding and buyers can concur—almost. Cellphone audiences activate access to agora of attachment. Absorption in "phonespace" (Johnsen, 2003: 168) cultivates consumership, citizenship and the close companionship of friends "always with you." Here we invest processually in the "idea of belonging" (ibid.: 163). We hold and (in turn) are securely "held" by hand phones.[5]

# 6 Mall-eable Media Marketing

## "Give Reality the Slip?"

*With Tan Huey Pyng and Rabaah Tudin*

Remember Who You Are,
Forget Who They Want You To Be.
Sleep past midday.
Take two hours for lunch.
Spend three hours on your hair.
Give reality the slip.
Give in to yourself.
Live more, worry less.
        The Gardens At Mid Valley
            ... it's about you.[1]

Media marketing may be malled. Advertising's agora or gathering spaces and times for the gregarious on screen can be written into concrete formations as places not only for sipping Coke but for shopping. A mall's echoing architecture is regularly occupied by persons pursuing purchases and pleasure, by friends and family "outings" which as well as being intrinsic immersive fun are instrumentally functional. Visiting The Spring, Sarawak, some find the supermarket meets needs.

Yet shopping malls are represented as sites for the ludic set wholly apart from the laborious, as pure postmodern places for minds engaged in elevating, enjoyable materialism. Addressing an individualistic, assertive anticipation (" ... it's about you"), some brand elongated spaces and times ("Take two hours for lunch") are able to absorb audience consumers in play ("Give reality the slip"). Their wall-mounted poetry propositions us to cultivate the self ("Spend three hours on your hair") and its stories ("Live more, worry less"). In the midst of materialism, we are told, the mind can escape "their" mundane expectations, recovering instead its own identity: "Remember who you are".

Concentrating on such escapism, celebrating its space, we are said to be rescued from other-centered obsession and "give in" to ourselves. "Live more, worry less." But here we shall distance ourselves a little to consider such purportedly absorbing experience of the mall as a rich subject for consumer culture (or interpretive marketing) theory—tested qualitatively by talking to visitors rather than quantitatively established through enumeration of their responses to questionnaires. For malls are "geographies of consumption" (Jackson and Thrift, 2001) peopled by producers of meaning.

The structure of shopping malls (e.g. as web-like) is prefigured in the screen media which bear their marketing, the programs and pages which shape understanding of product. Citizens, advertising format and content make the frequent crossing between television or the Internet's virtual landscape and the town's more material layout, where some of us stroll, shop and catch a movie at the mall. In such substantial spaces people, those who persuade us and purchasers meet and make sense of one another in the cognitive processes or continuum of selling and consuming.

Malls are analogous in format and functioning to media. On the brands-caped mall like the television or Internet screen there are genres (of shops and stores rather than programs or websites), addressing (often noisily) and attracting varying crowds. As in malls, media carry global product, distributing it in diverse ways to the locally situated audience, even addressing us appropriately. Consumer citizens view—and with anticipation become absorbed in the content of products in shops as well as programs or sites on screens. They articulate accounts of both and in moments of appropriation apply these narratives to themselves. In the agoric gathering places of material malls or simulated shopping spaces on screen we position ourselves immersively amid product of interest. But in both we can be epistemologically stretched between the intrinsic ludic focus of an "outing" and an instrumental concern with a necessary purchasing for dutiful domestic labor—the "diffusion of consumer culture presents" "dilemmas for the world's peoples" (Classen and Howes, 1996: 179).

## THE MALL AS A MEETING PLACE FOR CONSUMER AND COMMUNICATION THEORY

Quantitative questionnaires generally omit qualitative detail—the defining cultural aspects of a locality which are expressed in focus group speech or authored weblogs. A passing moment of eating at a cafe mall may be an "epiphany." Yet such subjective specificity can be accommodated and preserved within a structured narrative of how people perceive the world. Detailed cultural references may be placed within categories of seeing as a process (e.g. as more than meeting expectations) which form the focus of a questionnaire whose answers can be counted with accuracy. "Is visiting the mall ever more than anticipated? If so, tell us your story."

"Malaysian Shopping Mall Behavior: An Exploratory Study" (Ahmed et al., 2007) concludes:

> Malaysian students were motivated to visit malls primarily by the interior design of the mall; products that interested them; opportunities for

socializing with friends; and convenient one-stop shopping. Further analysis showed that younger respondents have more favorable dispositions or shopping orientations towards malls than somewhat older respondents. (...) Generally, the observed Malaysian shopping behavior was similar to that observed of Western shoppers in prior shopping studies. (Abstract)

These banal and culturally dispossessed conclusions are the product of a quantitative research method which generalizes about the world omitting specific human perceptions. Even the authors admit in acknowledging the limitations of this research that, "consumers' shopping-related perceptions and expectations are likely to differ across countries or cultures throughout the world."

Unfortunately, positivist accounts of different expectations and perceptions remain at the level of the nomological. Driven by inductivist logic, after all, the goal of these researchers is to establish conclusions which are as general or wide ranging as possible, with the character of scientific laws and cultivating causes of attitudes to malls buried not far beneath. Ambitiously world-wide in focus, these assertions leave little space for detailed reason-giving from those immersed in local culture.

Customers from many countries or backgrounds, we are told, including Hispanics living in Florida (Nicholls et al., 1997), Generation Y in the mid-Western area in the USA (Martin and Turley, 2004), Hungarian (Millan and Howard, 2007), as well as Chinese and Chilean (Nicholls et al., 2000; Li et al., 2003, 2004), appeared to come malling with an instrumental shopping purpose rather than a more intrinsically focused goal of deriving pleasure from simply being in these places of considerable architecture. On the other hand, large proportions of the shoppers in Florida, USA (52.6%) indicated that they came to look and browse (Nicholls et al., 2002).

In paradigmatic positivist marketing studies of mall and media culture, connections between shop or screen content and its consuming audience are considered reductively as observed stimulus and response [research subjects completing "anonymous scaled attitude measures" (Belk,1995: 62)]. We have noted little mention is made of local cultural detail, the particularities of place and time embedded in people's stories of why they go shopping. Instead, media content and consumer are quantitatively compared as variables: research hypotheses make connections between, for instance, increased television marketing and augmented purchasing. We have discussed such views (as that repeating screen images of succulent pizza prompt/promote customer salivation and sales).

Conceptualized within this prevailing paradigm for consumer studies, advertising "targets" audiences: its effects on them, their reactions, are causal consequences. A recent monograph, we noted, describes as its focus "unintended effects of ethnically targeted advertising on ethnic groups that are not targeted but who are still likely to see the advertising" (De Run, 2008: 1).

From the alternative perspective of marketing reception theory with which we have engaged, product advertising is said to "address" consumers with a "preferred reading." Selling a nation in a celebratory or tourist television advertising positions its intended audience not as salivating for sensation but as making sense of events alongside narrative agents on screen. We share the search for meaning and hence (if we do not resist) its preferred and proffered resolution.

More widely, in marketing reception theory both screen media and shopping mall can be regarded as "edited" to absorb viewers without hindrance ("cuts" between characters are covered by continuous dialogue: in the modern mall, doors are often absent). But a place is left for (relatively autonomous) actual audiences or people passing by to respond to what they see "actively"— to decide to immerse themselves in media or mall space, scenario or shop, to try out their anticipation of a pleasurable program or purchase, and then to (in)form themselves accordingly. In this model, there is no chain of cause and effect passivity between mall, media image or marketing content and consumer conduct. Rather, culturally specific reactions by its visitors or viewers are considered akin to reading, as instantiating a universal cognitive process of constructive consumption.

Visiting the mall or viewing media, in this second paradigm, is analyzed by reception theory as constructing meaningful narrative, an activity of intrinsic or instrumental interest to those engaged in the process. "Give reality the slip" in a slow stroll around shops/programs—or swiftly gather materials to enable eating or educated living in "real life" outside these agora of acquisition, tubular corridors for refreshing identities and reconnoitering for goods. The mall has been with us always, under other names and in different forms (Underhill, 2004: 3). As Ancient Greek agora, it was gathering place for exercising citizenship and subsequently a market place for consumption. This civic and suburban shopping space continues to immerse its consumer citizen visitors as a "site of communication and interaction," "community," a "surrogate town square" (Shields, 1992: 5).

Modes of mall immersion are considered here by drawing on the phenomenology of play and thereby modeling or representing them for analysis as ludic. These extended spaces of outdoor/indoor occupation support a "synthesis of leisure and consumption activities" for participants as an absorbed "audience" (Shields, 1992: 6, 7). "Malling" is structurally goal-directed activity with an intrinsic focus on establishing a narrative of one's immediate surroundings: here "private spaces of subjectivity" are related to "changing spatial contexts" (ibid.: 1) But a pleasurably playful immersion is stretched and undercut by accommodating dutiful extrinsic or instrumental concerns.

Farrell's discussion of "Just Looking" (2003) furthers the distinction between "intrinsic" and "instrumental" looking in malls. Shoppers who are "just looking" are not directly or instrumentally relating their gaze to a dutiful purpose beyond (or extrinsic to) the mall. Instead, their immersive interest is "visual spectacle," the "visual feast" that "beckons us invitingly." "From the soaring arches at the entrance to the intricate tile-work in the restrooms, the mall is meant to impress us" (ibid.: 139) The intrinsic interest in "looking for meaning" accompanies even the most instrumentally oriented.

When people go to the mall "looking for stuff," on the other hand, their investigative shifting gaze is instrumental albeit in doing so necessarily constructing accounts or making sense of their complex surroundings. Here, a shopper's looking can be far from guided by immediate interests external to her or his malling but accompanied by an imagined (counterfactual) auto-biography of buying one day. "Americans routinely fantasize about things that we might purchase some day."

Shopping actuality (or fantasy) is a real (or imagined) narrative of present (or future) self-defining appropriation of goods. Changing identity in buying can be a planned consequence or merely coincidental. "We produce the self by consuming stuff (...) Often we're looking for stuff that helps us define and express ourselves (...) I can become myself" in the mall (ibid.: 140–4).

Malls are explorative gathering places—spaces and times for making our narrative sense out of items seen and searching out goods. Whenever "we shop with other people, we simultaneously explore our relationship with them." In short, because it can claim to be particularly ludic in its play-like escapism, malling is "an activity that requires focus, mental energy" (ibid.: 155). Malls have "taken on a lot of the burden of keeping suburban America diverted" (Underhill, 2004: 85).

"Malls cannot be thought of apart from the mass-mediated images of television" (Langman, 1992: 49). "Malling" like media consumption is shaped by past shopping experience or screen use in our continually anticipating and articulating a meaningful dalliance ("Give in to yourself") or dutiful visit. As we have emphasized throughout this volume, in contradistinction to positivism, the generation of knowledge is generic. Perceiving place from our horizons of understanding, seeing screen media or shopping mall content, we relate memory of type to recognized instance in our projecting and production of an account, of being there. Expecting chosen vistas, to see particular programs or potential purchases, our goal in such understanding and use is placing them within a coherent narrative of self or another's satisfaction. Consumption is embodied "active, committed production of self and of society" (Shields, 1992: 2).

Some consumers align, or identify with, while others are antagonistic to (their perceptions of) media marketing's preferred reading of a product to purchase. Immersed on screen, "consumption-based selfhood" can "see itself as the key figure of a TV program, movie or commercial" (Langman, 1992: 56). Likewise, both viewers and visitors "circling the mall" (Williamson, 1992) appropriate or are alienated by screen tag lines or shopping thoroughfares presented as guiding them to gain. Thus audience-consumer-citizens read and recruit (or perhaps ridicule) narratives in the mall.

Looking more widely at consumer studies, we noted that the subject has pursued separate accounts of consumption from communication studies.

These disciplines have constructed distinct intellectual trajectories of research. While the former more recently foregrounded the structured cognitive process of consuming (e.g. as reading), the latter has historically focused on eliciting the structured content of programs. Communication theory could productively mobilize not only its substantial research insight into screens mediating the world through narrative or story telling but accounts of viewing as reading, particularly in the context of analyzing Asian responses to Western popular media constructions of space, time and occurrence. On the other hand, consumer studies would be enhanced by focusing more on marketing screen narrative (Cayla and Arnould, 2008).

In mall studies, methodological integration of communication and consumer studies is possible: shop fronts can be productively theorized as screens just as shoppers may equally be paradigmatically relaunched as readers. As Morris remarks in "Things to Do with Shopping Centers" (1993), malls are "minimally readable to anyone literate in their use" (393). Emerging from literary studies, reader reception theory [associated, we have noted, with Iser (1978) and Jauss (1982)] has played a pivotal role in consumer studies: this European approach to our making sense of media (marketing and malls) was developed by way of phenomenology and hermeneutics.

Consumers read and recognize culturally close malls and marketing from informed horizons of understanding in a process which has been seen as "marketplace metacognition" (Wright, 2002) or drawing on "cultural schemas" (Singh et al., 2005: 131) for comprehending. Reception theory's active constructivism is far from cultivation theory's passively acquiescent audience. In the latter paradigm, while "causality cannot be definitively established" in searching for the media genesis of attitude it is an appropriate goal for research (O'Guinn and Shrum, 1997: 290). Even if not committed to theorizing audience evaluative beliefs as effects of media use, at least for some cultivation theorists, people viewing television involves their being in a "passive cognitive state," "regularly suspending their disbelief" (ibid.: 280).

Reception theory, on the other hand, asserts that the audience is active and always attached to the actual world. Consumers are cognitively involved in a process of interpreting mediated content as instantiating known narrative precisely because they are continually able to recognize it from their culturally-historically located horizons of understanding. Indeed, for two earlier but future-oriented theorists of reading and recognizing advertising, "recognition accuracy can serve as a valid indicator of processing strategy" (Meyers-Levy and Maheswaran, 1991: 63).

From a consumer reception theory viewpoint we read malls and the commodified meaning of advertising texts knowledgeably as following formats or instantiating types. Negotiating these spaces and their selling is enabled by our memory of screen signifiers and shopping complexes. Selfhood becomes thereby "expressed in everyday practices and typifications" (Langman, 1992: 45). Malls are experienced as instantiating generic patterns. Even on first entry, we recognize brands and reconnoitre accordingly from a horizon of expectation. Audiences draw on wide cultural knowledge to see and synthesize a particular world of consumption.

We consider the structure of consumer responses to global advertising, the "social uses of advertising" (Ritson and Elliott, 1999) in media marketed meaning, rather than the structure of that advertising culture itself. The latter's representing of social relationships is discussed elsewhere. [A recent instance is Moon and Chan's (2005) comparison of Hong Kong and Korean advertising. Their investigation of marketing's cultural dimensions makes use of Hofstede's (1980) typology of societal features in classifying advertising's address to its audiences: individualism/collectivism, masculinity/femininity, power distance and uncertainty avoidance.]

Affirming the habitual horizons from which we engage with the world, the familiarity of mundane patterns of acting (not least our apprehending of known media content), consumption activity is important to both the "maintenance and the development of a stable, harmonious self-concept" (Schouten, 1991: 412). Alternatively, appropriating the screen based "idealized images of advertising" (Richins, 1991) can lead to disharmony in comparisons with the self.

Audiences do become alienated from advertising. Distinct from the hermeneutics of consumers processing textual understanding and persuasion, a depth hermeneutics can explore responses distancing selves from powerfully prescriptive marketing. (We noted Chinese audiences criticizing a transnational telecommunications branding narrative of phone calls disrupting family reunions.) Such negativity shows the commercial and cultural necessity of attending to an "ethics of representation" for international marketing communication (Schroeder and Borgerson, 2005).

In short, "advertising theory must extend its horizons beyond oversimplistic cause-and-effect models of advertising response": its perspective on consumer perception needs to take into account the qualitatively "subtle influences created by the social contexts that exist between reception and purchase" (Ritson and Elliott, 1999: 274). Milling around in malls, audiences activate meaning.

Reception theory's presentation of "understanding" as a prolonged activity spatially as well as temporally positioned is particularly apposite when investigating the shopper's cultural responses to visiting and immersing herself or himself in a mall. Consumers read walls, windows and walking in to purchase, reconciling expectations and events, forming their coherent stories of being absorbed in screen enjoyment and shopping expedition. From the perspective of reader reception theory, we can understand their discourse of "understanding" with its minutiae of accomplishment and failure.

Responding to enigmatic marketing (albeit on the "windows" of screen media rather than the "walls" of shopping malls), a Chinese respondent in earlier research, we saw, reflected on her subjective sustained search for sense as process: "you won't know what happens next. So that you have to imagine first (...) you will think many things, 'Eh, what (are) they going to do?'"

Reception theory represents a qualitative approach to studying the forms of comprehension engaged with by mall users which emphasizes the latter's conceptualizing of their circumstances as foundational. Here (as distinct from following a positivist route to sociological insight) the categories and insights of the social scientist are secondary: they are to be logically derived from and shaped by the horizons of understanding or perspective of the ordinary mall participant.

> The "organization of everyday social life is *presupposed* in the practice" of professional sociologists "appropriating their understandings from the members of the society at least as much, if not much more so, than from their formal sociological doctrines. (...) The simple point about 'social actions' is that the relevant criteria of identity belong to the social settings in which those actions occur, and are not contrived by or taken from the theories of social science. (...) The 'intelligibility' of social life derives from the understandings indigenous to the social setting in question." (Hutchinson et al., 2008: 94–96, 101) (emphasis in the original)

Developing the reception model further in consumer studies as a schematic account of the activity through which people immerse themselves not only in screen media but shopping malls we can point to the following structuring moments patterning perception in stories of milling around in such elongated space and time. Independent of ethnicity, these aspects of the "shopper's gaze" form a "cross-class," "trans-gender" "common construction" (Shields, 1992: 13, 12) of our subjectivity walking in these sometimes gargantuan gathering places:

becoming *absorbed*(1) in buying or just being there, already experienced ("regular") consumers simultaneously *anticipate*(2) events which they *articulate*(3) into an account of "malling"; *appropriating*(4) the narrative (e.g. as "outing"), aligning with *others*(5) or finding it *alienating*(6) and hence *analyzing*(7) content, we generate from these stories a renewed horizon of understanding self.

From immersion emerges invention. People play and purchase in modes intrinsic to the mall space—or plan instrumentally (perhaps presents for others).

Following philosophical hermeneutics, reception theory, we noted, considers understanding itself to be play-like. The consuming process of producing meaning is immersive, involving our attention in moving "to and fro" across the concrete text, as well as being goal-oriented in achieving sense. It is thus appropriate to apply accounts of the ludic [Caillois, 1961; Hans,1981; Huizinga, 1970] to thinking through our discursive response to malls. In their indivisible social-economic role as lively citizen-consumers, people engage in game-like mode with such "familiar foreign places," these always recognizable but "set apart" agora (gathering places) prefigured in advertising.

Consumers bring shared cultural perspectives to interpreting marketing or view branded space and time from common horizons of understanding. "Hanging out" ["mallingering" (Kowinski, 1985)] in malls or heavily encumbered by duty, we absorb ourselves actively in these marketed gathering places for subjectivity in shopping. Becoming immersed, consumers simultaneously initiate and subsequently integrate (assemble) accounts of pleasurable play and buying. Relating expectation to event, we can linger and be ludic in malled space, forming stories of place and persons met as well as purchase made. When completed, these narratives are consensually appropriated to inform our identities—or alienate potential purchasers into critical analysis.

Using their introduction to a monograph (*Shopping, Place and Identity*) about building a sense of self and surroundings in the mall, Miller et al. argue for identity construction ("elicitation" of person and place) as a "practice" in "contested" narratives of "interactive" "creative appropriation" or "oppositional" alienation: stories involve the establishing of meaning "bounded" by a gathering place so "often about others as it is about self." A varied "sense of place is increasingly played to" in malls with their "display of difference." Shoppers "identify with their respective site" (1998: 27).

Mall immersion with its intrinsic focus on narratives of the here and now may become subordinate to (or in tension with) an instrumental sense of externally related duty or "tiresome obligations," fulfilled as "often hard and tedious graft." Shopping can be "as much an obligation and a chore as a pleasure," "relatively rarely for the purpose of play" (ibid.: 29). Yet the story of the "chore" is immersively produced in a goal-directed to-and-fro articulating of subjective narrative.

Qualitatively positioned in conceptually sensitive descriptive studies, Miller et al. argue that quantitative methods of measuring consumption can be sclerotic, ossifying or reducing shopper identities to membership of a single category (e.g. "reluctant shoppers") in a "simple typology."

> Such categorical approaches may be a necessary prelude to statistical analysis but they bear little relation to the shifting and complex nature of social identities where we rarely think of ourselves as one thing at all times and in all places. Instead, identity is flexibly formed as a "*discursively* constituted social relation, articulated through narratives of the self and accessed empirically through focus group" as well as ethnographic research [emphasis in original]. (1998: 22–3)

"Data" from our local mall interviews in these enclosed spaces and times of proposed purchase is able to put discursive flesh on a global skeletal model of consumer reception. By drawing on both consumer and communications studies, screen media theory and a phenomenology of reading as cultural projection we exhibit the rich relationship between shopping malls and their users.

We can reflect from the perspective of such consumer culture or interpretive marketing theory on mall user narratives, the brief stories associated with interviews and more extended accounts in (web)logs. Systematic analysis of the latter is now a "new addition to the qualitative researcher's toolkit" (Hookway, 2008: 91). Of course, interviewees usually can be identified reliably in terms of ethnicity, gender (and so on), which is not always true of bloggers. And research participants are addressing different audiences (other contributors and investigators) from those who write online for (they hope and aspire to) global reading. Moreover, the self presented locally to an academic investigator can be quite different from that constructed for a global weblog audience.

Nonetheless, drawing on these various sources of data or talk about the branded agora of acquisitive shopping and assertive self in the mall does permit a focus on how persons milling around in that mall "recognize the artifice, and welcome the play it gives us, the holes, the lacunae, we can fill with our various imaginings" (Small, 2006: 318). For shopping malls, like screen media, from an interpretive marketing perspective informed by reader reception theory, can be discerned as texts replete with indeterminate meaning able to be rescued, identified and transformed into a certain understanding of self by those who perceive, play and purchase productively within them.

## CATCH UP! SCREEN MEDIA AND SHOPPING MALL AS IMMERSIVE AGORA

> Catch Up With Your Friends. Catch Up With Yourself.
> Make small talk, share big dreams.
> Make up for lost time, make it up to yourself.
> Feed your imagination.
> Feed your soul.
> Listen to your heart.
> Hear yourself.
> > The Gardens At Mid Valley
> > ... it's about you.

Shopping malls are secured pleasure domes for the "management of fantasy" (Kowinski, 1985), piled-high pyramids to persuade consumers in seriously playful mode of possibilities to culturally "negotiate" (Salcedo, 2003: 1084) a meaning for themselves in narratives of perception and purchasing. Frequently recycling brands available elsewhere, a limited postmodern pluralism of address to audiences is on view. Selectively signaled in the "virtual geographies" (Currah, 2003) to be found on the relatively small screens showing television and Internet advertising, these shopping zones are vast motif bearing material brandscapes. Explored with a wondering/wandering gaze akin to a tourist's, mediated malls are extended corridors concretely positioning contemplated and consummated consumption (Ozdemir, 2008: 238), conceptually and spatially shaping people's purchasing for others' profit. Rendering this space as place, we buy, meaningfully and materially.

Our narratives of shopping in the mall can re-align in purpose from the less to the more detailed in their goal-attaining focus, in constructing a meaningful account, seeking a sense-making product. Moving from individually attuned to extended research analysis of ludic or goal-directed activity it is "becoming clear" that individuals define their goals initially in more general and abstract terms and later in more specific and concrete ways (Lee and Ariely, 2006: 60–1).

Whatever our focus, we consumer citizens are located on cultural horizons of understanding: they are defining measures of our "discursive agency" (Athique, 2008: 29). We perceive brands of coffee and culinary treat from our media informed perspectives. So positioned, we are *inter alia* intensely addressed by materialism, called to augment our appetite by the increasing construction of new malls and the proliferation of television channels (Cayla and Eckhardt, 2008: 223). Through our extended mall and media consuming of content we are involved in "two contexts of spatial appropria-tion" (Jansson, 2002: 429). For cyberspace itself is a "sprawling mall" (Olson, 2005: 11).

As in clicking on a media screen, gazing not glancing, we cross a mall's loosely defined thresholds with explorative expectation to envelop ourselves in a segment of promoted lifestyle. Recognition of familiar product supports projection, a culturally located anticipation of enjoyment. Escaping daily monotony in this "dreamland" (Salcedo, 2003: 1087), we become absorbed in play-like speculative consideration of likely goods, articulating stories of self-focused consuming, albeit intermittently distracted by remembered exter-nal other-centered obligations. Do we—released from duty—also aim to "catch up with (our) friends" or families, "catch up with (ourselves)"?

Entering the mall, albeit subject to surveillance, we join an intangible agoric "imagined community" (Anderson, 1983) of circumscribed consumer citizens "constructing self and doing community" (Hookway, 2008: 91). We appro-priate products (even a cinema ticket) in extended narratives of gaining a purchase, (in)forming our identities immersively as intrinsic pleasure seekers or (more instrumentally) perhaps with a focus stretched somewhat by serving an equally extended family. "For mall developers and managers, the mall is a dreamland aimed at rescuing citizens from the problems of everyday life" (Salcedo, 2003: 1087). Recover yourself through shopping! Thereby cultivating remarkable if relatively passing detachment, being a part not of the mundane but of the mall supports our storied synthesis of self and shopping in its "dream-like atmosphere" (ibid.: 1088). This elongated space is thus a "true gathering place" (ibid.) for personhood and product, quasi-religious release from the everyday (Varman and Vikas, 2007: 125).

Yet accounting for the process of perceptual immersion must not exclude politically inflected judgment. Liberated in its "produced space" (Ryan, 2005) we are "in play." But what are the mall's "exigencies of place" (Cook, 2008b: 3), its restrictive rules for gamely engaging with people in the positive process of gaining our purchase on its meaning and product? Can the poor play in malls?

Equally, should we "counter-play" (Bradshaw and Holbrook, 2008: 25) or distance ourselves from this ludic urban layout? Can we resist its multiple (less than subtle) persuasion to share far-flung identities as international, regional or global consumers (Cayla and Eckhardt, 2008: 216) of product in "transnational consumerism" (Murdock, 2004: 28)? Do we see the mall's promissory notes of pleasure in entering universal coffee shop brands as cultural imperialism (Christophers, 2007) impervious to local voices or merely recruiting minds for profit? For some perceive and vigorously critique a suspect "secular litany of salvation through purchase" implicit in the mall's self-marketing (imbued in The Gardens prose poetry celebrating the material of individualism):

> critics discern a "reinvigorated master ideology of consumerism, which invited people to think of themselves first and last as individual actors in the marketplace with a sovereign right (even a duty) to remake themselves and realize their aspirations by purchasing goods and services."
>
> (Murdock, 2004: 30, 34)

Resisting international branding, we can cultivate the more locally focused experience of distinctive corner or "dry market" shopping. These diminutive establishments are physically and often psychologically distant from air-conditioned hyperreal constructions of space and spectacle—the elongated shopping mall's "strangely familiar" (Cayla and Eckhardt, 2008: 226) constantly echoing (re)"semblance" of branded places replayed from elsewhere. Within the latter's gigantic geography, we form our identities from the "retailed and the retold" (Small, 2006, 317).

With her or his ability to choose as centrifugal, the mobile postmodern consumer "transforms from someone who *belongs* to a culture, a society, or a lifestyle" to become "someone who actively *negotiates* one or more communities; a cultural constructor, and a *player*" (Firat and Dholakia, 2006: 129) (emphasis in original). We articulate selves, slipping, perhaps with politicized purpose, from universal shopping mall to urban street markets, "shopping for subjectivity" (Langman, 1992).

Can we "give reality the slip" as citizen consumers playing (cognitively and constructively) in the mall? Crossing the disciplinary bridge between literary theory and media studies (Murdock, 2004: 21) and drawing upon the former's insights into the mental activity of audiences, we are able to analyze shopper discourse about immersive malls as navigational reader responses to the three-dimensional texts shaped and substantiated by these postmodernist thoroughfares. We propose a "cultural psychology" (Ratner, 2008) of mall guided (or malled) consumption as productive process.

Quantitative methods of measuring marketing and shopper consumption assume a "relatively culturally homogeneous" focus of study "responsive to conventional survey instruments" (Cayla and Arnould, 2008: 89). Instead, we emphasize consumer and mall culture as a "symbolic repertoire for the construction of identities" in "co-created" if countable stories (ibid.: 101, 98) told off/online. "I go to Gardens (mall) for the children," "they learn to talk more" a Chinese father informed us.

In Kuching, Sarawak, Malaysia, on a wet Saturday in January 2009 around noon just before Chinese New Year, one of the authors (RT) spoke briefly to small groups of youthful passers-by in the subterranean mall section of the Riverside Shopping Complex (ten persons of varying ethnicity and gender). Our contributors knew responses were being recorded (in a small digital machine).

Readings by these consumer citizens of their mall presence (their passing or prolonged immersion) suggest not only the pursuit of an instrumental or extrinsic purpose (e.g. a male Bidayuh government servant purchasing a present for his girlfriend) but an intrinsic pleasure in playfully milling around. While these extended spaces and times can serve functionally as gathering places for material goods they also maintain the more subtle good of gathered friendship.

For a female Malay student, the mall is "our usual" ludic gregarious place: "we just want to meet our friends here," "we can gather here," "we can act more freely" than at home. Being at the mall ("watching movies," "bowling"), they enjoy the day more. Distanced from duty, equally at play, another female Malay student mall sojourner (a *flaneuse*) is "just walking around," just being there.

In similar mode, approximately six months later in August, at a new Kuching suburban mall two authors of this chapter (RT and TW) interviewed three Malays (two male, one female, youthful and apparently on their own) and three Chinese families (parents, a grandparent and children). One of our participants described The Spring mall as "very small" (father). Be this as it may, usually seen by our respondents as more Western than Asian, The Spring food court where these short cross-cultural exchanges occurred is resolutely postmodern in its Malaysian offerings of food with which to cultivate a varying ethnic identity (Halter, 2002) to buy and go or quickly consume.

Absorbed in its consumption, the male Malay visitors were enjoying its "many types of food" (as breakfast or lunch) as well as "window shopping" or purchasing branded products whose authenticity was more likely than outside the mall. One had discovered difficulty in articulating or navigating his way around the shops, getting a "bit lost": the "direction (signage) is not very clear." The mall failed to meet their horizons of expectation: "I am less satisfied," it "can't compete." While still a "comfortable" experience for them, the female Malay maller regretted the lack of cinema.

Like the Riverside Shopping Complex, visiting The Spring was clearly an immersive narrative for the single and young. But the Chinese families balanced an intrinsic enjoyment of being there as temporarily different from the (dry?) everyday with perceiving it as more instrumental time.

Although the mall more or less met shopping "needs" (mother), that the Saturday visit was an "outing" was a theme repeated across genders and family groups. They experienced a brief if regular weekend pleasure of being absent together as families from the diurnal mundane. In their responses, "wants" signaling a ludic ambition (e.g. for a cinema) were nonetheless linked by references to "need" with the more laborious duty of attending to the week's supermarket shopping.

> "Every weekend I'll bring the family out," a "routine", it's a "good place to hang around" (with family) as well as "quite organized here" for shopping: culturally, it's a "mixture of everything" (father); "it's a family outing", "they have a very good supermarket" but "with the opening of the cinema it would be better", "just an outing" (father).
> "it's our usual outing"; materially the shops instantiated the mall genre, "they're all here," "it's got everything that I need here"; though The Spring curtailed her immersive involvement with "all I want here (…) except the cinema" (mother).

While our family visitors to The Spring in regional East Malaysian Borneo engaged with its space to articulate a narrative of both intrinsic collective pleasure and instrumental shopping duty, strollers at The Gardens mall, Kuala Lumpur, were mostly exercised by immersive gazing. "Remember who you are, forget who they want you to be," philosophical people not purchasers?

On a Sunday morning (16th August 2009) two of the chapter's authors (THP and TW) sought to speak to a few reluctant folk. For distinctly different from Kuching, whether because of social class or civic paranoia (not least in the midst of an H1N1 pandemic), we found people less than enthusiastic contributors to our research at this upmarket shopping space adjacent to a more functional and much more crowded Mid-Valley mall located across a walkway. Seen talking into our recorders, a female Filipino tells us after some minutes, "I'm shaking already!" (laughs).

Our only volunteer family group (the female Filipino accompanied by Malaysian Chinese husband and children) shared with the single people visiting this visually rewarding mall as individuals or in groups a largely ludic intrinsic enjoyment of its towering open walkways. "We come here to give my daughter and son (the experience?), to look around and see what we want to buy, or something" and we "feel happy" (female Filipino). "I go to Gardens for the children," "they learn to talk more" (male Chinese). Only subsequently, if at all, do they shop. Other than in basement food courts displaying the customary diversity, purchasing was a secondary activity.

Likewise, a young female Chinese visitor to The Gardens has a "date with a friend today." Talking about the variety of food and beverage available ("there are a lot of choices"), she informs us: "we just have a gathering over here, not thinking of buying anything today." "It's a good place for friends to gather together because the location (of this 'high end' mall) is quite centralised." "I come up to meet my friends" confirmed another youthful female Chinese subsequently, munching on food, with a gesture towards a more instrumental purpose: "just walking around, then you find what you want." But "for me," the mall is "more to high end, instead of the normal one, lah." She "seldom" buys: here, "just for window shopping, it's OK, lah!", "just for walking around."

Local research participant accounts of visiting the (Malaysian) mall as being immersive rather than instrumental are extended in often named contributions to the global blogosphere. These were located here by means of Google Blog Search (*http://blogsearch.google.com*) and Technorati (*http://technorati.com*) using an advanced keyword search in weblogs about Kuala Lumpur and Malaysia with the word "mall." Clearly blogging is a rich source of narrative phenomena.

Sharon Bakar, a resident of Kuala Lumpur, describes herself as a "totally book-addicted Brit in Malaysia!" Visiting the mall on Sunday is seen as a ludic outing or "tremendous fun." Through representing it as being "guilt free" she detaches this happy experience from everyday duty. "Sunday is the day to visit Amcorp Mall—the flea market is tremendous fun and provides a great excuse to visit BookXcess to buy a guilt free pile of books."[2] Sharon articulates this narrative of immersive shopping, appropriating an account of the mall to confirm her identity as "totally book-addicted." This story's focus is on intrinsic pleasure far from the "self-sacrifice of thrift" (Miller, 1998: 108).

"Boo_licious," we are informed, is "just a crazy gal living" in "Kay-El, Malaysia" "who is obssessed [*sic*] with food."[3] Despite an ironic gesturing in the direction of duty, her intrinsic enjoyment of weekend playing in the 1 Utama mall "to r & r away" is said to be focused on food: "confession time again!" But even before entering this shopping centre, she strives competitively in the sport-like activity of locating a parking space. Her fun is seriously involving, almost an extreme sport of "battling with loads of people for a carpark space and jostling with others when the mall is packed" with "this minefield of people." Yet events in this story of a competition to consume more than meet her expectation: "we found our epiphany with the very unusual funnel cake" sold in the mall. Boo_licious' immersive inventory of eating enables her to affirm her initial self-definition as "obsessed with food," a ludic distraction which is subsequently identified with by a respondent to her blog, "kwazymonkey": "this is my 'snack-between-work' place when I'm in the mall."

But malling can go wrong. Immersion in their sometimes complex corridors of consumption can resemble incarceration, with lost souls unable to complete a coherent project. A failure to articulate an acceptable narrative of being there can only be appropriated as diminishing the self.

Jaya S (who is otherwise anonymous and of unspecified age, ethnicity or gender) blogged on 5th August 2009 about meeting a male Dutch tourist "wandering" in KLCC (Kuala Lumpur City Centre) Mall located immediately beneath the towering Petronas Twin Towers, briefly the tallest building in the world ("When Romanticism Meets Pragmatism"):[4]

> He looked around and, I am not sure what came into his mind all of a sudden, asked where the twin towers were. When we explained to him that he had in fact been wandering in the mall under the towers, he was perplexed and extremely disappointed. He complained he'd been walking through the "stupid mall" trying to find an exit, and all the while there he was, right by the towers. How he could have missed something as obvious as the nose on his face, I'm not quite sure, but it was a pretty amusing bit of confusion, and I wish I could have captured his priceless expression.

Absorbed in a hermeneutic circle not of constructing sense but rather of "confusion," this tourist went "walking through the 'stupid mall' trying to find an exit." Anticipation of a way out was followed, not by positioning himself as the potential source of a successful story, but rather self-excoriating failure: "he was perplexed and extremely disappointed."

### "MAKE THAT 'SOME DAY' TODAY"

> Have a good laugh.
> Have a good cry.
> Lose yourself in a sad story.
> Find yourself in a happy song.
> Shrug the weight off your weary shoulders.
> Slip into something light.
> Heed neither rhyme nor reason.
> Make that 'some day' today.
> > The Gardens At Mid Valley
> > ... it's about you.

In this inquiry we have applied media marketing reception theory to gain insight into those who visit, view and (homeward bound) subsequently vacate the mall. In testing theory against talk, our approach has emphasized a multiple making of meaning by shoppers and sight-seekers, fore-grounding the formation of sense. Intelligible connections between moments of mall visitation are established by their conceptualization of activity as (for instance) "just walking around." Quasi-philosophical inquiries in focus groups or interviews yielding criteria for applying social description generate definitional insight or "empirical measures," data "adequate to establish the generality of connections between one aspect of social life and another" (Hutchinson et al., 2008: 101). Defined like games by a distance from wearying reality, family "outings" can yet incorporate the functional.

"Television not only socializes consumption" but structurally "predisposes later mall-based seeing and being seen" (Langman, 1992: 37). We mirror media immersion in "malling." Like screen texts, these shopping thorough-fares offer visitors passing opportunities to enjoy the ludic loss of their every-day selves, albeit besmirched by semi-awareness of duties elsewhere. Paradoxically, seclusion in "malling" can be shaped (or nuanced) by obliga-tion to others outside. Viewing media or visiting a mall merges private and public space and time. Locating ourselves ("I'm lost!") in text or thoroughfare can require our investigating of mall or media to understand our circumstances.

Funneled (or tunneled) by a shopping mall into speculative if not specious freedom we walk together, parading in more or less abstracted mode through sometimes novel media-structured geographies of communication (Jansson, 2004: 553) and consuming. Malling constructs behavioral narratives producing a "dialectic between doing something and being someone" (Langman, 1992: 54). Here predictable "social structures exert considerable control over human subjectivity" (Ritzer, 1999: 239): indeed the postmodern mall is read by con-cretely positioned people engaged (implicitly or explicitly) in self-formation not *ex nihilo* but always with materially informed memories.

Marketing screens and shopping malls convey the same to consumers—products. But while frequenting the latter, we can evaluate the content immediately, tangibly and probably more slowly. The "high end" mall for a minority is "beyond the mundane spaces of the life-world" (Jansson, 2002: 441), a place of immersive time when privileged purchasers, credit-card equipped consumer citizens can anticipate, articulate and appropriate materi-ally focused narratives of a shopper self in agoric "communities of consump-tion" (Ryan, 2005). "Shrug the weight off your weary shoulders," rebuild an identity in purchasing. The rest, the many, well, they refresh by "just walking around."

# 7  Banks, Blogging and Reflexive Branding

In *Global Advertising, Attitudes and Audiences*, we have considered the process wherein our consumers respond to the mediatization of marketing, branding's narratives on screen and malls. While this cognitive activity diverges culturally at a local level, its structure is identical—and global. In hermeneutic terms (the theory of understanding), it moves through seven moments (phases). In this seventh chapter, we review these phenomena in the context of bank branding. We add to our critique in Chapter One, dismissing as conceptually incoherent the pervasive but pernicious myth that "marketing stimuli affect product attitudes" (Bloemer et al., 2009: 66).

As we saw in Chapter One, positivism defines as a core axiom the deductive-nomological model of scientific explanation. In this philosophy of research method, explaining an occurrence by referring back to an observable earlier causal event is presented as logically symmetrical with the future-oriented prediction of that occurrence on the basis of the preceding event (Hunt, 1991: 4).[1]

Both rendering occurrence intelligible and inferring the likelihood of its happening rest on the same universal law taking the form, "Whenever X (e.g. heating a gas) occurs, then (other things being equal) Y (it expands)." In view of the event-focused nature of prevailing positivist explanation and prediction in marketing studies, it is hardly surprising that research participant attitudes cannot function in this subject as a basis of successfully anticipating behavior. For, as we have observed, attitudes as beliefs are of the wrong logical character to count as events.

So-called "marketing science" academics have written about the "many failed attempts in previous literature to predict the buying behavior of individual consumers from measures of their attitudes" (Riley et al., 1999: 85). But as we have just outlined, within the positivist deductive-nomological model of explanation as symmetrical with prediction, events bring other subsequent events about in accordance with universal laws which it is the continual task of physical and social scientists to determine. From this perspective, failure to predict purchasing should not be in the least unexpected given the logical incoherence of attempting to anticipate such behavior on the basis of beliefs, states of mind ("attitudes") rather than earlier causal events.

Despite De Houwer et al.'s speculation to the contrary, attitudes are not subjective events or "immediate, automatic affective reactions that stimuli evoke." Hence logically they cannot in their turn be "causal factors" or have a "causal role" in explanations or predictions [claiming, for instance, the "maintenance of smoking behavior" (De Houwer et al., 2006: 1274) by marketing]. Departing from marketing's reductive privileging of audience "attitude," O'Shaughnessy and O'Shaughnessy (2004) prefer the more culturally embracing concept of consumer "perspective." Corresponding closely to the core hermeneutic idea of an audience regarding the screen from informed horizons of understanding, a "person's perspective on an issue constitutes his or her point of view" (18).

As we have seen, media marketing sketches its own prescriptive perspectives on products (the branded horizons of happy understanding) through elliptical stories on screen. In a frequent fusion of culturally global and local horizons, consumers articulate these into fully fledged narratives with which they find favor (align) or from which they distance themselves (or become alienated).

Pursuing this progressive phenomenologically oriented path to interpreting their own research participant behavior, for instance, Lawlor and Prothero (2008) argue for a reader reception approach to exploring children's "understanding of television advertising." Their consumer research "requires the researcher to put to one side the stimulus-organism-response (SOR) approach which arguably has informed many of the extant studies on children and advertising. The latter have tended to ask 'what does advertising do to children?' (…) This research takes a different approach by asking 'how do children read advertising?'" (1207). Here, interpretive reading replaces induced response.

> [During their research] children presented themselves as active and goal-directed audiences for advertising. This contrasts [*sic*] an image of children as passive, sponge-like viewers, which tends to prevail in the debate over advertising regulation in countries such as Ireland and the UK.
>
> (Lawlor and Prothero, 2008: 1219)

## ENGAGING WITH MALL AND MARKETING MEDIA

Visiting the mall, as we discovered from Malaysian interviewees in the last chapter, is characterized by not only utilitarian but hedonic moments or aspects of experience. "Hedonic value is more subjective and personal than its utilitarian counterpart and results more from fun and playfulness than from task completion" (Babin et al., 1994: 646). For families, a morning spent at these "cathedrals of consumption" (Abaza, 2001: 98) involves their shopping at the supermarket yet is also an immersive "outing" and narrative articulation of being together each weekend. But we further wish to argue, their time out from the mundane week, whether focusing on buying or burger, is an extended episode of being perceptually involved, engrossed in finding their way around or eating food. They are engaged by/in a prolonged process of ludic cognitive absorption albeit curtailed by dutifully meeting needs set by a world external to the mall.

Walking or watching, making sense of mall shops and marketing screens, consumers project their narratives of determinate meaning wherein (their) purchases and (other people's) profits are invariably central themes. Absorbed and anticipating these shopping stories, we cross the cognitive "lower threshold" (Scolari, 2009: 131) of perceiving material or virtual content in three and two dimensional packaging for actual or imagined consumption. Active audiences, we engage with these ludic spaces in a goal oriented cognitive play of perception as visual fields in which collectively or individually we construct sense processually from our surroundings.

> As cultural theorizing has shifted focus to the performative, participatory, and playful uses of new technologies, and toward the "interior", domestic, and subjective experiences of new media users, engagement with media has also been reconceptualized in terms of articulations and the co-production of public and private.
>
> (Lievrouw, 2009: 315)

We perceive from a platform, positioned upon and informed by the public culturally located horizon of looking from which we make our individual private world intelligible. Our projection of meaning is thereby guided by a shared awareness of genre and typical content initiating our expectation and subsequent engagement with media and their branded landscapes. We continually revisit our earlier ways (horizons) of understanding the world in the process of comprehending screen content with its shaping of everyday identity (Malpas, 2009). Essentially future oriented, projection is furthered by readers anticipating a story of mall visit or media event to be made actual through the process of articulating perceived content within space and time.

Cultures are practiced. Consumers share horizons of understanding marketing narratives which brand (e.g. believing that telecommunications advertising will feature cellphones). As given assumptions underwriting our everyday comprehension of the world, these views are almost too familiar for reflection. But because based on such cultural boundaries shaping our expectations, sharing a similar perspective, people perceive and project developments on screen alike. These common and cognitive trajectories of anticipating and articulating content may be considered in "consensus analysis"—analyzing the "structure of informant agreement" (Horowitz, 2009: 51).

Allowing statistical evaluation of their responses, research participants can be asked: do they agree with audience perceptions of a narrative type invoked in anticipating content? Do they share a conception of "advertising genre" implicit in consumers recognizing events on the screens of media marketing to be appropriate? Do they consent to accounts of probably occurring content (e.g. fast food's likely advertising as warm, welcoming and contributing to customer wellbeing)? The "totalized narrative" (Gould, 2008: 410) emerging from a viewer's articulating an advertising story must fit such a shared definition if it is to be recognized by consumers as typical content.

Positivist "nomothetic research," Horowitz tells us, holds that its methodology of using "statistical estimation constructs [*sic*] reduces the role of a researcher's subjective judgment or interpretation" (2009: 55). But constructs used or interpretations brought to a study of consumer response are not guaranteed by rendering them more general. On the contrary, they need to be justified by relating their unavoidably selective ways of seeing the world (or their slant on the social) to local participant concepts. Why should the researcher think along a particular semantic route? Why be limited (for instance) by a presumption about consumer citizen ethnicity or "whiteness" (Burton, 2009) as a cultural horizon of understanding appropriation of branding?

Gabriel and Lang, indeed, assert against inductivism a "virtual impossibility of generalizing about consumers" (2008: 322). We, on the other hand, have sought to construct an abstract model of their cognitive practice in responding to screen media and shopping mall—a skeletal but not sclerotic structure which can be specially clothed in the cultural particulars of local context enabling the passage and production of individual points of view on perception. In our audience voices can be heard the constitution of self through consuming, "people's creative appropriation" (Trentmann, 2009: 206) or contestation of brands in "self-fashioning" (ibid.: 211). For research "itself establishes positions from which it become possible for participants to 'speak'" (Buckingham, 2009: 635).

The agora of advertising (these media or mall spaces and times of branded selling and buying by consumer citizens) are appropriated by audiences, domesticated or individuated in identification. Acquisition involves a fusion of horizons in which our perception of cultural types (e.g. families) and their activity in a televised or Internet marketing text (such as those associated with telecommunications) informs a renewed sense of who we are, as role-embodying individuals (e.g. siblings maintaining cellphone contact). Consumer appropriation of advertising and its brandscapes revises our interpretation of typical cultural formations and practices as patterns of social belonging or familiar forms of life (e.g. in tourism or university membership).

People's identities develop across time (Shankar et al., 2009: 76), shaping selves. Choices and constraints on our occupying and appropriating—or alienated analysis of—the potential roles articulated in mediated marketing are important. Critical distancing and its insights are almost always at least implicitly political or focused judgmentally on perceptions of power in a text. The model (or implied and preferred) audience of the video "marketing" the Malaysian Identity Card in Chapter Three comprehends and consents to (identifies with) its prescriptive narrative. But a Chinese Malaysian distanced herself, dismissive of the powerful male Malay presenter.

Through interpretive "episodes" or synthesizing moments in their screen use, consumers maintain and mould their identities. Brands thereby both inform and subsequently form our everyday lives, supporting "dynamic and complex" audience readings (Nairn et al., 2008: 628). Given ubiquitous product branding, most of us spend much of our time in brandscapes.

Consumers appropriating branding on screens of cinema, television and Internet can be said to "objectify" (Borgerson, 2009: 155) their narratives. Walking in the mall, we materialize or render brandscapes "real." Occupying agoric spaces and times (albeit often shaped for corporate profit) can establish critical awareness of ethical citizenship, a rationally justified alignment with or alienation from eco-tourist or political marketing (Henneberg et al., 2009; Smith and French, 2009). Convinced consumers not only share alignment with the brand vision but may enter associated altruistic moral communities (Utz, 2009), trusting one other in a double polarity of felicitous "feel-good" attachment demonstrating an "individual-group identification" (Cutcher, 2008: 372).

Alcoholics Anonymous members discover cellular brandscapes to be therapeutic, sending each other messages with "bonding properties of relational glue" (Campbell and Kelley, 2008: 916). More negatively, video marketing terror may align viewers in a subversive scenario, the absorbing alternative politics of counter citizenship (O'Shaughnessy and Baines, 2009).

Marketing theory, then, guided by a process model of consumer identities as "'playful' subjectivities" (Roig et al., 2009: 90) regards media use as an audience actively appropriating narrative, thereby shaping self in a fusion of textual type and reader's social role. For positivism, however, events on an advertising screen, consumer attitude and then action come together in a mythical relationship as a cause and effect (or stimulus–response) sequence involving passive percipients. Media effects research when conducted on marketing becomes attitude studies.

But this renders advertising-related human action analogous to impulsive behavior, an effect caused by an urge (the attitude): "such behavior is typically characterized by a spontaneous urge to engage in an approach action with respect to the tempting object" (Mukhopadhyay et al., 2008: 587). Responses are reduced to involuntary reactions akin to noting a product's country-of-origin, "said to arouse a purely emotional reaction in the consumer" (Bloemer et al., 2009: 63).

"Rational thinking," assert Novak and Hoffman definitively, is "logical, cause and effect, rule based" (2009: 57). However their claim is fundamentally contradictory. For if a person's thinking is rational and rule based he or she acts as they judge appropriate in a given context [e.g. following the "behavioral norms" of a class culture (Henry and Caldwell, 2008: 388)]. We thereby infer (logically) "correct" conduct from our interpretation of the situation, a "reading" which can be a complex reconciling of global media guidance and local edict. "Appropriate" action is thus conceptually and materially distinct from a behavioral response caused by a stimulus, for the latter simply instantiates the pattern in the physical world of one event bringing about—effecting—another.

The relationship between screen and user, more widely, is one of active meaning creating appropriation by audiences rather than that of a designed technology with designated passive effect. As Harrison and Barthel remind their readers, the "history of email has taught us that users may appropriate computer-mediated technologies and fashion them for their own purposes, which sometimes supersede or are at odds with the original purposes of designers" (2009: 156).

## BRANDING BANKING

In a final empirical contribution to establishing and evaluating consumer responses to branded landscapes, we visited the mediated construction of banks. The Malaysian nation's largest bank, Maybank, brands itself across geographical horizons (such as between that country and Indonesia) with a black tiger icon on a yellow background and marketing narratives to match. Remarking on the connotative dimension of these images, a group of Chinese students commented that invoking ideas of luxury and trust, the color yellow could call on local consumer associations with the "Yang Di-Pertuan Agong" (King of Malaysia) and Sultans or Rulers of State. A widely circulating instance (available on YouTube[2]) of the bank's beckoning brandscape seemed an appropriate choice for our research on its reception during a global financial crisis.

The bank uses maybank2u as a mantra to name its popular website. A digital denotation of this nature can be read as authored to create cultural closure, as a statement intending to signify intimate identification with (serving) customer interests. Absorbed and aligned in this shared position, located on a semantic horizon of articulating the narrative of Maybank corporate activity as typifying reliable support, the model website visitor has reason to appropriate the banking service as integral to her or his life, and become (if not already) a Maybank customer.

Yet the very identity of this avowedly secure website is contested in email bearing the address of competing phishing sites seeking customer account and login details.

> "I received a weird email this morning from Maybank, saying that my maybank2u account is either inactive or due to several failure attempts of logging in [*sic*]. But the fact is, I just log in to maybank2u yesterday. Instead of clicking on the link given in the email, I open another browser and key in the link because I remember reading a lot of emails on this kinda spam act" underwriting his hermeneutics of suspicion.[3]

As has been noted throughout *Global Advertising*, the branded landscapes of media marketing can include as generic features not only corporate icon and associated product but political prescription: "Don't you just love this country?" (Petronas) Maybank is no exception to such incorporation of civic address in branding: the "true secret of our country" is that:

> we all share 1 rice bowl—the one filled, grain by grain, by the sacrifice, hard work and unity of those who came before us. And we share 1 responsibility to continue filling it, together, for those who will come after.[4]

But its message of Malaysian unity (1Malaysia) on National Independence Day (Merdeka) can receive an alienated analytical or resigned and resentful response. It is interesting to:

> see the amount of money being pumped in by the GLC's (Government Linked Companies) to advertise the 1 Malaysia slogan. It's been in the papers every day. Maybank certainy [*sic*] has been leading the charge. The saying is, if you say it enough times, people will believe it. So I guess that is exactly what Najib (Tun Razak—the Prime Minister) is trying to do, say it enough times so people will believe it.[4]

Alienated analysis was also a characteristic of consumer responses to Maybank's marketing in Iban employing the tiger icon in a narrative of (patriarchal) power and protection on television when the latter was discussed by Sarawak students. Local undergraduates possessed linguistic cultural capital supporting their challenging deconstructive (analytical) responses that the language was poorly pronounced by an actress. "In my opinion as a Sarawakian myself, I don't find the video real, the actress that portrays the daughter doesn't have the local accent" (female Chinese).

Can such reactions in cyberspace or the classroom be reduced to attitudes—behavioral dispositions lacking culturally rich and subjective reference? Are they marketing's screen-effected, allegedly powerfully produced, hence passive mental consequences among consumers? Which of these audience-centered phenomena do quantitative statistical accounts of responses measure anyway? Here one should indeed ask interviewees before adding and assembling an inventory of reactions. Can one then discern a correlation between identification and ethnic identity, or psychological and physical positioning across nations? How does subjectivity relate to statistics?[5]

## BRANDSCAPES IN THE BLOGOSPHERE: PERCEPTUAL PHENOMENA

Philosophical analysis of focus group contributions reveals the horizons of understanding within which people contribute (e.g. their perception of an "outing" as ludic). In the last chapter, consumer weblogs were considered at length as an additional source of narrative "data" where active audiences were reflecting on their own absorbed experience in materialized brandscapes—or agora made actual, as is so often the case, in shopping malls. Seen from the perspective of hermeneutic consumer culture theory, immersive fast food consumption, whether anticipated and projected on screen or actually partaken in the city, is (marketed as) a structured process of self renewal which we can open to analysis. "Pull Open the Glass Door, Feel the Rush of Cool Air!"

In "blog scholarship" (Garcìa-Gomez, 2009: 611) student web logging on university brandscapes can be viewed as exploring the connections and contradictions between advertising-enhanced aspiration and actuality. Their stories articulate and appropriate narratives of serious play intrinsic to academic space—stretched instrumentally by the extrinsic task-oriented goals (Robinson, 2009: 492) of future employment. Cellphone users who blog equally measure expectations derived not least from the marketing of mobile "network capital" (Larsen et al., 2008: 656) against material reality: immersed, they evaluate their capacity to connect and celebrate alignment with advertising or announce analytical alienation. Likewise, "mommy blogging" (Lopez, 2009) can be critically detached from the mall's branded spaces and times, announcing disillusionment and the early intention to depart.

Albeit with a source sometimes less defined than focus group interviewees, blogosphere narratives are rich in detail as "user agency" (Van Dijck, 2009: 42) accounts of brandscapes accessed, articulated and actualized. Bloggers contribute their stories within a narrative horizon of ethical commitment (Cenite et al., 2009) and demonstrate political involvement (De Zúñiga et al., 2009).

A person's day-to-day authorial presence, albeit only somewhere in the space and time of the blogosphere, can affirm her or his continued identity despite changing locations across vast distances of the real world through travel or more permanent diasporic movement (Mitra, 2008). Web logs carve out a "specific identity narrative that is rooted in real space while at the same time expressing the voice in cyberspace" (ibid.: 457). Such writing is able to signal immersion in media or mall, marking out the cultural horizons of a journey placing brandscape in cyberspace.

Traveling consumers can enjoy the extended immersion of articulating brandscapes on mobile TV (Orgad, 2009: 204). Like the sojourner and tourist mall bloggers we encountered earlier in Chapter Six, these earnest voyagers communicate in weblogs to maintain a screen "connected presence" (Christensen, 2009) amidst audiences. Their narratives are available as an absorbing focus for readers in the process of articulating a coherent sense for websites (Brügger, 2009) thereby furthering their alignment and appropriation or analytical alienation from content.

## REFLEXIVE BRANDING: WHAT DOES IT LOOK LIKE?

A "phenomenologically-based hermeneutical approach provides a description of the interpretive process" (Borgerson and Schroeder, 2002: 573). Here, consumer interpretation has been presented as a seven stage cognitive process located upon and shaped by cultural horizons of understanding media marketing in screen and shopping mall. Often, audience absorption in the agora of advertising involves immersion in branded space and time. Brandscapes can be the well considered work of a single source or collectively "co-created" (Van Dijck and Nieborg, 2009: 855). Both producing and consuming such meaning in marketing involves author or audience in playlike, goal oriented interpreting, sometimes stretched to address external need.

Reflexive branding constructs a profit oriented product life-world—phenomenology's encircling horizon of cultural horizons—to accommodate the model citizen consumer in an extended agora of retailing and reckoning. We have considered extensively cognitive conditions or moments of the latter's informed immersion in processing their absorbed anticipation and articulating of otherwise indeterminate content.

Aligned audiences appropriate the branded landscape's prescriptive narrative: others, aware of their alterity, vigorously assert distanced analytical alienation. Either reader furthers their sense of themselves as an ethnic, gendered or generational identity.

Branded landscapes extend beyond the virtual screen content of cellphone, television and Internet to material everyday life. For branding icons shaping the interpretation of space and time are everywhere—and particularly in shopping malls. Brandscapes in this book range from fast food restaurants to nations, telecommunications linkages to university campuses. They are not only public but private (e.g. the personal branding of the self as a subject to trust on Facebook).

The images and logo of brands blur boundaries between media, malls and consumer responses, informing our familiar frameworks or cultural horizons of understanding sights and shopping. We may identify spaces for meeting as places called McDonald's or Starbucks: when much used, we cultivate them as familiar close material horizons of being or living about which we need not think too much if negotiating their environments for eating, consumption and coffee.

Mediated branding, then, is appropriated not only by an audience in daily viewing but in visiting the mall. Collective consumer memory is shaped by branded horizons of understanding the world. Marketing culture is thereby drawn into everyday life: our response to its scripts as "embodied beings" involves putting into encultured practice, as well as perceiving, its engaging prescriptive narrative. Analyzing specific consumer involvements can thus be understood in media marketing terms. Both people seeing and immersing themselves in shops and the very spaces of selling are structured to conform to horizons of profit-oriented perception (Pereira, 2009). Thereby exercising corporate power, brandscapes can be viewed as agora where (not least when they believe they have rights to services) consumers can nonetheless respond as citizens.

# Conclusion
## Note for a Method of Marketing Research

"Ultimately, the methodology a researcher (in business communication) chooses represents a world view."

(Cross et al., 1996: 106)

*Global Advertising, Attitudes and Audiences* has engaged in a critique of inductivist-causalist theory wherein consumer attitude formation is a (passive) consequence of television's content. Seen through the distorting prism of marketing positivism, attitudes as complex evaluative beliefs are reduced to mental events. They are argued here to be otherwise as modes of sharing or separating ourselves from prescriptive narratives in branded space and time.

We have considered an interpretive-inductivist model in which audiences (actively) articulate and appropriate branding narratives from screen media and shopping mall—or find them alienating. Always already informed in viewing, knowing about types (genera) of aesthetic content, consumers draw on their cultural circumstances to infer (project) narrative development. Audiences, we have seen, overcome antinomies of advertising (paradoxes of product promotion) by inserting contradiction resolving content, and thereby can be seen to produce branding narrative themselves.

Consumer voices have been heard in offline focus groups and interviews and read in their weblogs online. Research could synthesize these investigatory approaches in focus groups online, albeit that the "technologically mediated environment prevents researchers from directly observing research participants and often makes the interaction anonymous" (Garcia et al., 2009: 52).

The Appendix to this volume sets out a research exemplar informed by hermeneutic theory and the phenomenology of consumer understanding as cognitive play. Audiences not only align with and appropriate but engage in alienated analysis below the surface of globally local branding. Immersing themselves in the latter's space and time or growing irritated, consumers celebrate close proximity or discover distance between self and the screen's horizons of understanding the world.

# Appendix

## Constructing Marketed Meaning from Consumer Culture  Two Television Advertisements: A Reception Study

Watching a program is a process of projecting and positioning narrative meaning on screen. We have seen this to be a cognitive-expressive creative play or plasticity of audience interpretation (in)formed by viewers' cultural horizons of understanding, their knowledge of typical television. The following exemplar of consumer reception research explored from this perspective readings of two Malaysian television advertisements. While the responses were brief but intense, our later interpretation is both more prolonged and draws on communication, cultural and consumer theory.

Our purpose is to apply the conceptual framework developed earlier in this volume and articulated from ideas such as "identification," "distanciation" and "projection" as they are interpreted in post-structuralist screen studies (e.g. the Brechtian account of the alienated audience) and hermeneutic phenomenology (Gadamer and Heidegger). We analyze the process of Chinese, Indian and Malay consumers reacting to television advertising, their achieving meaning. Global media marketing which is successful (despite a distant source) contains a prescriptive narrative which is culturally close to consumers, thereby supporting their *double* alignment. Audiences are enabled to move from informed absorption in anticipating advertising content to articulating (their understanding of) the text's story line. Sharing this identification (or construction) of meaning with narrative agents, consenting consumers equally identify (or align) *with* the latter's instantiating of persuasive discourse. Consequently, they appropriate its glorious terms to shape the self. In this way, identification leads to importing marketing's mediated life-worlds to (in)form one's being.

One advertisement in our investigation showed basketball being played in a Kuala Lumpur city centre street (Jalan Sultan) accompanied by the consumption of Coca-Cola; the other promoted a Malaysian Chinese children's music CD. On 30th June 2004, audience (student) readings of this promotional programming were investigated in two focus groups facilitated by two of the authors in this volume who were then located at Universiti Tunku Abdul Rahman, Kuala Lumpur (Wilson et al., 2006). Here, in order particularly to display the prolonged consumer interpretive process in play we discuss individual readings of the advertisements which were shown to the groups: these audience interpretations took written form. No respondent was aware of the present theory.

Ten Malaysians took part—the female Chinese co-author who co-ordinated this discursive experiment and nine students of varied ethnicity and gender (see below). Importantly, those participating in Group 1 spoke English at home (as a "domestic discourse" acquired early in life), while for those in Group 2 it was a second language (developed in the "public sphere" of education). Students who joined the first discussion were likely to have attended Malaysian government schools, while those in the second were probably educated at Chinese Malaysian institutions. Contributors in the two groups, in other words, had a different relationship to the language they used in responding to questions, in which discussion was conducted/constructed. Below, we classify participants in the first group as "/edd" (acquiring English as a domestic discourse), and those in the second as "/eps" (learning English in the public sphere). This is a cognitive-linguistic distinction in terms of educational experience. Misunderstanding between those facilitating and those facilitated in focus groups occurred in responses by participants for whom English was a secondary public sphere discourse. This could be heuristic (e.g. pointing to the epistemological complexity of viewers "identifying" as identification *of* as well as *with* narrative agents).

We posed three questions for contributors to consider, providing their reactions with a broad structure. As noted, these queries were answered by our participants both individually on paper, and in the two focus groups. The questions concerning their interpretive readings were:

(i) *Indicate the Content*—outline the narrative or story line of each advertisement: what do you see and hear and how is this related to what you understand to be the "message" of the advertisement?
(ii) *Identification with Characters*—do you identify with any of the people shown, and if so, why?
(iii) *Intention to Consume*—if you do identify, does it increase your intention to consume the product, and if so, why?

Below, we set out a ludic cultural logic of media-focused consumption, foregrounding responses of identification and distanciation underwritten by consumers' constructive readings of the advertisements as providing (respectively) instantly immediate/ intensely mediated access to content. Our reception study of a global/local text (the US Coca-Cola advertisement) shows consumer consent, or audiences aligning with advertising. On the other hand, responses to a local/global text (the Malaysian Music advertisement) manifest consumer contestation, our audience's alienation or distancing of self from this television marketing.

# THE PROCESS OF CONSUMERS INTERPRETING

## The Coca-Cola Advertisement and Consumer Alignment

### (i) Audiences Articulating the Prescriptive Narrative

Participant reports of viewing the Coca-Cola advertisement record completed narrative projections, a success in accurately actualizing stories which distinguishes these readings from later responses to the Malaysian music CD. Narrative fulfillment aligns audience and actants (see ii):

> The ad(vertisement) starts off with a question: "Perlukah ada gelanggang?" (The Malay on screen is "Mesti ada gelanggang ke?" or "Must there be a court?") Then it shows a bunch of guys playing street basketball and the ball bounces in front of a girl. She picks up the ball and scores a basket. Then the question is answered: "Tidak sangat!" ("Guess not!"). [The Malay on screen is "Tidak juga!" or "Not really!"]
>
> (female Indian/edd)

> "Some people are playing basketball on the street but not at the basketball court. They do not have the basket for them to shoot the basketball into the basket. They just use the useless (?) basket and put it at the building wall."
>
> (female Chinese/eps)

In detailed written responses, students offered absorbed or immersive transparent readings of the Coca-Cola advertisement. These are reproduced below, providing a focus for our theorizing. No analytical reference was made to its highly elliptical (music video style) edited compilation of shots or to aesthetic elements of the text other than there being "nothing special with the music." Youthful audience audio-visual horizons of expectation were not challenged by screen narrative.

> "Many young people gather on the street, it's an old town street, there are old buildings—old Chinese shop houses. The people seem happy, to have fun, both male and female youngsters are playing basketball. The final scene—two young ladies (a Malay and a Chinese) look like college students, the Chinese female (has?) a bag while the Malay female is drinking a bottle of Coke. Nothing special with the music."
>
> (male Chinese/eps)

> "A group of young boys (are) having fun on the street," "playing basketball by hanging a 'basket' on the wall, they gain lots of passengers' [sic] attention. Then, two of the boys have Coca Cola. They seem like (they) enjoy the Coke. Later, a Malay girl who wears *baju kurung* joins the

team, she has a beautiful shot. (This) shows that girl can play basketball well too. And the girls drink Coca Cola too."

(female Chinese/eps)

"The advertisement starts with a long shot of a busy street. People walking. Vehicles lining on the road. A group of teenagers playing basketball in front of a row of shops. A girl appears and joins in playing the game after the ball reached her. She succeed to throw the ball in the basketball net (rattan basket). Lastly, the Coca Cola logo appears."

(male Malay/eps)

Most readings of the Coca-Cola advertisement articulated its prescriptive narrative to be the drink's alleged capacity to produce unconventionally creative behavior: "The message behind the ad(vertisement) is that if you drink Coke, you can do anything, anytime. Conventional rules are broken if you drink Coke" (female Indian/edd). Coca-Cola consumers can "challenge the norms," its purchase is progressive, supporting "experiment," Youthful creativity is "encouraged."

The advertisement:

"questions the need for a proper court to play basketball with. It also shows two girls outplaying two guys at basketball. The message to me was 'challenging the norms' where proper courts are not needed to have a good game, and girls can be good at basketball too! 'Cuba!' 'Try!' is their challenge to consumers to beat the norm."

(male Chinese/edd)

"'Cuba!' 'Try!'—the company's 'Shout Out'—proves effective with its message in urging youths to experiment with the drink. It encourages youths like us to be more creative, vibrant and exciting—to make us think out-of-box. Playing basketball in the streets and using the waste basket as a rim is a way of creative thinking."

(male Chinese/edd)

Addressing advertising's consumers more widely, "this scene shows that if we want to drink Coca Cola, we can drink it (everywhere?). There are no geographical boundaries (...) we can enjoy drinking Coca Cola anywhere, anytime."

(female Chinese/eps)

Here, Coca-Cola's promotional messages concern high energy motivation from breaking the rules. "The 'message' would be telling us—Coke for young people, for motivation" (male Chinese/eps). "I interpret the 'message' of the advert(isement) as: Break the rules, enjoy Coca Cola, it brings you freedom and energy" (female Chinese/eps). The "Malay girl who wears *baju kurung* and plays the basketball, she looks cool and really 'breaks the rules'" (female, Chinese/eps).

### (ii) Advertising's Address and Audience Alignment

Television advertising's mode of address to consumers seeks their comprehension (identification *of* prescriptive narrative) and conviction (identification *with* prescriptive narrative). Model purchasers are aligned in building and buying both persuasive narrative and product therein. Audiences are asked to assemble and accept a particular evaluative account of action on screen.

A Chinese male contributor responded to Coca-Cola's text analytically. He signaled his capacity to make an identification of its "elements" as contributing connotatively to the "culture" of the beverage ("I was able to identify the culture"). This clearly precedes one's acceding to narrative alignment or identification with (those elements in) its characters' evaluative articulation of a story. The advertisement showed the "concept" of Coca-Cola to be "lively", "vibrant":

> "As for the Coca Cola advert(isement), I was able to identify the culture that was set upon." "The Coca Cola advert(isement) uses young and vibrant youths as the models of their advert(isement). Two girls and two guys were used in showing the excitement of the youths of today. It also shows the two girls outplaying the two guys and furthermore these two girls are dressed in *baju kurung*—an attire deemed not suitable for sports.
>
> However, the music used in this advert(isement) is very fun and lively. The elements in this advert(isement) do indirectly show or represent the concept of the Coca Cola company."
>
> (male Chinese/edd)

On the other hand, if interpreted correctly, a female Chinese consumer for whom English is a second language acquisition claims her failure in identification *of* people (her inability to describe them) in the Coca-Cola advertisement results in an inability to identify *with* them. "No, I can't identify any of the people in the ad(vertisement)s. Because the most (that) catch my attention is the big basket" (female Chinese/eps).

But otherwise, Coca-Cola's prescriptive "Try It!" crosses cultural distance, appropriately addressing its "target" consumer groups inclusively and straightforwardly ("simply" "both boys and girls," both basket ball players and beverage drinkers). Identification of/with its highly evaluative narrative is supported. "The advertisement definitely works" for a female Indian consumer:

> [It] "is very interesting as it targets both boys and girls around my age. As a girl who believes that I can do anything as good as the boys, the

advertisement definitely works for me. The slogan 'Try It!' also is simple but managed to stick in my mind."

(female Indian/edd)

"Coca Cola uses the teenagers playing basketball in their TV advertisements. Maybe their aim/target audience is the teenager. The teenagers playing basketball, they need to replace a lot of energy, then they may try Coca Cola. That's why they have the slogan, 'Cuba!' 'Try!'"

(female, Chinese/eps)

The Coca-Cola advertisement "is a straight-to-point advertisement. Its focus (is) to teenagers and the active lifestyle."

(male Malay/eps)

Read as addressing a wider range of consumers, "the question raised— 'Mesti ada gelanggang ke?' ('Must there be a court?')—simply represents that one doesn't necessarily have to be in a high level class to consume Coca Cola. Anybody in the streets can actually just pop in to a stall nearby and purchase it."

(male Chinese/edd)

Absorbed in aligning/identifying, a female Indian student playfully "connected to" the hybrid cultural narrative in the Coca-Cola advertisement, to "the kids on the street playing basketball. I like to watch or sometimes play games. It makes me feel like I'm one of them" (female Indian/edd). A male Chinese participant agreed/sided with Coca-Cola consumers on screen contesting everyday assumptions, acknowledging (his perception of) the advertisement's persuasive support in going beyond conventional horizons of narrative expectation.

"I can identify with the Coke ad(vertisement) because it encourages people to challenge the norms. It also says that you can have a good time even if the environment is not as extravagant as you would've expected (i.e. the makeshift basketball ring)."

(male Chinese/edd)

Audience alignment subsequent to their articulating meaning is both specific and broadly focused. Identification emerges from the viewer's cultural construction of a shared youth [as "spirit(ed)"] and national identity ("Malaysian"): "I would identify myself with the two girls in the advertisement who managed to throw the ball into the basket. They are in my age (group) and they have the spirit in them. Besides that, they are both Malaysian" (female Indian/edd).

Displaying a creative purchase on (his production of) narrative content, a male Chinese participant identifies across both gender and ethnic difference/distance. He aligns himself with the "female playing basketball," "because her action and outlook are masculine," But he also identifies with the "Malay female drinking Coke" because of her demonstrable capacity for unconventional behavior, extending expectations, producing a coherent story despite conflicting dress and context:

> "it's controversial [the scenes before the female are 'outdoor' look—activism, while the Malay female looks like an 'indoor' girl, walking slow and wearing *baju kurung*, which (means) she can't play basketball like the other female does. However, she can still play it]—kind of breaking the rules."
>
> (male Chinese/eps)

Finally, for a Malay male student, the content of the Coca-Cola advertisement was close or recognizable, despite the unknown actors ("models"): the drink is a "famous brand," the music is "very familiar" as is the "multi-racial multi-culture" theme. This consumer could therefore "relate" to its narrative, identifying with the inventive (basketball) players on screen because "I (am) still young." Coke conceals the clash of civilizations.

> "The (Coca Cola advertisement) music is very familiar to the audience because it uses the theme song with a new composition." "I do not know the models they used, but I can relate to (the advertisement) because I (am) still young and Coke is such a famous brand": "they used multi-racial multi-culture as (their?) theme. Moreover, Coke is so famous and widely known."
>
> (male Malay/eps)

### (iii) Appropriating Advertising: Purchasing Narrative Products

The commercial and cultural logic of advertising narrative is to align consumers with characters in developing intelligible narratives formed by the product-enhanced pursuit of an unquestionable "good"—realizing youth, relieving thirst. Identifying with the basketball playing "youths" as the source of "cool" cultural construction (the "'in' crowd"), gives a male Chinese participant a "psychological reason" to share their purchase of Coca-Cola's "'young' kinda feeling":

> "Yes. In fact, it gives me a psychological reason that if I consume the product, I am actually being in the 'in' crowd and that I'm cool. Besides, by consuming the product after watching the advert(isement), you will have a more 'young' kinda feeling in you. In a way, it is all psychological play I shall say."
>
> (male Chinese/edd)

"The Coca Cola advert(isement) shows that once you are thirsty you can get Coca Cola (anywhere?)"

(female Chinese/eps)

"Yes, I would buy Coke." Consuming Coca-Cola was considered by a female Indian contributor to continue and enhance the experience of identification with the basketball players initially provided by the televised advertisement. Drinking would suppress the perceived distance between they who are—and she who was not—ludic. "I think that drinking Coke would make me feel alive, vibrant, and cool—just like the kids on the street" (female Indian/edd).

Advertisements can be read as narratives succeeding or failing to demonstrate product relevance to "my character" or "myself" on the basis of consumer identification with their use on screen. Purchase proceeds from counterfactual playful alignment: "This ad(vertisement) relates to my character and it does increase my intention to consume the product" (female Indian/edd).

Bringing its meaning home, a male Chinese student would purchase Coca-Cola to confirm his youthful identity as an addressee of the advertising text, to make desired sense of his life: "yes, to show my 'young' image, to show that 'I'm the target audience' because I'm young. Also, the product shows that it's special—like the Malay girl" (male Chinese/eps). The Coca-Cola advertisement has "increased my desire to buy it" (male Malay/eps).

While the story which they tell is identified, these screen images are not appropriated by all our participants however. Refusing the advertisement's prescription to "Try!", a female Chinese consumer rejects this narrative of a drink's elevating and entrepreneurial effects. She "buys" neither its sense nor its claim to satisfy. "No. Because it does not fulfill my desire. The advert(isement) didn't focus on the product itself, but it focuses on the image of Coca Cola" (female Chinese/eps). Failure to identify with those in the Coca Cola advertisement means remaining unconvinced: "maybe I will buy to try whether it really works" (female Chinese/eps).

Likewise, the Coca-Cola advertisement is read by a male Chinese student as having a neutral effect on his purchasing behavior. While he identifies with the innovative activity it elliptically narrates, he resists the connection between identification and investment. For the advertisement does not augment the drink's existing association of "sophistication" with consumption. Nor does it establish (as if Coke were an "unknown" product) enhanced creativity as a consequence of buying:

"Coke has already had a reputation for being associated with sophistication. Identification with characters of the ad(vertisement) will not influence my purchase decision for this product. If the characters were promoting a new and unknown product, I would not be likely to purchase it."

(male Chinese/edd)

## The Malaysian Music CD and Consumer Alienation

On the Malaysian children's music CD, which formed the other focus of our discussion, there were three songs in Mandarin:

> Song 1: "Xiao xing xing wo ai ni. yue liang oh yue liang oh, ni bie sheng qi." ("Little stars, I love you. Oh, little moon, please don't be angry.")
>
> Song 2: "Say hay, say hay say hah. qian jin hou tui, bu guo shi yi nian zhi cha. you yu de ren hen nan zhang da." ("Say, hey, hah, there is only a very little difference between making a decision to go ahead and to stay back. It's hard for an indecisive person to be mature.")
>
> Song 3: "Oh ai yi ya ae ya oh ai yo, mamak dang." ["Oh ai yi ya ae ya oh ai yo (sounds), mamak stall."]

### (i) Audiences Articulating the Prescriptive Narrative

Consumer audiences of this advertisement's story appear to gain transparent immersive access to events via veridical (seemingly truthful) images on screen. "The five little girls wearing the sari sing the 'mamak stall.' The scene shows that they are so cute wearing the sari, singing and dancing" (female Chinese/eps). But when contributors turn to consider their alignment with narrative actants (below), an alienated, distanciated reading of content and presentation is evident.

Like the Coca-Cola advertisement, the children's music CD promotion tells its story using a culturally hybrid set of signifiers. It "was very colorful and musical" (female Indian/edd). However, here a local Malaysian product is thematized against a backdrop of changing global horizons. This audio-visual text displays a group of:

> "little girls singing and dancing throughout the ad(vertisement). They go through many countries—Paris (Eiffel Tower), America (Mount Rushmore). Then they show a bunch of kids singing and clapping along, while watching these girls on TV."
>
> (female Indian/edd)

> "children (who) sing and dance in different places. Their costumes are different in different scenes. The advert(isement) has played some songs from their album. The (...) five girls are very active singing, dancing, and one of the backgrounds is in Paris."
>
> (female Chinese/eps)

The music CD advertisement constructs a ludic space: children are "singing in the garden (children's playground), then they dance, look energetic and funny. Then, they are taking a trip to (go) round the world (maybe part of the world), because some of the world land-marks are shown" (male Chinese/eps). "Five of the cute little girls use their 'cute' voices to present some famous song. The advert(isement) is full of energy and melody."

(female Chinese/eps)

The prescriptive recommendation (message) to purchase implicit in the music CD narratives is construed by a female Indian viewer to focus on buying as achieving parallel possibilities of involved identification for audiences within/ watching this visual text. Purchasers perform/produce meaning with participants. She points to the way "looking" is relayed from children to consumer, supporting audiences in absorption and alignment with narrative agents.

On the viewers' screen, the "bunch of kids singing and clapping along" energetically empathizes with the singing and dancing "girls" they watch on TV. The intended consumer can become similarly absorbed in the advertisement role of performer. So the "message is that if you buy the CD, you'll be a star. You can see yourself on TV and you'll have lots of fun" (female Indian/ edd). "The 'buy CD, free CD' promotion slogan was to gain the audience's attention to buy this product" (female Chinese/eps), "to sell the kids' group album" (male Malay/eps).

### (ii) Audience Alienation from the Advertising

In responses to the music CD advertisement, Coca-Cola's earlier alignment of potential consumers becomes alienation. While a male Chinese student contributor personally lacks the age-related cultural positioning to identify with the CD promotion's "childish" narrative construction ("the girls"), he acknowledges that it "might actually capture the interest of children." Nevertheless, it is articulated from fragmented "childish like kinda elements":

"As for the music CD (advertisement), I was unable to identify with myself with any of the girls." "(It) uses the same concept with Coca Cola by involving youngsters to promote their product. This advert(isement) also uses cartoons, childish like kinda elements and lots of multimedia editing effects as its colorful and interesting background of the advert. This might actually capture the interest of children and even some adults to purchase the product."

(male Chinese/edd)

Readings by other participants were more forthright in rejection. Identification with Coca-Cola purchasers and players was replaced by her "disconnected" distanciation from performers in a female Indian consumer's dismissive response to the music CD advertisement. Alignment gave way to analysis. Not perceiving its content as familiar (or as exhibiting cultural proximity) beyond being "just a bunch of kids," she deconstructed the "made up" text as visually "unrealistic."

"I feel disconnected. I don't identify with any of the characters in this ad (vertisement). To me, they are just a bunch of kids and there's nothing special about them. Also, I can't stand the way they look in the commercial—they're so made up and unrealistic."

(female Indian/edd)

Likewise, a male Chinese contributor perceives the music CD promotion as generic ("very typical") and responds to this instance of advertising popular entertainment with a deconstructive distanced reading, alienated from identifying by its lack of "attractive" features. His analysis is dismissive: "this advert(isement) is very typical of a music CD promo—using cartoons and graphics. The ad(vertisement) is not the least bit attractive to me and the visual images do not leave a lasting impression." "I cannot identify with the music CD ad(vertisement)" (male Chinese/edd).

Realizing her distance in years and "language" from children singing in Chinese prompts another female Indian viewer's alienated reading of the advertisement. Here, the difference between a consumer's and "characters" culturally separate horizons of understanding the world subverts both the former's ludic achievement of textual intelligibility (identification of narrative) and her identification with the actors: "The problem in understanding the advertisement is the language." "I couldn't identify myself with any of the characters in the advertisement. They are all children and they were singing songs in Chinese" (female Indian/edd).

A Chinese male viewer is sufficiently culturally close to the dancers on screen to engage in the interpretative process necessary to comprehend this audio-visual promotion. But he resists alignment by its blurred images with those physically and pleasurably at play, a "crowd shouting" at/of the world. Instead, our participant offers an identification of the music CD advertisement in an alienated descriptive reading, vaguely remembering a "disturbing" "group".

"The (music CD) background music, I consider it disturbing, like the crowd shouting": "five children—I remember all five, but not a single one can be impressive. I remember all five because all five people look like a group of dancers. I remember the 'group' image, but not a 'single' image of any one of them."

(male Chinese/eps)

Likewise, two female Chinese focus group participants considered their identification of the narrative (the issue of its recognition) rather than identification with its characters. "I can't really memorize the girls because they look similar whether (considering) the fashion or faces. But I can identify the song" (female Chinese/eps); "there are five kids in the ads. I can identify them because they are singing the other singers' song" on TV (female Chinese/eps).

Finally, the male Malay consumer's response to the music CD advertisement lacked even identification of content or recognition beyond noting its "straightforward" story of a "group singing and dancing." Without deeper narrative involvement, he could not "relate to it," failing to identify *with* those on screen because "their music is for children." His reading was distanced indeed:

> "we can see the video-clip of the group singing and dancing. Very straightforward, but I do not know what group is that." "I have no idea who are the group members. Maybe they are school-children-cum-artist. I cannot relate to it because they are not my favorite artist, and their music is for children."
>
> (male Malay/eps)

### (iii) Alienated Analysis of Advertising: Not Purchasing Meaning/Media

At best, a female Chinese viewer considered the CD's relevance to other audiences ("children," younger "sisters") rather than herself a reason for purchase. Counter-factually identifying with such customers, she considered the "product is most suitable for children" who could align with the on-screen audience in pleasurably engaging with its "cute" "five little girls":

> "I will also consider to consume the children's CD because the advert (isement) shows that the five little girls are so cute. I will just consider to buy it if I have sisters, because I have not listened to the children's song. I think the product is most suitable for children."
>
> (female Chinese/eps)

Otherwise, "no, I won't buy the CD" (female Indian/edd) was a characteristic response to the advertisement. Its audio-visual invitation to align with an on-screen audience and appropriate/purchase the music as life-enhancing prompted only a perception of irrelevance and irritation.

> "The (music CD) ad(vertisement) doesn't have any relevance to myself and therefore it doesn't provoke me to purchase it."
>
> (female Indian/edd)

> "I have no use for it. Plus, the ad(vertisement) makes me feel angry or irritated."
>
> (female Indian/edd)

Alienated and analytical, distanced by the advertisement's "disturbing" aesthetics, tedium (it "can't attract my attention") or tendency towards the "cute," other Chinese do not count themselves amongst the CD's potential purchasers:

> "No. I don't like (the) children singing. It's a disturbing tone of voice."
>
> (male Chinese/eps)

"I'm not interested in the children's album. The advert(isement) can't attract my attention. Although I have a strong impression of their singing, but I didn't have the intention to consume."

(female Chinese/eps)

"I (do) not really like the kids' singing style. Their MTV just seems cute."

(female Chinese/eps)

The Malay male consumer concludes: "I will never buy the (music CD) album because I am not their target market." An appropriate audience—the "target market"—would possess the cultural capital enabling recognition of group and music, a closeness supporting identification with its screen images of pleasurable viewing and purchase. "I don't know them. Cannot relate to them. Not my favorite group or music. So, I don't care and I will never buy the album" (male Malay/eps).

We should reflect on the platform of understanding provided by this research exemplar. Successful glocal advertising practice meets multiple consumer horizons of understanding, supporting their easy crossing by an audience to advance/align with marketed meaning. Intended purchasers engage in creative identification *of/with* characters as "like us." Representing consumption of an American global product within the locally signified space of Malaysia's capital city, the Coca-Cola advertisement positioned its clearly implied and our actively accommodating actual audience in immersive, playfully engaged, positive response.

The advertisement for the Malaysian music CD, on the other hand, succeeded in alienating almost everyone. Reading responses, it was evident that this is not occasioned by its use of distant French and American global signifiers (background images of the Eiffel Tower and US Presidents carved in stone). Rather it occurs because of consumers' self-distancing or distanciated reaction as "disconnected" from the text's audio-visually excessive ("unrealistic") cultural construction of the local within the advertisement's hybrid horizons of understanding youth on screen. An audience's narrative anticipation is now met by media marketing experienced as fragmented, whose disparate alienating "childish like kinda elements" cannot be coherently articulated as a story: thus "I feel disconnected. I don't identify with any of the characters in this ad(vertisement)," "I can't stand the way they look in the commercial—they're so made up and unrealistic" (female Indian/edd).

Ludic reception theory focuses on meaning emerging from the cognitive-expressive processes in play during the formation of personal and program identity in an audience's projection of narrative on screen. Viewed from a hermeneutic perspective, "the question raised—'Mesti ada gelanggang ke?' ('Must there be a court?')" (male Chinese/ edd) at the outset of Coca-Cola's advertising sketch is the source of intra-diegetic participant scrutiny of their location, taking shape as the investigative story of the basketball game. Equally, establishing this enigma enables the intended extra-diegetic consumer to initiate an "answer"—projecting from transparently accessible (veridical) narrative parts a holistic "storied" resolution of screen content. "Mesti ada gelanggang ke?", that is, aligns Malaysian audience with actants in the *process* of expecting and establishing an outcome to the game—of unusual basketball and textual understanding.

In immersively reading this anticipated and actualized narrative on screen, our participants' cultural horizons of understanding content are clearly close to the text's, enabling their development of a prescriptive story with which the convinced can identify and thus appropriate to inform lives: "The 'message' would be telling us—Coke for young people, for motivation" (male Chinese/eps). "I interpret the 'message' of the advert(isement) as: Break the rules, enjoy Coca Cola, it brings you freedom and energy" (female Chinese/eps). Consumer identification, then, is two-fold. It involves hermeneutic positioning, a participatory aligning with someone else's—transparently accessible—sense-making project of product purchase as both narrative processing and normative proposition.

# Notes

## Introduction

1 The term "brandscape" was first used by John Sherry in his paper "Cereal Monogamy: Brand Loyalty as a Secular Ritual in Consumer Culture" at the 1986 annual conference of the Association for Consumer Research held in Toronto, Canada (according to the online dictionary Word Spy).

2 For an earlier account of audiences immersing themselves in screen narratives see: T. Wilson and F. Thang (2007) "The Hermeneutic Circle of Cellphone Use: Four Universal Moments in a Malaysian Narrative of Continuing Contact," *New Media and Society* 9(6): 945–63.

3 The Ancient Greek agora was a gathering (or meeting) place for citizens and subsequently (a market place for) consumers. In the earlier phase, it was defined architecturally by impressive public buildings and thereafter by shops. Drawing on this productive ambivalence, in the following chapters, it is a space and time primarily on screen and secondarily in material reality of consumer citizen communication (whether located in McDonald's or media supported on cellphones).

4 Construing branding narratives as underwriting consumers' projected stories of self confirmation is consistent with Miller's neo-Hegelian theory of consumption developed in *Material Culture and Mass Consumption* (1987). Consuming as "objectification" is "concerned with the development of a given subject through its creation, or projection on to, an external world, and the subsequent introjection of these projections" (178).

5 Analyzing the discourse of Internet users, we can conclude that web logging (blogging) is a shared and socially situated genre of new media practices. Nonetheless, writing occurs within and is shaped by contested authorial and reader horizons of expectation. Perspectives are challenged. Governments may seek a disputed definition of reasonable content. As readers we carry semi-conscious expectations, projecting and assembling coherent content where not encountering in the text irresolvable contradiction: we appropriate or grow alienated from the very narratives we have produced, positioning ourselves politically and more widely as persons. Blogging is Internet immersed play, yet tethered to (commenting on) the everyday, an online practicing of genre knowledge as "situated cognition" (Berkenkotter and Huckin, 1993).

## Chapter 1

1 Brecht's concept of "alienating" the spectator is a political term used to refer to deliberately disrupting or fragmenting events in his theater (the "elements" of the production). By means of such techniques (e.g. speaking directly to the audience

from the stage) he considered he could reach his desired dramatic goal of an actively socially aware audience rather than the customers of bourgeois theatre who merely identified with those on the stage and passively accepted their worldview. By using "alienated" to refer here to critical consumers who distance themselves from the brandscapes of marketing I am not implying that the latter are deliberately constructed to achieve such a result. Nonetheless, as I hope is demonstrated here, such audiences are analytical in Brechtian mode.

2 Conceptual complexity within consideration of media and marketing effects is considerable. For instance, in an initial discussion (from which I have omitted bibliographical references) Bilandzic and Busselle link the "mechanism" involved in cultivation effects to "transportation":

> Despite four decades of cultivation research demonstrating a reliable, albeit small, cultivation relationship, questions remain about the mechanisms that link exposure to perception. This study investigates the role of transportation—losing one's self in a narrative as an explanatory mechanism in cultivation. It also extends research into the relationship between content categories and cultivation effects by focusing on recurring narrative patterns in genres, patterns that contain typical plots and suggest a specific view of reality.
>
> (Bilandzic and Busselle, 2008: 508)

Relating "recurring narrative patterns" to "cultivation effects" by "explanatory mechanisms" suggests an inductivist statistical analysis (ISA) exhibiting caused *passive* "effects." But "transportation" refers to an audience's *actively* absorbing themselves in a narrative which I have argued to be the first moment (stage) of the cognitive process associated with the interpretive model. In audience and consumer studies, "mechanisms" of screen response need to be categorized as observable or unobservable and associated (or linked) with a cognitive account of viewers as active or passive. What is to be made of the conflicting claims that on the one hand, "readers are psychologically transported into the narrative world where they cognitively and emotionally relive the fictional events" but on the other, "while engaging with a narrative, one may lose conscious awareness of oneself and the surroundings and take on the perspective of the characters"? Who then are "they"? "Active viewing may be too ambiguous a concept for cultivation research" (ibid.: 510) *indeed*.

Likewise, Nabi and Sullivan (2001) attempt to integrate a cultivation analysis approach in accounting for (media caused) attitudes to crime with a theory of (active audience) reasoned action in accounting for subsequent self-protective behavior.

> Although cultivation research has, to varying degrees, established links among television exposure, beliefs, and worldviews, the further connection to behaviors has been left rather unexplored, as have the processes through which television exposure might ultimately lead to certain behavioral outcomes.
>
> (Nabi and Sullivan, 2001: 802)

Whether this conjunction of passive audience attitude formation and active later behavior can be sustained seems doubtful in the face of these authors' subsequently referring to the "thrust of cultivation theory's impact" lying in the possibility that the "behaviors of mass audiences will be shaped by their television exposure" (805) in a thoroughly passive response sequence. For the theory of reasoned action holds that "attitudes are composed of groups of salient beliefs regarding behavioral outcomes and (active) evaluations of those outcomes" (807). "Also questionable is the argued causal order between prevalence beliefs and mean world attitude" (817) *indeed*. Difficulties abound from cultivation theory's dilemma: "another causal order issue relates to proving that amount of television viewing is a predictor rather than an outcome variable in the model" (ibid.).

3 Prediction of behaviour from attitude need not assume they are entirely causally connected. The "theory of reasoned action posits a causal sequence of events in which actions with respect to an object follow directly from behavioral intentions, the intentions are evaluatively consistent with the attitude towards the object, and this attitude derives reasonably from salient beliefs about the object" (Ajzen, 1988: 33).

4 Potter and Wetherell (1987) refer to a similar tendency within positivist social psychology to suppress cultural variety through exclusive emphasis on the investigator's conception of behavior and refusal to acknowledge that the investigated construct their own accounts of the world: the "procedures psychologists regularly use for dealing with discourse have, often inadvertently, acted as management strategies for suppressing variability (...) all respondents are supposedly reacting to the same object of thought" (39, 52).

5 The present account of consumers draws on two non-positivist traditions of studying audiences and readers—those of screen theory and reception theory. Within the former somewhat contested category, I would include work as diverse as that of Bertold Brecht (1978; see MacCabe, 1974) and David Morley (1980), both of whom have sought to provide accounts of active audience responses to the theatre and television respectively, but who paid little attention to the cognitive intricacies (e.g. of alignment) involved. Reception theorists, on the other hand, such as Hans-George Gadamer (1975, 1976, 1985) and Wolfgang Iser (1978), discuss their view of the process wherein the reader constructs and arrives at a meaning for a text. Screen theory preferred politics to psychology.

6 In experimental social psychology, attitudes also "are taken to cause behavior" (McKinlay and McVittie, 2008: 113). However, within the conceptual framework of the scientific positivist's deductive-nomological model of explanation, where events bring about other events on the basis of universal laws, attitudes cannot have such a causal role. For they are "evaluative beliefs" (ibid.)—that which is the case about a person—not events taking place. In short, social psychology has to utilize another model of accounting for behavior (e.g. involving discursive reason-giving) if the latter is to be linked to attitude in narratives offering intelligible interpretation of action.

7 Hermeneutics' "horizons of understanding" content have a subsequent history of use as "framing" theory, often within accounts of agenda setting. "Framing reveals the potential of political rhetoric and news media to structure the world and make sense of events. But one event can be framed in many ways, with a great impact on its meaning" (Al Saed, 2009: 172).

## Chapter 2

1 An exemplary example is a colleague's recently published (and thought provoking): *Targeted Advertising Unintended Effects* (VDM, Saarbrucken, Germany: 2008). This scholarly research monograph examines the "unintended effects of ethnically targeted advertising on ethnic groups that are not targeted but who are still likely to see the advertising" (ibid.:1). Are recipients (whether intended or unintended) of advertising to be considered (passively) causally stimulated to purchase? Such Causalist discourse sits alongside the book's concern with the ethnic diversity of Malaysian consumers (actively) comprehending printed advertising: "issues of language, culture and cultural knowledge stand out. A reader must be able to encode advertisements to his or her own understanding before being able to react" (ibid.: 21).

2 In preparation for this volume, focus groups and interviews took place in Malaysia during 2007–2009 in which participants spoke of their responses to malls and media branding (from fast food to telecommunications, nations to universities). These discussions involved university student classes, mall visitors, self-selected walk-in customers at centers operated by a telecommunications company, and in one case, a promotional events organizer. Methodological and theoretical issues emerging from and supporting this research are discussed in the pages of this monograph.

3 When the first author entered media studies from philosophy in 1980, there was lots of talk in communication theory about "reading the screen" but the prevailing narrative of that process was psycho-analytical, an implausible account of present day small screen Internet viewing.

4 As noted earlier, the term "brandscape" may have been first used in a 1986 paper written by John Sherry. It is subsequently deployed in Sherry (1998).

5 Visited on 13th May 2008, corporate websites constructing these "fast food" brandscapes are:

Coffee Bean *http://coffeebean.com.my/* ("everyone's favourite 'time out' place")
Kentucky Fried Chicken *http://www.kfc.com.my/*
McDonald's *http://www.mcdonalds.com.my/*
Pizza Hut *http://www.pizzahut.com.my/* ("One Nation One Number")
Starbucks *http://starbucks.com.my/en-US/*

6 Coffee Bean Malaysia *http://www.fusionview.co.uk/2008/05/coffee-or-kopi/*
7 Kentucky Fried Chicken Malaysia *http://www.technorati.com/posts/*1jGdlgO7F%2BeKwRDGYZGR7vSCkPiHYKKoc%2BR3bwtIb7c%3D
8 McDonald's Malaysia *http://puretabby.blogspot.com/2008/05/*kat-tun-dont-you-ever-stop.html
9 Pizza Hut Malaysia *http://k0ks3nw4i.blogspot.com/2008/05/*20-glimpses-of-jodhpur-through-my-eyes.html
10 Starbucks Malaysia *http://www.technorati.com/posts/i9eAqRtn2Zxr2gnEKNT5hy60wqODal9Ececq5Ruszq8%3Ds*
11 McDonald's Malaysia *http://www.technorati.com/posts/%2BacXr9OcqD%2FUgz2xR6EJGuFc%2FJV7R4msuk4HQdC46Lg%3D*
12 Coffee Bean Malaysia *http://niknurehan.blogspot.com/2008/05/breakfast-at-oriental-kopitiam-kb.html*
13 Kentucky Fried Chicken Malaysia *http://iilovesyouus.blogspot.com/2008/05/don-know-why-i-just-open-blogger-and.html*
14 Kentucky Fried Chicken Malaysia *http://culinarycravings.blogspot.com/2008/05/flnger-lickin-good-factor.html*
15 McDonald's Malaysia *http://www.technorati.com/posts/Xb3YTVh4F9dvQEu6JDp17q5oPXwSyj33ulipZIA4Z%2Fo%3D*
16 McDonald's Malaysia *http://www.technorati.com/posts/cliAacqigpHAU1omew7%2Bg3UGojGO26hs9nFhZBzK%2BrM%3D*
17 Pizza Hut Malaysia *http://www.technorati.com/posts/jHDPz2StAaAnnWuN%2BgkytXLRSeesyCgjkB4fh5s%2FIRs%3D*
18 Starbucks Malaysia *http://www.technorati.com/posts/trAIM25hnuQlDTEM%2BjXYiojDvEBj%2F%2Ble5Dspiwz2VAw%3D*
19 Two Malaysians co-ordinated these focus groups, the female co-author of this chapter and a research assistant who recorded the television advertising and to whom we are immensely grateful for taking time out from her peripatetic music pedagogy. We likewise appreciate the hospitable research environment and support from academic colleagues at the University of Science, Penang, Malaysia: College Damansara Utama (KDU), Penang: Taylor's College (Bandar Sunway): and University

Malaya (Professor Azizah Hamzah). There were twenty-eight (mostly full-time) student participants meeting in the four groups which varied in ethnicity and gender of membership: we appreciate their vigorous "voicing out" of responses to website and television brandscape building. After viewing Internet sites and TV videos projected on a large screen, discussion was more or less loosely structured around the questions:

(i) describe the content of the website or video—what's taking place (if anything)?
(ii) can you identify with what you see—do you find it "culturally close"?
(iii) do you think the website or advertising gives you reason(s) for buying the product?

## Chapter 3

1 A recent example of engaging with consumer perceptions through the perplexing prism of positivist "cause and effect" discourse would be Chandon and Janiszewski's assertion that: "an alternative cause can generate the consequent independent of the antecedent, hence it can cast doubt on the necessity of the antecedent" (2009:104). Where there are alternative possible causes of an event, none of them need be regarded as necessary?

## Chapter 4

1 As indicated, ancient Greek agora were sites for citizen consumer assembly. In this volume "agora" is a preferred concept to "public sphere" since it links rather than severs the connection between purchasing and politics. See: *http://en.wikipedia.org/wiki/Classical_Athens*.
2 Audience reception theory's producerly consumer citizen can be heard in *Understanding Media Users* (Wilson, 2009) responding to telecommunications branding on television. Even "after you know it, it's still (of) interest for me," the brandscape's "still got some space for us to think about the story" (female Chinese reflective citizen).
3 Brandscapes are "corporate brand cultures" (Balmer, 2004) written into life as ludic landscapes of purportedly well formed and regulated reliable promise within (and out of) which we move and have our being as consumer citizens or persons placed in agora.
4 Leicester University Undergraduate Prospectus *http://www.le.ac.uk/admissions/ugprospectus/*
Limkokwing University of Creative Technology *http://www.limkokwing.edu.my/v6/*
Monash University My.Monash Student Portal *https://my.monash.edu.au/*
Ohio University Home Page *http://www.ohio.edu/*
University Technology MARA Undergraduate Page *http://www.uitm.edu.my/uitm/index.php?option=com_content&task=view& id = 85& Itemid = 376*
University of Malaya Undergraduate Page
*http://www.um.edu.my/undergraduates/index_undergraduates.php?intPrefLangID=1&*
(all first accessed 22nd June 2008, and then shown in focus groups on 8th and 11th July 2008)
Malaysian Open University Television "Infomercial" (2007)
5 The relationship between cognitive inquiry and citizenship is not instrumentally unidirectional since modes of citizenship can themselves be understood as maintaining philosophical ideals.
6 We wish to express our gratitude to our researcher who searched the airwaves for relevant television advertising and sustained our energy and enthusiasm.

7 Accessed on 22nd July 2008: *http://isuhangat.blogspot.com/2008/06/scandal-of-lim-kok-wings-university.html*

8 Accessed on 22nd July 2008: *http://blackpoliticalthought.blogspot.com/2008/07/being-black-in-america-what-does-it.html*

9 Accessed on 22nd July 2008: *http://www.technorati.com/posts/%2FG1X3Xro M9O1eZ0gdMQbshH89filAk%2FAbbIeVSAMXds%3D*

10 Accessed on 22nd July 2008: *http://crime-heaven-malaysia.blogspot.com/2008/05/um-thetrusted-university-no-more.html*

11 Accessed on 30th August 2008: *http://dzulnida.blogspot.com/2008/08/ive-been-extremely-busy.html* and *http://uknoewho.blogspot.com/2008/08/university-and-me.html*

12 Accessed on 20th August 2008: *http://educationmalaysia.blogspot.com/2008/08/spotlight-on-uitm-issues.html*

13 Accessed on 20th August 2008: *http://lavished.wordpress.com/2008/08/20/on-university-life/*

14 Accessed on 30th August 2008: *http://ambertanny.wordpress.com/2008/08/25/reflections/*

15 Accessed on 30th August 2008: *http://www.teddy-o-ted.com/daily-life/mixing-the-unlikely/*

16 Accessed on 21st August 2008: *http://axeile.com/2008/08/21/here-have-a-bucket/*

## Chapter 5

1 The phrase "electronic agoras" is used by William J. Mitchell in *City of Bits* (1995).

2 We noted earlier an exemplary example: *Targeted Advertising Unintended Effects* (VDM, Saarbrucken, Germany: 2008). In discussing the effects of advertising on unintended recipients, this monograph draws on the language of both causation and consumer comprehension. Are recipients (whether intended or unintended) of advertising to be considered invariably (passively) causally stimulated to purchase or potentially cognitively shaped in (actively) understanding a product? People can say that they were "brought" or "forced" to act by advertising: does this mode of expression support synthesizing causal stimulus and cognitive shaping models of marketing?

3 As noted, in early 1980s media studies there was much talk about "reading the screen" but the dominant view of that prolonged process was psycho-analytical, an implausible narrative of extra-cinematic small screen viewing as it has now emerged on cellphones.

4 In the ludic model of reading or viewing an advertisement as *play*, the audience participates in "cognitive operations," a "merging of (mental) action and aware-ness." Assembling meaning, their focus turns frequently to-and-fro from expecta-tion to establishing the advertisement: guided by a memory of marketing, viewers move from anticipating content to further articulating its narrative.

> There is in everyone the "knowledge" that play involves transition from one realm of being to another realm of being (...) even if it isn't always without material interest, without profit, and is seldom not serious, it is truly an "otherness". It would be our preference to say that the true locale for all these connotations has to be in the fact of framing (by the screen, by horizons of understanding) and in the maintenance of that primacy.
>
> (Sutton-Smith and Kelly-Byrne, 1984: 318)

5 We wish to thank our researcher without whose sustained commitment these con-versations and conceptual analyses would have been neither commenced nor

completed. She also undertook translation into English of a Malay interviewee's comments (as indicated by "tr.").

We gratefully acknowledge Digi Telecommunications Sdn. Bhd. as the agoric transnational telecommunications provider in Malaysia (with its Yellow Coverage Fellow) who enabled and supported our access to customer citizens.

## Chapter 6

1 Prose poetry spotted at *The Gardens*, a large, upmarket shopping mall, central Kuala Lumpur.
2 *http://thebookaholic.blogspot.com/2009/08/bookxcess-turns-2.html* visited 4th August 2009.
3 *http://masak-masak.blogspot.com/2009/06/funnel-cake-churros-molten-lava-1-utama.html* visited 7th August 2009.
4 *http://wandering-brook.blogspot.com/2009/08/weekend-in-malaysia-kuala-lumpur.html* visited 7th August 2009.

## Chapter 7

1 The Positivist desideratum that data be observable can include speech revealing subjectivity. Thus "attitudes" are said to be "latent, hypothetical dispositions (to 'overt behaviour') that are inferred from a variety of observable responses. Information about an individual's responses can be provided by the individual in the form of self-reports" (Ajzen, 1988: 23).
2 The two minute YouTube video of Malaysia's largest bank, Maybank, branding itself in the Iban language as a bank with tiger characteristics of strength and sustainability can be located at: *http://technorati.com/videos/youtube.com%2Fwatch%3Fv%3D86oOmUCGgv4* (accessed 9th September 2009 as were the sites listed below in Notes 3 and 4).

Maybank is a government linked company (GLC). "A government-linked company or GLC refers to a corporate entity partially or wholly owned by the government through a holding corporation. A GLC can be a private or a public listed company, operating independently through its own business indicators and KPIs (Key Performance Indicators)."
*http://technorati.com/posts/Vwd8oIF2OlqZzMfV2vfHUsLq%2B6bDS6YDM_Orh8GDBg8%3D*
The bank's website is the most frequently accessed in Malaysia.

"A look at the top Malaysian sites in June revealed that Maybank2U.com led as the most visited local site with more than 1 million visitors, reaching nearly 12 percent of all Malaysians online. (…)

> 'comScore's findings confirm Maybank2u.com's position as Malaysia's most popular Internet banking destination and local site,' said Lim Hong Tat, senior executive vice president and head of consumer banking, Maybank (in a discourse further articulating closeness to consumers). 'The online channel continues to play a crucial role in our strategy as we strive to provide customers with the best online banking solutions and technologies to enhance their online experience and increase convenience.'"
> *http://www.lowyat.net/v2/latest/maybank-leads-as-the-most-visited-local-site-in-malaysia-4.html*

3 Many weblogs complain of receiving email phishing for account details. Two examples:
   *http://technorati.com/posts/OhyHpgjoF1MBo1s38NOVhLmyIC34aNYJZ*
   *Sg2m9uQCkg%3D*
   *http://www.mrmrsimran.com/2009/09/03/on-maybank-phishing-website-usana-dia-*
   *betes-testimonial/*
4 Alienated readings of Maybank's political prescription of national unity are located
   at: *http://hopeipoh.wordpress.com/2009/09/01/merdeka/*
   *http://mindacergas.wordpress.com/2009/09/01/1-malaysia-najibs-i-had-a-dream/*
5 A research project on Bank Branding and Consumer Response involving transnational banks such as HSBC and its construction of locality is being conducted
   funded by RMIT (Royal Melbourne Institute of Technology, Australia).

# References

Aakhus, M. (2003) "Understanding Information and Communication Technology and Infrastructure in Everyday Life: Struggling with Communication-at-a-Distance" in J. E. Katz (ed.) *Machines that Become Us: The Social Context of Personal Communication Technology*, pp. 27–42. New Brunswick, NJ: Transaction Publishers.

Abaza, M. (2001) "Shopping Malls, Consumer Culture and the Reshaping of Public Space in Egypt," *Theory, Culture and Society* 18(5): 97–122.

Admin (2008) "Watch Out, Your Cellphone Could Be Giving You a Rash," URL (consulted 17th October, 2008): *http://officialtechblog.com/2008/10/17/watch-out-your-cellphone-could-be-giving-you-a-rash/*

Ahmed, Z.U., M. Ghingold and Z. Dahari (2007) "Malaysian Shopping Mall Behavior: An Exploratory Study," *Asia Pacific Journal of Marketing and Logistics* 19(4): 331–48.

Ajzen, I. (1988) *Attitudes, Personality, and Behaviour*. Milton Keynes: Open University Press.

Albrecht, S. (2006) "Whose Voice is Heard in Online Deliberation? A Study of Participation and Representation in Political Debates on the Internet," *Information, Communication and Society* 9(1): 62–82.

Alexander, N. (2009) "Brand Authentication: Creating and Maintaining Brand Auras," *European Journal of Marketing* 43(3/4): 551–62.

Allen, D.E. (2002) "Toward a Theory of Consumer Choice as Sociohistorically Shaped Practical Experience: The Fits-Like-a-Glove (FLAG) Framework," *Journal of Consumer Research* 28 (March): 515–32.

Al Saed, A.R. (2009) "Words: Political Discourse from Shaping to Framing," in T.J. Riyanto, L.S. Limanta, and D. Setiawan (eds) *Proceedings: International Conference Media in a Fast-Changing World*, pp. 161–73. Surabaya: Petra Christian University.

Anderson, B. (1983) *Imagined Communities: Reflections on the Origins and Spread of Nationalism*. London: Verso.

Anon (2008) "1001 Uses for a Cellphone (Mail and Guardian)" URL (consulted 17th October, 2008): *http://twitterpig.com/twitter/twitter-sms/27718/1-001-uses-for/*

Arnold, M. (2003) "On the Phenomenology of Technology: the 'Janus-Faces' of Mobile Phones," *Information and Organization* 13: 231–56.

Arnold, S. J. and E. Fischer (1994) "Hermeneutics and Consumer Research," *Journal of Consumer Research* 21(June): 55–71.

Arnould, E.J. and C.J. Thompson (2005) "Consumer Culture Theory (CCT): Twenty Years of Research," *Journal of Consumer Research* 31(4): 868–82.

Askegaard, S. (2006) "Brands as a Global Ideoscape," in J. E. Schroeder and M. Salzer-Morling (eds) *Brand Culture*, pp. 91–101. London: Routledge.

Askegaard, S. and D. Kjeldgaard (2007) "Here, There, and Everywhere: Place Branding and Gastronomical Globalization in a Macromarketing Perspective," *Journal of Macromarketing* 27(2): 138–47.

Athique, A. (2008) "Media Audiences, Ethnographic Practice and the Notion of a Cultural Field," *European Journal of Cultural Studies* 11(1): 25–41.

Babin, B.J., W. R. Darden and M. Griffin (1994) "Work and/or Fun: Measuring Hedonic and Utilitarian Shopping Value," *Journal of Consumer Research* 20 (4) March: 644–56.

Bajde, D. (2006) "Other-Centered Behavior and the Dialectics of Self and Other," *Consumption, Markets and Culture* 9(4): 301–16.

Balakrishnan, M.S. (2009) "Strategic Branding of Destinations: a Framework," *European Journal of Marketing* 43(5/6): 611–29.

Balmer, J.M.T. (2004) "Initial Reflections on the Notion of Corporate Brand Cultures and Communities," Working Paper No 4/44, Bradford University School of Management.

Baudrillard, J. (2000) "A New Language?" in M.J. Lee (ed.) *The Consumer Society Reader*, pp. 233–40. Oxford: Blackwell.

Bauman, Z. (2007) "Collateral Casualties of Consumerism," *Journal of Consumer Culture* 7(1): 25–56.

Beckett, A. and A. Nayak (2008) "The Reflexive Consumer," *Marketing Theory* 8(3): 299–317.

Belk, R. W. (1995) "Studies in the New Consumer Behaviour," in D. Miller (ed.) *Acknowledging Consumption: A Review of New Studies*, pp. 58–95. London: Routledge.

Belk, R.W., T. Devinney and G. Eckhardt (2005) "Consumer Ethics Across Cultures," *Consumption, Markets and Culture* 8(3): 275–89.

Belk, R.W. and G. Tumbat. (2005) "The Cult of Macintosh," *Consumption, Markets and Culture* 8(3): 205–17.

Bell, G. (2005) "The Age of the Thumb: A Cultural Reading of Mobile Technologies from Asia," in P. Glotz, S. Bertschi and C. Locke (eds) *Thumb Culture. The Meaning of Mobile Phones for Society*, pp. 67–87. New Brunswick, NJ: Transaction Publishers.

Benezra, K. (1995) "KFC Mulls Mega-4-1," *Brandweek* 36(2).

Bennett, T. (2007) "The Work of Culture," *Cultural Sociology* 1(1): 31–47.

Berkenkotter, C. and T. N. Huckin (1993) "Rethinking Genre from a Sociocognitive Perspective," *Written Communication* 10(4): 475–509.

Bermejo, F. (2009) "Audience Manufacture in Historical Perspective: From Broadcasting to Google," *New Media and Society* 11(1 and 2): 133–54.

Beyes, T. and C. Steyaert (2006) "Justifying Theatre in Organizational Analysis: A Carnivalesque Alternative?" *Consumption, Markets and Culture* 9(2): 101–9.

Bilandzic, H. and R. W. Busselle (2008) "Transportation and Transportability in the Cultivation of Genre-Consistent Attitudes and Estimates," *Journal of Communication* 58: 508–29.

Bloemer, J., K. Brijs and H. Kasper (2009) "The CoO-ELM Model A Theoretical Framework for the Cognitive Processes Underlying Country of Origin-Effects," *European Journal of Marketing* 43(1/2): 62–89.

Boase, J. (2008) "Personal Networks and the Personal Communication System Using Multiple Media to Connect," *Information, Communication and Society* 11(4): 490–508.

Borgerson, J.L. (2005) "Materiality, Agency, and the Constitution of Consuming Subjects: Insights for Consumer Research," *Advances in Consumer Research* 32: 439–43.

——(2009) "Materiality and the Comfort of Things: Drinks, Dining and Discussion with Daniel Miller," *Consumption, Markets, Culture* 12(2) June: 155–70.

Borgerson, J. L. and J. E. Schroeder (2002) "Ethical Issues of Global Marketing: Avoiding Bad Faith in Visual Representation," *European Journal of Marketing* 36 (5/6): 570–94.

Bradshaw, A. and A. F. Firat (2007) "Rethinking Critical Marketing" in M. Saren et al. (eds) *Critical Marketing: Defining the Field*, pp. 31–43. New York: Elsevier.

Bradshaw, A. and M. B. Holbrook (2008) "Must We have Muzak Wherever We Go? A Critical Consideration of the Consumer Culture," *Consumption Markets and Culture* 11(1): 25–43.

Brecht, B. (1978) *On Theatre* (tr. and ed. by J. Willett). London: Methuen.

Brewis, J. and G. Jack (2005) "Pushing Speed? The Marketing of Fast and Convenience Food," *Consumption, Markets and Culture* 8(1): 49–67.

Brian Jones, D.G. and D.D. Monieson (2008) "Early Development of the Philosophy of Marketing Thought" in M. Tadajewski and D. Brownlie (eds) *Critical Marketing: Contemporary Issues in Marketing*, pp. 45–65. Boston: Wiley.

Brockmeier, J. and R. Harre (2001) "Narrative: Problems and Promises of an Alternative Paradigm," in J. Brockmeier and D. Carbaugh (eds) *Narrative and Identity Studies in Autobiography, Self and Culture*, pp. 39–58. Amsterdam: John Benjamins Publishing.

Brodie, R.J. and L. De Chernatony (2009) "Towards New Conceptualizations of Branding: Theories of the Middle Range," *Marketing Theory* 9(1): 95–100.

Brown, S. (2003) "No Then There Of Time, Space, and the Market" in S. Brown and J.F. Sherry (eds) *Time, Space, and the Market*, pp. 3–16. Armonk, New York: M.E. Sharpe.

——(2004) "Theodore Levitt: Ultimate Writing Machine," *Marketing Theory* 4(3): 209–38.

——(2006) "Ambi-Brand Culture," in J. E. Schroeder and M. Salzer-Morling (eds) *Brand Culture*, pp. 50–66. London: Routledge.

Brown, S., E.C. Hirschman, and P. Maclaran (2001) "Always Historicize! Researching Marketing History in a Post-Historical Epoch," *Marketing Theory* 1(1): 49–89.

Brownlie, D. and P. Hewer (2007) "Concerning Marketing Critterati: Beyond Nuance, Estrangement and Elitism," in M. Saren et al. (eds) *Critical Marketing: Defining the Field*, pp. 44–68. New York: Elsevier.

——(2007b) "Prime Beef Cuts: Culinary Images for Thinking 'Men,'" *Consumption, Markets and Culture* 10(3): 229–50.

Brownlie, D., P. Hewer and S. Horne (2005) "Culinary Tourism: An Exploratory Reading of Contemporary Representations of Cooking," *Consumption, Markets and Culture* 8(1): 7–26.

Brügger, N. (2009) "Website History and the Website as an Object of Study," *New Media and Society* 11(1–32).

Buckingham, D. (2009) "'Creative' Visual Methods in Media Research: Possibilities, Problems and Proposals," *Media, Culture and Society* 31(4): 633–52.

Burke, B. (1994) "Position, Personality, not Price should Frame Consumer Messages," *Brandweek* 35(36).

Burmann, C., S. Hegner and N. Riley (2009) "Towards an Identity-Based Branding," *Marketing Theory* 9(1): 113–18.

Burton, D. (2009) "'Reading' Whiteness in Consumer Research," *Consumption, Markets, Culture* 12(2) June: 171–201.

Caillois, R. (1961) *Man, Play and Games*. New York: The Free Press.

Caldwell, M.L. (2004) "Domesticating the French Fry McDonald's and Consumerism in Moscow," *Journal of Consumer Culture* 4(1): 5–26.

Campbell, S.W. and M. J. Kelley (2008) "Mobile Phone Use among Alcoholics Anonymous Members: New Sites for Recovery," *New Media and Society* 10(6): 915–33.

Carter, D. (2005) "Living in Virtual Communities An Ethnography of Human Relationships in Cyberspace," *Information, Communication and Society* 8(2): 148–67.

Cayla, J. and E. J. Arnould (2008) "A Cultural Approach to Branding in the Global Marketplace," *Journal of International Marketing* 16(4): 86–112.

Cayla, J. and G. M. Eckhardt (2008) "Asian Brands and the Shaping of a Transnational Imagined Community," *Journal of Consumer Research* 35 August 216–30.

Cenite, M., B. H. Detenber, A.W.K. Koh, A.L.H. Lim and N.E. Soon (2009) "Doing the Right Thing Online: a Survey of Bloggers' Ethical Beliefs and Practices," *New Media and Society* 11(4): 575–97.

Chandon, E. and C. Janiszewski (2009) "The Influence of Causal Conditional Reasoning on the Acceptance of Product Claims," *Journal of Consumer Research* 35 April: 1003–11.

Charters, S. (2006) "Aesthetic Products and Aesthetic Consumption: A Review," *Consumption, Markets and Culture* 9(3): 235–55.

Cherrier, H. and J.B. Murray (2007) "Reflexive Dispossession and the Self: Constructing a Processual Theory of Identity," *Consumption, Markets and Culture* 10(1): 1–29.

Chin, E. (2007) "The Consumer Diaries, or, Autoethnography in the Inverted World," *Journal of Consumer Culture* 7(3): 335–53.

Christensen, T. H. (2009) "'Connected Presence' in Distributed Family Life," *New Media and Society* 11(3): 433–51.

Christodoulides, G. (2009) "Branding in the Post-Internet Era," *Marketing Theory* 9(1): 141–4.

Christophers, B. (2007) "Ships in the Night Journeys in Cultural Imperialism and Postcolonialism," *International Journal of Cultural Studies* 10(3): 283–302.

Cinderella Jane (2008) "Once Upon a Time," URL (consulted 16th October, 2008): *http://ethelwenn.com/2008/03/midnight-rant*

Classen, C. and D. Howes (1996) "The Dynamics and Ethics of Cross-Cultural Consumption," in D. Howes (ed.) *Cross-Cultural Consumption: Global Markets, Local Realities*, pp. 178–94. London: Routledge.

Connolly, J. and A. Prothero (2003) "Sustainable Consumption: Consumption, Consumers and the Commodity Discourse," *Consumption, Markets and Culture* 6(4): 275–91.

Cook, D.T. (2003) "Agency, Children's Consumer Culture and the Fetal Subject: Historical Trajectories, Contemporary Connections," *Consumption, Markets and Culture* 6(2): 115–32.

——(2008) (ed.) *Lived Experiences of Public Consumption: Encounters with Value in Marketplaces on Five Continents*. Basingstoke, England: Palgrave Macmillan.

——(2008b) "Introduction: Dramaturgies of Value in Market Places," in D.T. Cook (ed.) *Lived Experiences of Public Consumption: Encounters with Value in Marketplaces on Five Continents*, pp. 1–10. Basingstoke, England: Palgrave Macmillan.

Corner, J. (2007) "Mediated Politics, Promotional Culture and the Idea of 'Propaganda,'" *Media, Culture and Society* 29(4): 669–77.

Couldry, N. (2008) "Mediatization or Mediation? Alternative Understandings of the Emergent Space of Digital Storytelling," *New Media and Society* 10(3): 373–91.

Couldry, N. and T. Markham (2008) "Troubled Closeness or Satisfied Distance? Researching Media Consumption and Public Orientation," *Media, Culture and Society* 30(1): 5–21.

Cronin, A.M. (2004) "Regimes of Mediation: Advertising Practitioners as Cultural Intermediaries?" *Consumption, Markets and Culture* 7(4): 349–69.

Cross, G.A. C.S. David, M. B. Graham and C. Thralls (1996) "Thinking and Rethinking Research Methodology," *Business Communication Quarterly* 59(3): 105–16.

Csaba, F.F. and A. Bengtsson (2006) "Rethinking Identity in Brand Management," in J. E. Schroeder and M. Salzer-Morling (eds) *Brand Culture*, pp. 118–35. London: Routledge.

Currah, A. (2003) "The Virtual Geographies of Retail Display," *Journal of Consumer Culture* 3(1): 5–37.

Cutcher, L. (2008) "Creating Something Using Nostalgia to Build a Branch Network", *Journal of Consumer Culture* 8(3): 369–87.

Daliot-Bul, M. (2007) "Japan's Mobile Technoculture: The Production of a Cellular Playscape and its Cultural Implications," *Media, Culture and Society* 29(6): 954–71.

Dawson, M. (2007) "Little Players, Big Shows: Format, Narration, and Style on Television's New Smaller Screens," *Convergence: The International Journal of Research into New Media Technologies* 13(3): 231–50.

De Certeau, M. (2000) "'Making Do': Uses and Tactics," in M.J. Lee (ed.) *The Consumer Society Reader*, pp. 162–74. Oxford: Blackwell.

De Chernatony, L. (2009) "Towards the Holy Grail of Defining 'Brand,'" *Marketing Theory* 9(1): 101–5.

Deetz, S. (1977) "Interpretive Research in Communication: A Hermeneutic Foundation," *Journal of Communication Inquiry* 3: 53–69.

De Gournay, C. and Z. Smoreda (2003) "Communication Technology and Sociability: Between Local Ties and 'Global Ghetto'?" in J. E. Katz (ed.) *Machines that Become Us: The Social Context of Personal Communication Technology*, pp. 57–70. New Brunswick, NJ: Transaction Publishers.

De Houwer, J., R. Custers, and A. De Clercq (2006) "Do Smokers have a Negative Implicit Attitude toward Smoking?" *Cognition and Emotion* 20(8): 1274–84.

De Run, E. C. (2008) *Targeted Advertising Unintended Effects*. Saarbrucken, Germany: VDM.

Devlin, J.F. and S. McKechnie (2008) "Consumer Perceptions of Brand Architecture in Financial Services," *European Journal of Marketing* 42(5/6): 654–66.

De Zúñiga, H.G., E. Puig-I-Abril and H. Rojas (2009) "Weblogs, Traditional Sources Online and Political Participation: an Assessment of How the Internet is Changing the Political Environ-ment," *New Media and Society* 11(4): 553–74.

Di Gennaro, C. and Dutton, W. H. (2007) "Reconfiguring Friendships: Social Relationships and the Internet," *Information, Communication and Society* 10(5): 591–618.

Dixon, T.L. (2008) "Network News and Racial Beliefs: Exploring the Connection Between National Television News Exposure and Stereotypical Perceptions of African Americans," *Journal of Communication* 58: 321–37.

Dubois, B. (2000) *Understanding the Consumer: A European Perspective*. Harlow: Pearson Education.

Du Gay, P. (2004a) "Devices and Dispositions: Promoting Consumption," *Consumption, Markets and Culture* 7(2): 99–105.

——(2004b) "Self-Service: Retail, Shopping and Personhood," *Consumption, Markets and Culture* 7(2): 149–63.

Dutton, W.H. and Shepherd, A. (2006) "Trust in the Internet as an Experience Technology," *Information, Communication and Society* 9(4): 433–51.

Eckhardt, G. M. and M. J. Houston (2002) "Cultural Paradoxes Reffiected in Brand Meaning: McDonald's in Shanghai China," *Journal of International Marketing* 10 (2): 68–82.

Elliott, R. and A. Davies (2006) "Symbolic Brands and Authenticity of Identity Performance," in J. E. Schroeder and M. Salzer-Morling (eds) *Brand Culture*, pp.155–69. London: Routledge.

Elovaara, P. and Mortberg, C. (2007) "Design of Digital Democracies Performances of Citizenship, Gender and IT," *Information, Communication and Society* 10(3): 404–23.

Evans, E.J. (2008) "Character, Audience Agency and Transmedia Drama," *Media, Culture and Society* 30(2): 197–213.

Faiola, A. and MacDorman, K.F. (2008) "The Influence of Holistic and Analytic Cognitive Styles on Online Information Design Toward a Communication Theory of Cultural Cognitive Design," *Information, Communication and Society* 11(3): 348–74.

Farrell, J. (2003) "Just Looking," in *One Nation Under Goods: Malls and the Seductions of American Shopping*, pp. 137–63. Washington, DC: Smithsonian Publications.

Feldman, C.F. (2001) "Narratives of National Identity as Group Narratives: Patterns of Interpretive Cognition," in J. Brockmeier and D. Carbaugh (eds) *Narrative and Identity Studies in Autobiography, Self and Culture*, pp. 129–44. Amsterdam: John Benjamins Publishing.

Ferraro, R., J. R. Bettman and T. L. Chartrand (2009) "The Power of Strangers: The Effect of Incidental Consumer Brand Encounters on Brand Choice," *Journal of Consumer Research* 35 (February): 729–41.

Firat, A.F. and N. Dholakia (2006) "Theoretical and Philosophical Implications of Postmodern Debates: Some Challenges to Modern Marketing," *Marketing Theory* 6 (2): 123–62.

Fischer, E., C.C. Otnes and L. Tuncay (2007) "Pursuing Parenthood: Integrating Cultural and Cognitive Perspectives on Persistent Goal Striving," *Journal of Consumer Research* 34 (December): 425–40.

Fischer, E. and J.F. Sherry (2007) "Introduction Explorations in Consumer Culture Theory: What are We Exploring Now?" in J. F. Sherry and E. Fischer (eds) *Explorations in Consumer Culture Theory*, pp.1–3. London: Routledge.

Fornäs, J. (2002) "Passages across Thresholds: Into the Borderlands of Mediation," *Convergence: The International Journal of Research into New Media Technologies* 8 (4): 89–106.

Fournier, S. (1998) "Consumers and their Brands: Developing Relationship Theory in Consumer Research," *Journal of Consumer Research* 24 (March): 343–73.

Foxall, G.R. (2001) "Foundations of Consumer Behavior Analysis," *Marketing Theory*, 1(2): 165–99.

Friend, L.A. and S.M. Thompson (2003) "Identity, Ethnicity and Gender: Using Narratives to Understand their Meaning in Retail Shopping Encounters," *Consumption, Markets and Culture* 6(1): 23–41.

Gabriel, Y. and T. Lang (2008) "New Faces and New Masks of Today's Consumer," *Journal of Consumer Culture* 8(3): 321–40.

Gadamer, H.G. (1975) *Truth and Method*. London: Sheed and Ward.

Gadamer, H.G. (1976) *Philosophical Hermeneutics*. Trans. by D.E. Linge. Berkeley: University of California Press.

Gadamer, H.G. (1985) "The Historicity of Understanding," in K. Mueller-Vollmer (ed.) *The Hermeneutics Reader: Texts of the German Tradition from the Enlightenment to the Present*, pp. 256–92. Oxford: Blackwell.

Gallagher, S. (2004) "Hermeneutics and the Cognitive Sciences," *Journal of Consciousness Studies* 11 (10–11).

Garcia, A.C., A. I. Standlee, J. Bechkoff and Y. Cui (2009) "Ethnographic Approaches to the Internet and Computer-Mediated Communication," *Journal of Contemporary Ethnography* 38 (1): 52–84.

Garcìa-Gomez, A. (2009) "Teenage Girls' Personal Weblog Writing Truly a New Gender Discourse?" *Information, Communication and Society* 12(5): 611–38.

Gerbner, G., L. Gross, M. Morgan, and N. Signorielli (1980) "The 'Mainstreaming' of America: Violence Profile No. 11," *Journal of Communication* 30(3):10–29.

Geser, H. (2005) "Is the Cell Phone Undermining the Social Order? Understanding Mobile Technology from a Sociological Perspective," in P. Glotz, S. Bertschi and C. Locke (eds) *Thumb Culture. The Meaning of Mobile Phones for Society*, pp. 23–35. New Brunswick, NJ: Transaction Publishers.

Glynn, M. (2009) "Integrating Brand, Retailer and End-Customer Perspectives," *Marketing Theory* 9(1): 137–40.

Goffey, A. (2008) "Abstract Experience," *Theory, Culture and Society* 25(4): 15–30.

Goggin, G. and C. Spurgeon (2007) "Premium Rate Culture: the New Business of Mobile Interactivity," *New Media and Society* 9(5): 753–70.

Gordon, J. (2007) "The Mobile Phone and the Public Sphere: Mobile Phone Usage in Three Critical Situations," *Convergence: The International Journal of Research into New Media Technologies* 13(3): 307–19.

Gould, S.J. (2008) "An Introspective Genealogy of My Introspective Genealogy," *Marketing Theory* 8(4): 407–24.

Grayson, K. (1999) "The Dangers and Opportunities of Playful Consumption," in M.B. Holbrook (ed.) *Consumer Value: A Framework for Analysis and Research*, pp.105–25. London: Routledge.

Grunig, J.E. (1982) "The Message-Attitude-Behavior Relationship," *Communication Research* 9(2): 163–200.

Gummesson, E. (2001) "Are Current Research Approaches in Marketing Leading Us Astray?" *Marketing Theory* 1(1): 27–48.

Habermas, J. (1985) "On Hermeneutics' Claim to Universality," in K. Mueller-Vollmer (ed.) *The Hermeneutics Reader*, pp. 294–319. Oxford: Blackwell.

Hall, R.T.H. (2006) "Culture and Consumption II: Markets, Meaning, and Brand Management," *Journal of Advertising Research*, September 347–48.

Halter, M. (2002) *Shopping for Identity: The Marketing of Ethnicity*. Schocken Books: New York.

Hamilton, C.A. and Schneider, R. (2002) "From Iser to Turner and Beyond: Reception Theory Meets Cognitive Criticism," *Research Library* 36(4): 640–58.

Hans, J.S. (1981) *The Play of the World*. Amherst, MA: University of Massachusetts.

Hare, M. (2004) "Trade Routes," *Global Cosmetic Industry*, April, 24–25.

Hargittai, E. and Walejko, G. (2008) "The Participation Divide Content Creation and Sharing in the Digital Age," *Information, Communication and Society* 11(2): 239–56.

Harindranath, R. (2009) "Media Audiences, Public Knowledge and Citizenship: an Indian Example." Paper presented at the ANZCA09 Communication, Creativity and Global Citizenship Conference, Brisbane, Australia.

Harre, R. (2004) "Discursive Psychology and the Boundaries of Sense," *Organization Studies* 25(8): 1435–53.

Harre, R. and P.F. Secord (1972) *The Explanation of Social Behavior*. Oxford: Blackwell.

Harrison, T. M. and B. Barthel (2009) "Wielding New Media in Web 2.0: Exploring the History of Engagement with the Collaborative Construction of Media Products," *New Media and Society* 11(1–78).

Hartmann, M. (2006) "A Mobile Ethnographic View on (Mobile) Media Usage?" in J. R. Hoflich and M. Hartmann (eds) *Mobile Communication in Everyday Life: Ethnographic Views, Observations and Reflections*, pp. 273–97. Berlin: Frank and Timme.

Hatch, M. J. and Rubin, J. (2006) "The Hermeneutics of Branding," *Brand Management* 14 (1/2) 40–59.

Hearn, A. (2008) "'Meat, Mask, Burden': Probing the Contours of the Branded 'Self,'" *Journal of Consumer Culture* 8(2): 197–217.

Hebdige, D. (2000) "Object as Image: The Italian Scooter Cycle," in M.J. Lee (ed.) *The Consumer Society Reader*, pp. 125–61. Oxford: Blackwell.

Heidegger, M. (1962) *Being and Time*. (J. Macquarrie and E. Robinson, Trans.) New York: Harper and Row.

——(1985) "Phenomenology and Fundamental Ontology: The Disclosure of Meaning," in K. Mueller-Vollmer (ed.) *The Hermeneutics Reader*, pp. 214–40. Oxford: Blackwell.

Heisley, D.D. and D. Cours (2007) "Connectedness and Worthiness for the Embedded Self: A Material Culture Perspective," *Consumption, Markets and Culture* 10(4): 425–50.

Henneberg, S.C., M. Scammell and N.J. O'Shaughnessy (2009) "Political Marketing Management and Theories of Democracy," *Marketing Theory* 9(2): 165–88.

Henry, P. and M. Caldwell (2007) "Headbanging as Resistance or Refuge: A Cathartic Account," *Consumption, Markets and Culture* 10(2): 159–74.

Henry, P. and M. Caldwell (2008) "Spinning the Proverbial Wheel? Social Class and Marketing," *Marketing Theory* 8(4): 387–405.

Hill, M.E. and J. Cromartie (2004) "That Which is 'Not:' Forgetting … ," *Consumption, Markets and Culture* 7(1): 69–98.

Hjorth, L. (2005) 'Postal Presence: A Case Study of Mobile Customisation and Gender in Melbourne' in P. Glotz, S. Bertschi and C. Locke (eds) Thumb Culture. The Meaning of Mobile Phones for Society, pp. 53–65. New Brunswick, NJ: Transaction Publishers.

——(2007) "The Game of Being Mobile: One Media History of Gaming and Mobile Technologies in Asia-Pacific," *Convergence: The International Journal of Research into New Media Technologies* 13(4): 369–81.

——(2008) "Being Real in the Mobile Reel: A Case Study on Convergent Mobile Media as Domesticated New Media in Seoul, South Korea," *Convergence: The International Journal of Research into New Media Technologies* 14(1): 91–104.

Hofstede, G. (1980) *Culture's Consequences: International Differences in Work-related Values*. London: Sage.

Hogg, M.K., C. F. Curasi and P. Maclaran (2004) "The (Re-)Configuration of Production and Consumption in Empty Nest Households/Families," *Consumption, Markets and Culture* 7(3): 239–59.

Hoijer, B. (2008) "Ontological Assumptions and Generalizations in Qualitative (Audience) Research," *European Journal of Communication* 23(3): 275–94.

Holden, T.J.M. (2001) "The Malaysian Dilemma: Advertising's Catalytic and Cataclysmic Role in Social Development," *Media, Culture and Society* 23: 275–97.

Holt, D. (1995) "How Consumers Consume: A Typology of Consumption Practices," *Journal of Consumer Research*, 22 June: 1–16.

——(1997) "Poststructuralist Lifestyle Analysis: Conceptualizing the Social Patterning of Consumption in Postmodernity," *Journal of Consumer Research* 23 (March): 326–50.

——(2004) *How Brands Become Icons: The Principles of Cultural Branding*. Cambridge, MA: Harvard University Press.

——(2006) "Toward a Sociology of Branding," *Journal of Consumer Culture* 6(3): 299–302.

Hookway, N. (2008) "'Entering the Blogosphere': Some Strategies for Using Blogs in Social Research," *Qualitative Research* 8(1): 91–113.

Horowitz, D.M. (2009) "A Review of Consensus Analysis Methods in Consumer Culture, Organizational Culture and National Culture Research," *Consumption Markets and Culture* 12(1): 47–64.

Huber, F., J. Vogel, and F. Meyer (2009) "When Brands Get Branded," *Marketing Theory* 9(1): 131–6.

Huizinga, J. (1970) *Homo Ludens: A Study of the Play Element in Culture*. London: Temple Smith [Published previously, London: Routledge and Kegan Paul (1949) and Boston: Beacon Press (1955)].

Hunt, S.D. (1989) "Reification and Realism in Marketing: In Defense of Reason," *Journal of Macromarketing* 9: 4–10.

——(1991) *Marketing Theory: The Philosophy of Marketing Science*. Homewood, IL: Irwin.

——(1991b) "Positivism and Paradigm Dominance in Consumer Research: Toward Critical Pluralism and Rapprochement," *Journal of Consumer Research* 18 June: 32–44.

Husserl, E. (1973) Experience and Judgement. London: Routledge and Kegan Paul.

——(1985) "The Phenomenological Theory of Meaning and of Meaning Apprehension," in K.Mueller-Vollmer (ed.) *The Hermeneutics Reader*, pp. 165–86. Oxford: Blackwell.

Hutchinson, P., R. Read and W. Sharrock (2008) *There is No Such Thing as a Social Science: In Defense of Peter Winch*. London: Ashgate.

Iacobucci, D. (2001) "Commonalities between Research Methods for Consumer Science and Biblical Scholarship," *Marketing Theory* 1(1): 109–33.

Ingarden, R. (1985) "On the Cognition of the Literary Work of Art," in K. Mueller-Vollmer (ed.) *The Hermeneutics Reader*, pp. 187–213. Oxford: Blackwell.

Iser, W. (1978) *The Act of Reading*. Baltimore: Johns Hopkins University Press.

Iversen, N.M. and L. E. Hem (2008) "Provenance Associations as Core Values of Place Umbrella Brands A Framework of Characteristics," *European Journal of Marketing* 42(5/6): 603–26.

Jackson, P. (2004) "Local Consumption Cultures in a Globalizing World," Transactions of the Institute of British Geographers 29: 165–78.

Jackson, P. and N. Thrift (2001) 'Geographies of Consumption', in D. Miller (2001) (ed.) *Consumption: Critical Concepts in the Social Sciences*, Vol. III, pp. 383–417. London: Routledge.

Jansson, A. (2002) "Spatial Phantasmagoria: The Mediatization of Tourism Experience," *European Journal of Communication* 17(4): 429–43.

——(2004) "Book Review: Nick Couldry, and Anna McCarthy (eds) *MediaSpace: Place, Scale and Culture in a Media Age*. London: Routledge (2004)," *European Journal of Communication* 19(4): 551–4.

Jauss, H.R. (1982) *Aesthetic Experience and Literary Hermeneutics*. Minneapolis: University of Minnesota Press.

Jenkins, H. (1992) *Textual Poachers: Television Fans and Participatory Culture*. New York: Routledge.

Jenkins, H. and M. Deuze (2008) "Editorial: Convergence Culture," *Convergence: The International Journal of Research into New Media Technologies* 14(1): 5–12.

JesuLalaine (2008) "3, 000 Ringgit Lucky Draw," URL (consulted 15th October, 2008): *http://www.jesulalaine.com/2008/10/3000-ringgit-lucky-draw.html*

Jin, D.Y. (2007) "Reinterpretation of Cultural Imperialism: Emerging Domestic Market vs Continuing US Dominance," *Media, Culture and Society* 29(5): 753–71.

Johnsen, T. E. (2003) "The Social Context of the Mobile Phone Use of Norwegian Teens," in J. E. Katz (ed.) *Machines That Become Us: The Social Context of Personal Communication Technology*, pp. 161–9. New Brunswick, NJ: Transaction Publishers.

Jubas, K. (2007) "Conceptual Con/Fusion in Democratic Societies: Understandings and Limitations of Consumer-Citizenship," *Journal of Consumer Culture* 7(2): 231–54.

Karppinen, K. (2007) "Against Naïve Pluralism in Media Politics: On the Implications of the Radical-Pluralist Approach to the Public Sphere," *Media, Culture and Society* 29(3): 495–508.

Katz, J. E. (2005) "Mobile Communication and the Transformation of Daily Life: The Next Phase of Research on Mobiles," in P. Glotz, S. Bertschi and C. Locke (eds) *Thumb Culture. The Meaning of Mobile Phones for Society*, pp. 171–82. New Brunswick, NJ: Transaction Publishers.

Kawashima, N. (2006) "Advertising Agencies, Media and Consumer Market: The Changing Quality of TV Advertising in Japan," *Media, Culture and Society* 28(3): 393–410.

Kazmer, M.M. and Xie, B. (2008) "Qualitative Interviewing in Internet Studies Playing with the Media, Playing with the Method," *Information, Communication and Society* 11(2): 257–78.

Kelly, A, K. Lawlor and S. O'Donohue (2005) "Encoding Advertisements: The Creative Perspective," *Journal of Marketing Management* 21: 505–28.

Kemper, S. (2001) *Buying and Believing: Sri Lankan Advertising and Consumers in a Transnational World*. Chicago and London: University of Chicago Press.

Kennedy, H. (2008) "New Media's Potential for Personalization," *Information, Communication and Society* 11(3): 307–25.

Khan, M. (2006) "Innovation Sans Frontieres," *Brand Strategy*, November.

Kirchberg, V. (2007) "Cultural Consumption Analysis: Beyond Structure and Agency," *Cultural Sociology* 1(1): 115–35.

Kjeldgaard, D. and J. Ostberg (2007) "Coffee Grounds and the Global Cup: Glocal Consumer Culture in Scandinavia," *Consumption, Markets and Culture* 10(2): 175–187.

Klein, N. (1999) *No Logo: Taking Aim at the Brand Bullies*. New York: Picador.

Knight J. and A. Weedon (2008) "Editorial: Patterns of Use and Exchange," *Convergence: The International Journal of Research into New Media Technologies* 14 (2): 131–33.

Kobayashi, T., Ikeda, K. and Miyata, K. (2006) "Social Capital Online Collective Use of the Internet and Reciprocity as Lubricants of Democracy," *Information, Communication and Society* 9(5): 582–611.

Kocamaz, I. (2009) "Reviews of *Critical Marketing: Contemporary Issues in Marketing*, edited by M. Tadajewski and D. Brownlie, Chichester, John Wiley and Sons

(2008) and *Critical Marketing: Defining the Field*, edited by M. Saren, P. Maclaran, C. Goulding, R.Elliott, A. Shankar and M. Catterall, Oxford, Elsevier (2007)," *Consumption Markets and Culture* 12(1): 85–98.

Kowinski,W. (1985) *The Malling of America: An Inside Look at the Great Consumer Paradise*. New York: William Morrow.

Kozinets, R. V. (2008) "Technology/Ideology: How Ideological Fields Inffluence Consumers' Technology Narratives," *Journal of Consumer Research* 34 April 865–81.

Krotz, F. (2006) "Ethnography, Related Research Approaches and Digital Media," in J. R. Hoflich and M. Hartmann (eds) *Mobile Communication in Everyday Life: Ethnographic Views, Observations and Reflections*, pp. 299–319. Berlin: Frank and Timme.

——(2007) "The Meta-Process of 'Mediatization' as a Conceptual Frame," *Global Media and Communication* 3(3): 256–60.

Laguerre, M.S. (2004) "Virtual Time The Processuality of the Cyberweek," *Information, Communication and Society* 7(2): 223–47.

Langman, L. (1992) "Neon Cages: Shopping for Subjectivity," in R. Shields (ed.) *Lifestyle Shopping*, pp. 40–82. London: Routledge.

Larsen, J., J. Urry and K. Axhausen (2008) "Coordinating Face-to-Face Meetings in Mobile Network Societies," *Information, Communication and Society* 11(5): 640–58.

Lasen, A. (2006) "How To Be in Two Places at The Same Time? Mobile Phone Use in Public Places," in J. R. Hoflich and M. Hartmann (eds) *Mobile Communication in Everyday Life: Ethnographic Views, Observations and Reflections*, pp. 227–51. Berlin: Frank and Timme.

Lawlor, M-A and A. Prothero (2008) "Exploring Children's Understanding of Television Advertising—Beyond the Advertiser's Perspective," *European Journal of Marketing* 42 (11/12): 1203–23.

Lee, H. (2005) "Implosion, Virtuality, and Interaction in an Internet Discussion Group," *Information, Communication and Society* 8(1): 47–63.

Lee, L. and D. Ariely (2006) "Shopping Goals, Goal Concreteness, and Conditional Promotions," *Journal of Consumer Research* 33 June: 60–70.

Lee, N. and G. Greenley (2008) "The Primacy of Theory," *European Journal of Marketing* 42 (9/10): 873–8.

Leidner, R. (1993) *Fast Food, Fast Talk: Service Work and the Routinization of Everyday Life*. Berkeley: University of California Press.

Levin, M. (1991) "The Reification-Realism-Positivism Controversy in Macromarketing: A Philosopher's View," *Journal of Macromarketing* 11: 57–64.

Levine, E. (2008) "Distinguishing Television: the Changing Meanings of Television Liveness," *Media, Culture and Society* 30(3): 393–409.

Li, D. and G. Walejko (2008) "Splogs and Abandoned Blogs: The Perils of Sampling Bloggers and their Blogs," *Information, Communication and Society* 11(2): 279–96.

Li, F., J.A.F. Nicholls, G. Zhuang, N. Zhou, T. Mandokovic, and G. Zhuang (2003) "A Pacific Rim Debut: Shoppers in China and Chile," *Asia Pacific Journal of Marketing and Logistics* 15 (1/2): 115–31.

Li, F., N. Zhou, J.A.F Nicholls, G. Zhuang and C. Kranendonk (2004) "Interlinear or Inscription? A Comparative Study of Chinese and American Mall Shoppers' Behavior," *Journal of Consumer Marketing* 21 (1): 51–61.

Licoppe, C. (2003) "Two Modes of Maintaining Interpersonal Relations Through Telephone: From the Domestic to the Mobile Phone," in J. E. Katz (ed.) *Machines That Become Us: The Social Context of Personal Communication Technology*, pp. 171–85. New Brunswick, NJ: Transaction Publishers.

Liddle, A.J. (2000) "McD's Stake in Food.Com Reveals Multibrand Online Strategy," *Nation's Restaurant News* 27th March, 39, 44.

Lievrouw, L.A. (2009) "New Media, Mediation, and Communication Study," *Information, Communication and Society* 12(3): 303–25.

Lillie, J. (2005) "Cultural Access, Participation, and Citizenship in the Emerging Consumer-Network Society," *Convergence: The International Journal of Research into New Media Technologies* 11(2): 41–8.

Lindridge, A.M., M.K. Hogg and M. Shah (2004) "Imagined Multiple Worlds: How South Asian Women in Britain Use Family and Friends to Navigate the 'Border Crossings' between Household and Societal Contexts," *Consumption, Markets and Culture* 7(3): 211–38.

Ling, R. and L. Haddon (2003) "Mobile Telephony, Mobility, and the Coordination of Everyday Life," in J. E. Katz (ed.) *Machines That Become Us: The Social Context of Personal Communication Technology*, pp. 245–65. New Brunswick, NJ: Transaction Publishers.

Livingstone, S., M. Bober and E.J. Helsper (2005) "Active Participation or Just More Information? Young People's Take-Up of Opportunities to Act and Interact on the Internet," *Information, Communication and Society* 8(3): 287–314.

Livingstone, S. and E. J. Helsper (2007) "Taking Risks when Communicating on the Internet: The Role of Offline Social-Psychological Factors in Young People's Vulnerability to Online Risks," *Information, Communication and Society* 10(5): 619–44.

Livingstone, S., P. Lunt and L. Miller (2007) "Citizens, Consumers and the Citizen-Consumer: Articulating the Citizen Interest in Media and Communications Regulation," *Discourse and Communication* 1(1): 85–111.

Lopez, L.K. (2009) "The Radical Act of 'Mommy Blogging': Redefining Motherhood through the Blogosphere," *New Media and Society* 11(5): 729–47.

Lüders, M. (2008) "Conceptualizing Personal Media," *New Media and Society*, 10(5): 683–702.

Lunt, P. (1995) "Psychological Approaches to Consumption Varieties of Research—Past, Present and Future," in D. Miller (ed.) *Acknowledging Consumption: A Review of New Studies*. London: Routledge, pp. 238–63.

Lury, C. (2009) "Brand as Assemblage Assembling Culture," *Journal of Cultural Economy* 2 (1 and 2): 67–82.

Lyons, J. (2005) "'Think Seattle, Act Globally.' Speciality Coffee, Commodity Biographies and the Promotion of Place," *Cultural Studies* 19(1): 14–34.

MacCabe, C. (1974) "Realism and the Cinema: Notes on some Brechtian Theses," *Screen* 15(2): 7–27.

Machin, D. and J. Thornborrow (2003) "Branding and Discourse: the Case of *Cosmopolitan*," *Discourse and Society* 14(4): 453–71.

Mackenzie, A. (2006) "Innumerable Transmissions: Wi-Fi from Spectacle to Movement," *Information, Communication and Society* 9(6): 781–802.

Maclaran, P. and M. Hogg (2008) "Rhetorical Issues in Writing Interpretivist Consumer Research," *Qualitative Market Research: An International Journal* 11(2): 130–46.

Malpas, J. (2009) "On the Non-Autonomy of the Virtual," *Convergence: The International Journal of Research into New Media Technologies* 15(2): 135–39.

Mansell, R. (2007) "The Problem of Internationalizing Media and Communication Research," *Global Media and Communication* 3(3): 283–88.

Martin, C. A., and L.W. Turley (2004) "Malls and Consumption Motivation: An Exploratory Examination of Older Generation Y Consumers," *International Journal of Retail and Distribution Management* 32 (10): 464–75.

Martin, E. (2005) "Food, Literature, Art, and the Demise of Dualistic Thought," *Consumption, Markets and Culture* 8(1): 27–48.

McGrath, M.A. (1998) "Dream On: Projections of an Ideal Servicescape," in Sherry, J.F. (ed.) *ServiceScapes: The Concept of Place in Contemporary Markets*, pp. 439–53. Chicago: American Marketing Association.

McKinlay, A. and C. McVittie (2008) Social Psychology and Discourse. Oxford: Wiley-Blackwell.

Medway, D. and G. Warnaby (2008) "Alternative Perspectives on Marketing and the Place Brand," *European Journal of Marketing* 42(5/6): 641–53.

Melewar, T. C., E. Badal and J. Small (2006) "Danone Branding Strategy in China," *Brand Management* 13(6): 407–17.

Mesch, G. S. and Talmud, I. (2007) "Editorial Comment: E-Relationships—the Blurring and Reconfiguration of Offline and Online Social Boundaries," *Information, Communication and Society* 10(5): 585–89.

Meyers-Levy, J. and D. Maheswaran (1991) "Exploring Differences in Males' and Females' Processing Strategies," *Journal of Consumer Research* 18 June: 63–70.

Millan, E. S. and E. Howard (2007) "Shopping for Pleasure? Shopping Experiences of Hungarian Consumers," *International Journal of Retail and Distribution Management* 35 (6): 474–87.

Miller, D. (1987) *Material Culture and Mass Consumption*. Oxford: Basil Blackwell.

——(1998) *A Theory of Shopping*. Cambridge. Polity Press.

Miller, D., P. Jackson, N. Thrift, B. Holbrook and M. Rowlands (1998) *Shopping, Place and Identity*. London: Routledge.

Miller, L.J. (2009) "Review of R. Sassatelli (2007) *Consumer Culture: History, Theory and Politics*. London: Sage," *Journal of Consumer Culture* 8(3): 419–32.

Mintz, S.W. (1997) "Afterword: Swallowing Modernity," in J.L. Watson (ed.) *Golden Arches East: McDonald's in East Asia*, pp. 183–200. Stanford, CA: Stanford University Press.

Mitchell, W. J. (1995) *City of Bits: Space, Place, and the Infobahn*. Cambridge, MA: The MIT Press.

Mitra, A. (2008) "Using Blogs to Create Cybernetic Space: Examples from People of Indian Origin," *Convergence: The International Journal of Research into New Media Technologies* 14(4): 457–72.

Moe, H. (2008) "Dissemination and Dialogue in the Public Sphere: a Case for Public Service Media Online," *Media, Culture and Society* 30(3): 319–36.

Mohammad, T., S. Barker and J. Kandampully (2005) "Multicultural Student Perceptions of Fast Food Restaurant Brands: An Australian Study," *Journal of Hospitality and Leisure Marketing* 12(4): 93–118.

Moisander, J. and P. Eriksson (2006) "Corporate Narratives of Information Society: Making up the Mobile Consumer Subject," *Consumption, Markets and Culture* 9(4): 257–75.

Money, A. (2007) "Material Culture and the Living Room: The Appropriation and Use of Goods in Everyday Life," *Journal of Consumer Culture* 7(3): 355–77.

Moon, Y.S. and K. Chan (2005) "Advertising Appeals and Cultural Values in Television Commercials. A Comparison of Hong Kong and Korea," *International Marketing Review* 22(1): 48–66.

Moor, E. (2003) "Branded Spaces: The Scope of 'New Marketing,'" *Journal of Consumer Culture* 3(1): 39–60.

Moreno, R.M.A. (2006) "Citizens and Media Cultures: Hidden Behind Democratic Formality," *Global Media and Communication* 2(3): 299–313.

Morley, D. (1980) *The Nationwide Audience: Structure and Decoding*. London: British Film Institute.

Morley, D. (1995) "Theories of Consumption in Media Studies," in D. Miller (ed.) *Acknowledging Consumption: A Review of New Studies*, pp. 296–328. London: Routledge.

Morley, D. (2000) *Home Territories: Media, Mobility and Identity*. London: Routledge.

Morris, M. (1993) "Things to Do with Shopping Centers," in S. During (ed.) *The Cultural Studies Reader*, pp. 391–409. London: Routledge.

——(2005) "Interpretability and Social Power, or, Why Postmodern Advertising Works," *Media, Culture and Society* 27(5): 697–718.

Mort, F. (2000) "The Politics of Consumption," in M.J. Lee (ed.) *The Consumer Society Reader*, pp. 271–81. Oxford: Blackwell.

Mueller-Vollmer, K. (1985) (ed.) The Hermeneutics Reader. Oxford: Blackwell.

Mukhopadhyay, A., J. Sengupta and S. Ramanathan (2008) "Recalling Past Temptations: An Information-Processing Perspective on the Dynamics of Self-Control," *Journal of Consumer Research* 35 December 586–99.

Murdock, G. (2004) "Past the Posts: Rethinking Change, Retrieving Critique," *European Journal of Communication* 19(1): 19–38.

Muzellec, L. and M. C. Lambkin (2009) "Corporate Branding and Brand Architecture: a Conceptual Framework," *Marketing Theory* 9(1): 39–54.

Nabi, R.L. and M. Krcmar (2004) "Conceptualizing Media Enjoyment as Attitude: Implications for Mass Media Effects Research," *Communication Theory* 14(4) November: 288–310.

Nabi, R.L. and J.L. Sullivan (2001) "Does Television Viewing Relate to Engagement in Protective Action Against Crime? A Cultivation Analysis From a Theory of Reasoned Action Perspective," *Communication Research* 28 (6): 802–25.

Nairn, A., C. Griffin and P. G. Wicks (2008) "Children's Use of Brand Symbolism: A Consumer Culture Theory Approach," *European Journal of Marketing* 42(5/6): 627–40.

Nicholls, J.A.F., F. Li, C.J. Kranendonk and S. Roslow (2002) "The Seven year Itch? Mall Shoppers Across Time," *Journal of Consumer Marketing* 19 (2): 149–65.

Nicholls, J.A.F., F. Li, T. Mandokovic, S. Roslow and C. Kranendonk (2000) "US-Chilean Mirrors: Shoppers in Two Countries," *Journal of Consumer Marketing* 17 (2): 106–19.

Nicholls, J.A.F., S. Roslow and S. Dublish (1997) "Time and Companionship: Key Factors in Hispanic Shopping Behavior," *Journal of Consumer Marketing* 14 (3): 194–205.

Novak, T.P. and D.L. Hoffman (2009) "The Fit of Thinking Style and Situation: New Measures of Situation-Specific Experiential and Rational Cognition," *Journal of Consumer Research* 36 June: 56–72.

O'Guinn, T.C. and L.J. Shrum (1997) "The Role of Television in the Construction of Consumer Reality," *Journal of Consumer Research* 23 March: 278–94.

Olney, T.J., M.B. Holbrook and R. Batra (1991) "Consumer Responses to Advertising: The Effects of Ad Content, Emotions, and Attitude toward the Ad on Viewing Time," *Journal of Consumer Research* 17 March: 440–53.

Olson, K. K. (2005) "Cyberspace as Place and the Limits of Metaphor," *Convergence* 11(1): 10–18.

Orgad, S. (2009) "Mobile TV: Old and New in the Construction of an Emergent Technology," *Convergence: The International Journal of Research into New Media Technologies* 15(2): 197–214.

O'Shaughnessy, J. (1987) *Why People Buy*. Oxford: Oxford University Press.

O'Shaughnessy, J. and N.J O'Shaughnessy (2002) "Postmodernism and Marketing: Separating the Wheat from the Chaff," *Journal of Macromarketing* 22(1): 109–35.

O'Shaughnessy, J. and N.J. O'Shaughnessy (2004) *Persuasion in Advertising*. London: Routledge.

O'Shaughnessy, N.J. and P.R Baines (2009) "Selling Terror: The Symbolization and Positioning of Jihad," *Marketing Theory* 9(2): 227–41.

Ouwersloot, H. and G. Odekerken-Schroder (2008) "Who's Who in Brand Communities—and Why?" *European Journal of Marketing* 42(5/6): 571–85.

Ozdemir, A. (2008) "Shopping Malls: Measuring Interpersonal Distance under Changing Conditions and across Cultures," *Field Methods* 20(3): 226–48.

Park, C. W. and D. J. MacInnis (2006) "What's In and What's Out: Questions on the Boundaries of the Attitude Construct," *Journal of Consumer Research* 33 June: 16–18.

Parvez, Z. and Ahmed, P. (2006) "Towards Building an Integrated Perspective on E-Democracy," *Information, Communication and Society* 9(5): 612–32.

Peñaloza, L. and A. Venkatesh (2006) "Further Evolving the New Dominant Logic of Marketing: From Services to the Social Construction of Markets," *Marketing Theory* 6(3): 299–316.

Pereira, C. (2009) "Inequalities on the Web: Strengths and Weaknesses of a Political Economy Analysis," *Media, Culture and Society* 31(2): 325–30.

Petrecca, L. and B. McDowell (1997) "McDonald's Puts Branding Effort Behind Breakfast," *Advertising Age* 68(5).

Pettinger, L. (2004) "Brand Culture and Branded Workers: Service Work and Aesthetic Labour in Fashion Retail," *Consumption, Markets and Culture* 7(2): 165–84.

Pickard, V.W. (2008) "Co-optation and Co-operation: Institutional Exemplars of Democratic Internet Technology," *New Media and Society* 10(4): 625–45.

Popper, K. (1963) *Conjectures and Refutations*. London: Routledge and Kegan Paul.

Postill, J. (2008) "Localizing the Internet beyond Communities and Networks," *New Media and Society* 10(3): 413–31.

Potter, J. and M. Wetherell (1987) *Discourse and Social Psychology: Beyond Attitudes and Behavior*. London: Sage.

Power, J. and S. Whelan (2008) "The Attractiveness and Connectedness of Ruthless Brands: the Role of Trust," *European Journal of Marketing* 42(5/6): 586–602.

Preston, P. (2006) "Internationalizing Cultural Studies," *Media, Culture and Society* 28 (6): 941–5.

Qian, W., M. A. Razzaque and K. A. Keng (2007) "Chinese Cultural Values and Gift-Giving Behavior," *Journal of Consumer Marketing* 24(4): 214–28.

Raju, S., H. R. Unnava and N. V. Montgomery (2009) "The Effect of Brand Commitment on the Evaluation of Nonpreferred Brands: A Disconfirmation Process," *Journal of Consumer Research* 35 (February): 851–63.

Ram, U. (2008) "Review of A. Arvidsson, *Brands: Meaning and Value in Media Culture*. London: Routledge (2006)," *Journal of Consumer Culture* 8(3): 430–2.

Ratner, Carl (2008) "Cultural Psychology and Qualitative Methodology: Scientific and Political Considerations," *Culture and Psychology* 14(3): 259–88.

Rauch, J. (2007) "Activists as Interpretive Communities: Rituals of Consumption and Interaction in an Alternative Media Audience," *Media, Culture and Society* 29(6): 994–1013.

Richins, M.L. (1991) "Social Comparison and the Idealized Images of Advertising," *Journal of Consumer Research* 18 June: 71–83.

Ricoeur, P. (1981) "Phenomenology and Hermeneutics,", in J. B. Thompson (ed.) *Paul Ricoeur: Hermeneutics and the Human Sciences*, pp. 101–30. Cambridge: Cambridge University Press.

Ricoeur, P. (1981b) "The Hermeneutical Function of Distanciation," in J. B. Thompson (ed.) *Paul Ricoeur: Hermeneutics and the Human Sciences*, pp. 131–44. Cambridge: Cambridge University Press.

Riley, F. D., L. Rink and P. Harris (1999) "Patterns of Attitudes and Behavior in Fragmented Markets," *Journal of Empirical Generalizations in Marketing Science* 4: 62–91.

Rindfleisch, A., J. E. Burroughs, and N. Wong (2009) "The Safety of Objects: Materialism, Existential Insecurity, and Brand Connection," *Journal of Consumer Research* 36 (June): 1–16.

Ringberg, T. and M. Reihlen (2008) "Communication Assumptions in Consumer Research: An Alternative Socio-Cognitive Approach," *Consumption, Markets and Culture* 11(3): 173–89.

Ritson, M. and R. Elliott (1999) "The Social Uses of Advertising: An Ethnographic Study of Adolescent Advertising Audiences," *Journal of Consumer Research* 26 December: 260–77.

Ritzer, G. (1999) "Assessing the Resistance," in B. Smart (ed.) *Resisting McDonaldization*, pp. 234–55. London: Sage.

——(2008) *The McDonaldization of Society* 5. Thousand Oaks, CA: Pine Forge Press.

Rizzo, S. (2008) "The Promise of Cell Phones: From People Power to Technological Nanny," *Convergence: The International Journal of Research into New Media Technologies* 14(2): 135–43.

Roach, C. (1997) "Cultural Imperialism and Resistance in Media Theory and Literary Theory," *Media, Culture and Society* 19: 47–66.

Roberts, D. and D. Rocks (2005) "Let a Thousand Brands Bloom," *Business Week*, 17th October, Issue 3955.

Robinson, L. (2009) "A Taste for the Necessary: A Bourdieuian Approach to Digital Inequality," *Information, Communication and Society* 12(4): 488–507.

Roig, A., G. S. Cornelio, E. Ardèvol, P. Alsina and R. Pagès (2009) "Videogame as Media Practice: An Exploration of the Intersections Between Play and Audiovisual Culture," *Convergence: The International Journal of Research into New Media Technologies* 15(1): 89–103.

Roudakova, N. (2008) "Media–Political Clientelism: Lessons from Anthropology," *Media, Culture and Society* 30(1): 41–59.

Roy, I. S. (2007) "Worlds Apart: Nation-Branding on the National Geographic Channel," *Media, Culture and Society* 29(4): 569–92.

Ryan, J. M. (2005) "Easton: A 21st Century (R)Evolution in Consumption, Community, Urbanism, and Space," University of Maryland: MA Thesis.

Salcedo, R. (2003) "When the Global Meets the Local at the Mall," *American Behavioral Scientist* 46(8): 1084–1103.

Salter, L. (2004) "Structure and Forms of Use: A Contribution to Understanding the 'Effects' of the Internet on Deliberative Democracy," *Information, Communication and Society* 7(2): 185–206.

Sandikci, O. and Holt, D.B. (1998) "Malling Society: Mall Consumption Practices and the Future of Public Space," in J.F. Sherry (ed.) *ServiceScapes: The Concept of Place in Contemporary Markets*, pp. 305–36. Chicago: American Marketing Association.

Schembri, S. and J. Sandberg (2002) "Service Quality and the Consumer's Experience: Towards an Interpretive Approach," *Marketing Theory* 2(2): 189–205.

Scherer, J. (2007) "Globalization, Promotional Culture and the Production/Consumption of Online Games: Engaging Adidas's 'Beat Rugby' Campaign," *New Media and Society* 9(3): 475–96.

Schlosser, E. (2001) *Fast Food Nation: The Dark Side of the All-American Meal.* Boston: Houghton Mifffiin.

Schoenbach, K. (2007) "'The Own in the Foreign': Reliable Surprise—an Important Function of the Media?" *Media, Culture and Society* 29(2): 344–53.

Schouten, J.W. (1991) "Selves in Transition: Symbolic Consumption in Personal Rites of Passage and Identity Reconstruction," *Journal of Consumer Research* 17 March: 412–25.

Schrøder, K.C. and L. Phillips (2007) "Complexifying Media Power: A Study of the Interplay between Media and Audience Discourses on Politics," *Media, Culture and Society* 29(6): 890–915.

Schroeder, J.E. (2002) *Visual Consumption.* London: Routledge.

——(2009) "The Cultural Codes of Branding," *Marketing Theory* 9(1): 123–6.

Schroeder, J.E. and J.L. Borgerson (2005) "An Ethics of Representation for International Marketing Communication," *International Marketing Review* 22 (5): 578–600.

Schroeder, J.E. and D. Zwick (2004) "Mirrors of Masculinity: Representation and Identity in Advertising Images," *Consumption, Markets and Culture* 7(1): 21–52.

Schwarz, N. (2006) "Attitude Research: Between Ockham's Razor and the Fundamental Attribution Error," *Journal of Consumer Research* 33 June: 19–21.

Scolari, C. (2009) "Digital Eco_logy: Umberto Eco and a Semiotic Approach to Digital Communication," *Information, Communication and Society* 12 (1): 129–48.

Scott, L. M. (1994a) "Images in Advertising: The Need for a Theory of Visual Rhetoric," *Journal of Consumer Research* 21 September: 252–73.

——(1994b) "The Bridge from Text to Mind: Adapting Reader-Response Theory to Consumer Research," *Journal of Consumer Research* 21 December: 461–80.

Shankar, A., R. Elliott and J.A. Fitchett (2009) "Identity, Consumption and Narratives of Socialization," Marketing Theory 9(1): 75–94.

Shelton, J.A. and C.L.O. Peters (2006) "Actions Speak as Loud as Products: Disposition as a Self-Perceptive Method of Identity Incorporation," *Consumption, Markets and Culture* 9(3): 207–33.

Shepherd, R. (2003) "Fieldwork without Remorse: Travel Desires in a Tourist World," *Consumption, Markets and Culture* 6(2):133–44.

Sherry, J.F. (1998) (ed.) *ServiceScapes: The Concept of Place in Contemporary Markets.* Chicago: American Marketing Association.

——(1998b) "Understanding Markets as Places An Introduction to Servicescapes," in J.F. Sherry (ed.) *ServiceScapes: The Concept of Place in Contemporary Markets,* pp. 1–24. Chicago: American Marketing Association.

——(1998c) "The Soul of the Company Store: Nike Town Chicago and the Emplaced Brandscape," in J.F. Sherry (ed.) *ServiceScapes: The Concept of Place in Contemporary Markets,* pp. 109–46. Chicago: American Marketing Association.

Shields, R. (1992) "Spaces for the Subject of Consumption," in R. Shields (ed.) *Lifestyle Shopping,* pp. 1–20. London: Routledge.

Silverstone, R. (1999) *Why Study the Media?* London: Sage.

Sinclair, J. (2008) "Branding and Belonging: Globalized Goods and National Identity," *Journal of Cultural Economy* 1(2): 217–31.

Singh, N., H. Zhao and X. Hu (2005) "Analyzing the Cultural Content of Web Sites: A Cross-national Comparison of China, India, Japan, and US," *International Marketing Review* 22(2): 129–46.

Slater, M.D. (2007) "Reinforcing Spirals: The Mutual Influence of Media Selectivity and Media Effects and Their Impact on Individual Behavior and Social Identity," *Communication Theory* 17: 281–303.

Small, R.G. (2006) "The Book of Ours: Consumption as Narrative," *Consumption, Markets and Culture* 9(4): 317–25.

Smith, B. and A. C. Sparkes (2008) "Contrasting Perspectives on Narrating Selves and Identities: An Invitation to Dialogue," *Qualitative Research* 8(1): 5–35.

Smith, G. and A. French (2009) "The Political Brand: A Consumer Perspective," *Marketing Theory* 9(2): 209–26.

Smith, S., D. Fisher and S. J. Cole (2007) "The Lived Meanings of Fanaticism: Understanding the Complex Role of Labels and Categories in Defining the Self in Consumer Culture," *Consumption, Markets and Culture* 10(2): 77–94.

Sooryamoorthy, R., B. P. Miller and W. Shrum (2008) "Untangling the Technology Cluster: Mobile Telephony, Internet Use and the Location of Social Ties," *New Media and Society* 10(5): 729–49.

Sperber, B. (2001) "KFC Branding Campaign to Spice Up Image," *Brandweek*, 42(27), 6–7.

Stankevich, D. G. (1997) "Branding the Burger," *Discount Merchandiser* 37(9).

Stensaker, B. (2005) "Strategy, Identity and Branding—Re-Inventing Higher Education Institutions." Paper presented at the City Higher Education Seminar Series (CHESS).

Stern, B.B. and C.A. Russell (2004) "Consumer Responses to Product Placement in Television Sitcoms: Genre, Sex, and Consumption," *Consumption, Markets and Culture* 7(4): 371–94.

Stewart, J. (2007) "Local Experts in the Domestication of Information and Communication Technologies," *Information, Communication and Society* 10(4): 547–69.

Strelitz, L.N. (2002) "Media Consumption and Identity Formation: The Case of the 'Homeland' Viewers," *Media, Culture and Society* 24: 459–80.

Suseela (2008) "Beware of this Con Woman!!!" URL (consulted 15th October, 2008): *http://johnny-ong.blogspot.com/2008/10/beware-of-this-con-woman.html*

Sutton-Smith, B. and D. Kelly-Byrne (1984) "The Idealization of Play," in P. K. Smith (ed.) *Play in Animals and Humans*, pp. 305–21. Malden, MA: Blackwell.

Swaminathan, V., K.L. Page and Z. Gurhan-Canli (2007) "'My' Brand or 'Our' Brand: The Effects of Brand Relationship Dimensions and Self-Construal on Brand Evaluations," *Journal of Consumer Research* 34 (August): 248–59.

Tadajewski, M. (2004) "The Philosophy of Marketing Theory: Historical and Future Directions," *The Marketing Review* 4: 307–40.

——(2006) "Remembering Motivation Research: Toward an Alternative Genealogy of Interpretive Consumer Research," *Marketing Theory* 6(4): 429–66.

——(2008) "Final Thoughts on Amnesia and Marketing Theory," *Marketing Theory* 8 (4): 465–84.

——(2008b) "Incommensurable Paradigms, Cognitive Bias and the Politics of Marketing Theory," *Marketing Theory* 8(3): 273–97.

Tharp, M. and L. M. Scott (1990) "The Role of Marketing Processes in Creating Cultural Meaning," *Journal of Macromarketing* 10: 47–60.

Thompson, C.J. (1997) "Interpreting Consumers: A Hermeneutical Framework for Deriving Marketing Insights from the Texts of Consumers' Consumption Stories," *Journal of Marketing Research* 34(4): 438–55.

Thompson, C.J. and Z. Arsel (2004) "The Starbucks Brandscape and Consumers' (Anticorporate) Experiences of Glocalization," *Journal of Consumer Research* 31 (December): 631–42.

Thompson, C.J. and G. Coskuner-Balli (2007) "Countervailing Market Responses to Corporate Co-Optation and the Ideological Recruitment of Consumption Communities," *Journal of Consumer Research* 34 (August): 135–52.

Thompson, C. J., H. R. Pollio, and W. B. Locander (1994) "The Spoken and the Unspoken: A Hermeneutic Approach to Understanding the Cultural Viewpoints that underlie Consumers' Expressed Meanings," *Journal of Consumer Research* 21 (December): 432–53.

Thompson, C.J. and K. Tian (2008) "Reconstructing the South: How Commercial Myths Compete for Identity Value through the Ideological Shaping of Popular Memories and Countermemories," *Journal of Consumer Research* 34 (February) 595–613.

Toffler, A. (1980) *The Third Wave*. London: Pan Books.

Trentmann, F. (2009) "Crossing Divides: Consumption and Globalization in History," *Journal of Consumer Culture* 9(2): 187–220.

Turner, P.K. and R. L. Krizek (2006) "A Meaning-Centered Approach to Customer Satisfaction," *Management Communication Quarterly* 20(2): 115–47.

Tutt, D. (2005) "Mobile Performances of a Teenager: A Study of Situated Mobile Phone Activity in the Living Room," *Convergence: The International Journal of Research into New Media Technologies* 11(2): 58–75.

Underhill, P. (2004) *Call of the Mall: Geography of Shopping*. New York: Simon and Schuster.

Utz, S. (2009) "'Egoboo' vs. Altruism: the Role of Reputation in Online Consumer Communities," *New Media and Society* 11(3): 357–74.

Van Dijck, J. (2009) "Users Like You? Theorizing Agency in User-Generated Content," *Media, Culture and Society* 31(1): 41–58.

Van Dijck, J. and D. Nieborg (2009) "Wikinomics and its Discontents: a Critical Analysis of Web 2.0 Business Manifestos," *New Media and Society* 11(5): 855–74.

Varman, R. and R.W. Belk (2008) "Weaving a Web: Subaltern Consumers, Rising Consumer Culture, and Television," *Marketing Theory* 8(3): 227–52.

Varman, R. and R. Vikas (2007) "Freedom and Consumption: Toward Conceptualizing Systemic Constraints for Subaltern Consumers in a Capitalist Society," *Consumption, Markets and Culture* 10(2): 117–31.

Veloutsou, C. (2009) "Brands as Relationship Facilitators in Consumer Markets," *Marketing Theory* 9(1): 127–30.

Venkatesh, A. (1998) "Cyberculture Consumers and Cybermarketscapes," in J.F. Sherry (ed.) *ServiceScapes: The Concept of Place in Contemporary Markets*, pp. 343–74. Chicago: American Marketing Association.

Viseu, A., Clement, A., Aspinall, J. and Kennedy, T.L.M. (2006) "The Interplay of Public and Private Spaces in Internet Access," *Information, Communication and Society* 9(5): 633–56.

Volkmer, I. (2008) "Conffiict-Related Media Events and Cultures of Proximity," *Media, War and Conffiict* 1(1): 90–8.

Watson, J.L. (1997) "Introduction: Transnationalism, Localization, and Fast Foods in East Asia," in J.L. Watson (ed.) *Golden Arches East: McDonald's in East Asia*, pp. 1–38. Stanford, CA: Stanford University Press.

——(1997b) "Preface: Transnationalism, Localization, and Fast Foods in East Asia," in J.L. Watson (ed.) *Golden Arches East: McDonald's in East Asia*, pp. v–xi. Stanford, CA: Stanford University Press.

Watson, M. (2008) "The Materials of Consumption," *Journal of Consumer Culture* 8 (1): 5–10.

Weatherall, A., B.M. Watson and C. Gallois (2007) *Language, Discourse and Social Psychology*. London: Palgrave Macmillan.

Wernick, A. (2000) "The Promotional Condition of Contemporary Culture," in Martyn J. Lee (ed.) *The Consumer Society Reader*, pp. 300–318. Malden, MA: Blackwell.

Wilk, R. (2009) "Review of P. Sunderland and R. Denny (2007) *Doing Anthropology in Consumer Research*. Walnut Creek, CA: Left Coast Press," *Journal of Consumer Culture* 9(2): 299–302.

Williamson, J. (1992) "Notes from Storyville North Circling the Mall," in R. Shields (ed.) *Lifestyle Shopping*, pp. 216–32. London: Routledge.

Wilson, J. (2006) "3G to Web 2.0? Can Mobile Telephony Become an Architecture of Participation?" *Convergence: The International Journal of Research into New Media Technologies* 12(2): 229–42.

Wilson, T. (1993) *Watching Television: Hermeneutics, Reception and Popular Culture*. Cambridge: Polity Press.

Wilson, T. (2009) *Understanding Media Users: From Theory to Practice*. Boston and Oxford: Wiley-Blackwell.

Wilson, T., H.P. Tan and M. Lwin (2006) "Television's Glocal Advertising in Veridical Product Narrative: A Southeast Asian Reception Study of Consumer Alignment/ Alienation," *Consumption, Markets and Culture* 9(1): 45–62.

Winchester, M., J. Romaniuk and S. Bogomolov (2008) "Positive and Negative Brand Beliefs and Brand Defection/Uptake," *European Journal of Marketing* 42(5/6): 553–70.

WMW (2008) "What A Friday It Was!" URL (consulted 15th October, 2008): *http:// ugwug.blogspot.com/2008/10/what-friday-it-was.html*

Wood, H. (2006) "The Mediated Conversational Floor: An Interactive Approach to Audience Reception Analysis," *Media, Culture and Society* 29(1): 75–103.

Wright, P. (2002) "Marketplace Metacognition and Social Intelligence," *Journal of Consumer Research* 28 (March): 677–82.

Yan, Y. (1997) "McDonald's in Beijing: The Localization of Americana," in J.L. Watson (ed.) *Golden Arches East: McDonald's in East Asia*, pp. 39–76. Stanford, CA: Stanford University Press.

Yoon, T-J. and M. Ok (2007) "Watching and Shopping: Television Audiences' Experiences with Home-Shopping Channels in Everyday Lives." Paper presented at the International Association for Media and Communication Research Conference, UNESCO, Paris.

Zhao, X. and R.W. Belk (2008) "Politicizing Consumer Culture: Advertising's Appropriation of Political Ideology in China's Social Transition," *Journal of Consumer Research* 35 August 231–44.

Zwick, D. and N. Dholakia. (2006) "The Epistemic Consumption Object and Post-social Consumption: Expanding Consumer-Object Theory in Consumer Research," *Consumption, Markets and Culture* 9(1): 17–43.

# Index